Social Assessment Theory and Practice

A multi-disciplinary framework

Derek Clifford
Senior Lecturer in Social Work
Liverpool John Moores University

Ashgate

ARENA

Aldershot • Brookfield USA • Singapore • Sydney

Published by
Ashgate Publishing Limited
Gower House
Croft Road
Aldershot
Hants GU11 3HR
England

Ashgate Publishing Company
Old Post Road
Brookfield
Vermont 05036
USA

British Library Cataloguing in Publication Data
Clifford, Derek
   Social assessment theory and practice : a
   multi-disciplinary framework
   1. Social service
   I. Title
   361.3

Library of Congress Cataloging-in-Publication Data
Clifford, Derek, 1954–
        Social assessment theory and practice : a multi-disciplinary
   framework / Derek Clifford.
        p.   cm.
        ISBN 1–85742–429–8 (hardcover)
        1. Social service—Methodology. 2. Human services—Methodology.
   I. Title.
   HV40.C616   1998
   361—dc21   98–22998
                                                                            CIP

ISBN: 1 85742 429 8

Printed in Great Britain by Antony Rowe Ltd., Chippenham, Wiltshire

Contents

List of figures

List of figures

Preface

This book has two closely connected objectives. The first aim is to present a framework of concepts in order to create a competent theoretical basis for social assessment – a common task in a number of professions in health, social welfare, law and education, and a vitally important area in which the differing professions need to gain some common understanding. The second is to explore the practical use of these concepts in differing contexts where various professions – social workers and various kinds of care staff; psychologists; nursing staff; general practitioners and various medical staff, including psychiatrists, paediatricians and geriatricians; teachers; lawyers; probation officers, and the police – are supposed to be working together, but are frequently exposed as divided in their understanding. This means the development of a methodology capable of providing a useful guiding framework for the various complex practical issues involved, but one which is also responsive to the theory generated by practice itself.

The first part of the book will draw on social theory and social research methodology, bearing in mind the need to relate this to a very wide range of micro-social situations where individual people, their lives and social relationships are studied. It will draw on a range of relevant academic and applied disciplines, principally in the social sciences, and will therefore be multi-disciplinary in orientation, but firmly centred on the social.

The second part of the book will show how the conceptual framework applies in specific areas of professional practice where individuals from various user groups are assessed, including children and young people, older people, disabled people, and people in mental distress. This part will focus on the kinds of methods and practices towards which the various groups of people involved should be working, and will thus be multi-professional in its implications, but will focus particularly on those responsible for making social assessments – principally social workers.

However, it should not be assumed that there is a simple one-way flow from theory to practice. On the contrary, sound practice in social assessment can be seen as being theorised in Part One. There is therefore a deliberate effort to draw upon the experience of social assessment – from my own practice and observation of others at work (see 'Autobiographical notes and acknowledgements' below), from research I have conducted into social assessment practice with a colleague (Clifford and Cropper, 1994; 1997a and 1997b), and from good practice as it is described in the literature.

The proposed framework for social assessment has particular reference to assessments done by social workers. However, the concept of social assessment is also relevant in many professional areas, either as part of their own discourse, or in formal consultation or in team discussion with others. For example, in the legal system, formal and informal social assessment is carried on all the time, principally by probation officers, but also by the police, magistrates, solicitors and barristers in the course of their work. They may either refer to formal social assessments, or may construct their own informal social assessments in the course of their evaluation of evidence, investigation or sentencing. In education also, the social assessment of children is carried out informally all the time as a part of teachers' attempts to understand and contextualise children's progress. But that becomes even more important for teachers with pastoral or home liason duties, and especially for teachers with special responsibility in relation to child abuse.

In health and social welfare, there is a similar pattern to the division of labour. Although social workers have the prime responsibility for a social assessment, health workers, from nurses to consultants, all make informal social assessments of their patients, whatever their speciality. They may also have need to refer to an 'official' social assessment, especially where a patient is being discharged, or to understand the background to the development of illness or disease. However, some health care professionals obviously make assessments which overlap a great deal with social assessments, for instance health visitors, GPs and paediatricians dealing with child abuse cases; community psychiatric nurses, and psychiatric consultants.

The book sets out a theoretical framework which explains and justifies social assessment as a principled and disciplined activity, drawing on the social sciences, especially the disciplines of sociology, history and psychology. This means it is *multi-disciplinary* in construction and *multi-professional* in orientation, aiming to inform other professions while drawing on good practice by those most involved with social assessment, offering a supportive but challenging theoretical base from which to work. The emphasis is upon *social* assessment, as distinct from other kinds of assessment, and my contention is that the theory applies to any social assessment for any user group in any setting or context. The latter are innumerable, but the areas of practice covered in Part Two will provide a basis for guiding assessment practice and theory in almost any setting, even if it is not specifically represented here. Two important settings involving specific kinds of service user groups not discussed in Part Two can be used as examples.

The areas of *probation and youth justice* are not discussed in Part Two. This is partly because they are not areas of which I have great knowledge. However, having had some involvement in youth justice, and also having supervised students on placement in such settings, and having read some of the literature on assessment in both these areas, my judgement would be that the general issues of social assessment that arise are not in principle different. Particular issues, and the details of application are certainly significantly different, and the practitioners and others who work in these areas deserve respect for their efforts to develop social assessments in the face of scepticism or reserve from professions with more power and status (Beattie, 1997; Kemshall, 1996 and 1997; Johnstone, 1997; McEwan and Sullivan, 1996; Williams, 1997). Nevertheless, the general principles of social assessment as set out in Part One apply to youth justice and probation in the same basic respects as to all other areas of social assessment. Much of the discussion of practice set out in Part Two is also highly relevant, especially Chapters 7 and 8, which deal with general issues of practice. In addition, the chapters about assessing children and families (Chapter 9) and mental health (Chapter 10) will also have great relevance to youth justice and probation. The other chapters may also overlap with assessing offenders, depending on the age and/or disability of the person(s) concerned. In addition, discussion of the assessment of adult offenders before release into the community, and adults as parents (and thus as potential offenders against children), is a significant part of Chapters 7 and 9.

For readers interested in the theoretical basis and justification of social assessment, the discussion in the first part of the book is the obvious focus for attention. However, my argument is that the theory should not be considered in isolation from practice. The book's two parts are therefore welded together in various ways. The full implications of the theory can only be grasped by looking at the chapters which discuss various aspects of practice. Each of the chapters on theoretical principles is concluded with a series of questions that illustrate the implications for practice which are discussed in relation to a case study in Part Two.

People interested in practice, and especially in a particular area of practice, will need to look at other chapters because there is deliberate and significant overlap between particular practice areas, and also between the first and second parts of the book. The theoretical framework draws on all the practice areas, and contributes to them all: the interconnections are thus very important. The reader may have a particular interest in one chapter or section of the book, but my aim and intention is to draw their interest to the rest of the book because of the interconnections, which both illuminate and extend the contours of the concept of social assessment.

There are many parts of the discussion where I have felt aware of my ignorance, and others where I would have liked to expand but could not sensibly do so. I apologise in advance for the inadequacies that specialists will inevitably find in particular areas. My intention and hope is that readers will understand the *logic* of the argument, and where it is insufficiently instanced, may be able to supply some of the detail themselves. In any case, I take it as read that because the proposed framework is general in nature, both its overall design and its practice in specific settings must necessarily be matters for discussion and debate. What seems essential is that the main thrust of the argument for a concept of social assessment based soundly on relevant social theory and relevant social values and practice should be seriously considered with equal regard to both the theoretical and the practice issues.

I particularly regret the absence of an extended discussion of the ethical and moral problems that arise from the kind of argument presented. The traditional Kantian and Utilitarian values of the liberal professions and semi-professions, based on respect for persons, still maintain some official and popular support, at least in theory. The recent recognition of the value of empowerment, with its multitude of meanings, has been firmly analysed, and its limitations exposed (Humphries, 1996b; see also Chapter 6). It is an important issue, since the methodology discussed here explicitly tries to take values into account. The concept of anti-oppressive values seems currently to be less acceptable in academic or official spheres. This is partly because it is associated with media-driven stereotypes of outdated political idealism, and partly because of postmodern academics promoting an anti-foundationalist pluralism which sometimes sits uneasily with notions of social justice.

The essential point to grasp here is that values and methodology inevitably interconnect. A 'commitment' to values is not always conscious or explicit (though it is probably better if it is the latter): they are presupposed by the concepts used to understand the social world by participants within it. This is a familiar argument in the philosophy of the social sciences. Perhaps one major contribution of the recent dominance of postmodernist thought is to have carried the weight of opinion in the social sciences towards accepting this in varying degrees. This being the case, there would be little point in taking up too much space defending the link with values. The discussion could certainly be carried forward in that direction, but there is plenty of justification for concentrating here on the issues of social theory and social research methodology in relation to social assessment, whilst accepting that the position represented does indeed have value implications which include but go beyond a liberal respect for persons.

The approximate outlines of this value position are made explicit throughout, and are consistently linked to the methodology. This position attempts to take seriously the complex memberships of major social divisions that affect individuals' perspectives and actions, and to which they respond in different ways. It assumes that a better understanding of the social structuring and construction of lives may (but not inevitably) enable better negotiation between users, carers and professionals, and more constructive and effective, but less oppressive interventions in people's lives. It implies that theorist academics and professional practitioners are both participants within the social world, and that their awareness of their own values and their efforts to understand and assess have ethical and political dimensions – whether they like it or not. It supports a critical stance towards dominant powers and concepts, and continual re-evaluation of established ideas, including its own.

Autobiographical notes and acknowledgements

There is growing agreement that it is good practice to make clear to readers where the author's views originate. This is also an integral part of the following discussion of assessment, where the character, position and circumstances of the assessing professional have to be seen as part of the equation. I therefore include some autobiographical notes so that readers can assess for themselves what my background is, and be in a position to construct the sense of the argument to their own satisfaction.

I frequently use the first person when writing, deliberately to indicate that the ideas expressed are specifically related to personal concerns and experiences, even (perhaps especially) when I am arguing that they have a wide relevance. This is not part of some traditional academic styles, but is consistent with the intellectual case presented here, and with contemporary accounts of qualitative research (Fine, 1994). In explaining myself, I have tried to take account of the principles I have considered in this book: historical location, reflexivity, power, interacting social systems and social difference.

My experience of making social assessments in social work is mainly in childcare in Stockport and Manchester through the 1980s. However, I had previously spent a year working with mainly older people in a hospital setting, and trained professionally at Manchester University during 1977–9, when systems theory was popular in social work education. My interest in values and methods dates back before this to the 1960s, when I was also at Manchester University studying for a first degree in history, politics and economics, and a PhD in political theory with reference to moral philosophy. As the first university student in my extended family, I wondered how differing methods of understanding social life and differing values were interconnected, particularly in the context of studying Hegel and Marx. Although often taken for granted at the time, being a white English male at a major UK university gave me access to positions of relative power. I spent several years teaching political and social theory in universities in Trinidad, Tasmania and New South Wales before returning to England to get involved in social work and in family life.

I worked as a hospital social worker in Salford before completing an MA in Social Work and Social Administration. After qualifying, working in a generic team with a strong childcare component at the same time as being married with two young daughters raised numerous feminist issues. My social work in Manchester brought me into close working relationships with teachers, psychologists and psychiatrists, and also with black and Asian colleagues and service users. I have been fortunate to have had black women as line managers, both in social work practice and in academia. I have been involved in teaching and research at Liverpool John Moores University since 1988, with particular interests in anti-oppressive practice and social divisions, and the range of assessment issues, especially in childcare. Health professionals will note that whilst I have worked in a hospital and in a child mental health setting, and have also taught social values and ethics to nurses, my background is primarily in social work. My understanding of other social divisions has grown fitfully over the years, often thanks to disabled, gay or lesbian colleagues and service users. My experience of ageing makes me realise how little I know of any of these things, and how much I owe to the various people with whom I have lived and worked, many of whom will not be in a position to publish anything. I hope some of their influence comes through, but I acknowledge my own responsibility and control for what follows.

I also gratefully acknowledge help from colleagues who have commented on earlier drafts. The Professor of Social Work at John Moores University, Michael Preston-Shoot, has been assiduous and thoughtful in his written comments. Beverley Burke and Peter Sharkey, colleagues at John Moores University, have also been particularly helpful in reading and commenting. Other colleagues have also been helpful, including those involved in the Liverpool Risk Assessment Project, and former research assistant Andrea Cropper (now of Central Lancashire University), and especially current staff members in my own School who have also shown forbearance with my preoccupation with writing. Joanna Bornat, editor of *Oral History* and lecturer at the Open University, has been helpful and critical, and I am grateful to Chris Knox, Child Protection Co-ordinator for Liverpool Social Services, and Doug Feery, Training Officer for the same organisation, with whom I have been able to discuss some of these ideas with practising social workers during training. I would like to thank Professor Liz Stanley, Director of Women's Studies at my old University of Manchester for encouraging the early stages of this book, as well as for the intellectual stimulation of her many writings, and I am grateful for good advice and support from Jo Campling and Kate Trew and others at Ashgate Publishing.

I am especially grateful to John Moores University Research Strategy and Funding Committee for granting me a Research Fellowship for the first semester of 1997, which greatly helped to make some space to research and write this book. My friend John Powell, Lecturer in Education at Manchester Metropolitan University, has often usefully discussed related issues; and not least, my family have to take credit for making me conscious of being in a gender minority of one, as well as putting up with my absences on the word processor. I have learnt most from those to whom this book is dedicated – especially my wife. This is a small token of thanks, for everything.

Notes on terminology

1 There is no satisfactory generic term to describe people who are being assessed. They may be patients, subjects, clients, customers or service users, but their actual position in relation to a social assessment varies enormously with its setting and purpose. I shall refer to 'users', well aware that the service on offer is sometimes not what the people concerned actually want to use at all, especially when they are legally required or otherwise socially constrained to submit to an assessment.

2 The methodology I am discussing here is described as 'critical auto/biography', for reasons which will be explained. Following its initial use and explanation in the first chapter, I will thereafter usually abbreviate it to CA/B.

3 'Multi-disciplinary' will normally be used to refer to the relevance of multiple academic disciplines, *not*, as is sometimes the case, to the involvement of differing professions, which will be described as 'multi-professional', in order to distinguish between these two related but distinct concepts. Occasionally, I will use 'multi-disciplinary' as some do, to refer to multi-professional issues, in which case I will enclose the word in inverted commas to indicate that I am deferring to their usage in the context of a specific discussion.

4 I am using 'social assessment' in a broad sense to refer to social as distinct from psychological or medical assessment – that is, assessment which is centred on *social* explanation – and will draw on social research and social science concepts. Social assessment may cover assessment of social needs on a community-wide or even larger scale, but here I am concerned mainly with social assessment of individuals and small groups.

5   I will regard 'social work assessment' as work carried out by employed social workers in voluntary and statutory settings, whose focus is usually on social assessment, but who may also draw on other kinds of assessment, in the same way as others who are not social workers may use social assessment. However, it is not normally useful to speak of others doing a social work assessment, since the social work assessment is inherently connected to *being* a social worker, representing an organisation, and having specific responsibilities for assessment.

6   I use the term 'anti-oppressive' sparingly because of its adoption as a term of abuse in some quarters. However, it seems useful in order to mark the range of structural social oppressions, rather than individual or local prejudice, for which 'anti-discriminatory' seems adequate (Phillipson, 1992, p.15)

7   There are numerous debates about terminology in the areas discussed in this book. I have tried to use terms acceptable to the oppressed social groups concerned, but given changing times and places, and my own limited knowledge, if I have failed in this, I apologise in advance.

Part One

Critical auto/biography: Social theory for social assessment

This part of the book attempts to set out a theoretical basis for social assessment under six inter-related headings, with reference to contemporary social science methodology and values. The first chapter argues that auto/biography and other related developments in qualitative social research can and should be used as a basis for social assessment, but offers a specific, value-based interpretation of auto/biography. The following chapters spell out that framework. It is not being offered in any sense as final: it is all too clear that the changing issues involved could be debated at great length.

I have chosen to write about both theory and practice in a specific area, and therefore can only *indicate* positions which are discussed more fully by others (especially white and black feminists and other social theorists – to which I will refer). The argument should therefore be considered in the light of a range of developing theories which link research methodology and practice to the complex nature of oppression and its implications for any possible understanding of social issues in relation to individual lives and professional practice.

Part One

Critical Auto/Biography: Social theory for social assessment

1 Values and methodology

Introduction

This first chapter highlights some basic arguments about the nature of social assessment, and sets the pattern for subsequent chapters in Part One.

It will firstly propose six interconnected methodological principles on which to ground the theory and practice of social assessment – a methodological framework which will be described as 'critical auto/biography (CA/B). It outlines general practical and professional implications – ideas that will be examined in Part Two in relation to specific user and social groups, where theoretically informed practice methods and procedures will be discussed.

This first chapter will also discuss the first principle being proposed, which is concerned with methodology and oppression. Subsequent chapters in Part One will discuss the other principles proposed, the justification for them, possible objections, and general implications for practice.

Historically, the task of social history assessment has often been associated with hierarchically subordinate gendered roles in various agencies, with (mainly) women being managed by (mainly) men. In health, the nurse or junior doctor has 'taken a history' from a patient in order to inform senior consultants, and in social services a significant part of the basic-grade social worker's role has been to construct a 'social history' for other professionals to use – either in the courts, or to inform psychiatrists or other medical personnel. This socially constructed position of subordination has been reinforced by a relative absence of theoretical input to what has often been seen as a practical task at which women are particularly good – except where, occasionally, it is done by higher-status professionals. Compare, for instance, the theoretical input by forensic clinical psychologists into the assessment of sexual abusers (McMurren and Hodge, 1994) with the evidence that probation officers, working with the same kind of offenders, work with little or no agreed theoretical framework (Kemshall, 1995).

Historically, major theoretical contributions have been made by various psychodynamic traditions interpreting individual lives in terms of psychological development. Given their status, it is not surprising that it is these theories which traditionally underpin the social history as it has been used particularly in some mental health areas, and in social work with children and families. Even so, women are again stereotypically seen as particularly useful at gaining access to information about feelings, hence the common division of labour in multi-professional teams between (usually) women nurses or social workers who relate directly to the user, and the (not always) male doctors and consultants who are responsible for interpretation and diagnosis. Recent developments in the bureaucratisation of assessment practices, particularly in community care, have again emphasised the relatively low-status work, and minimal training required for completing assessment checklists and forms (Dominelli, 1996a, 1996b). Here a more unambiguous medical model appears to dominate, involving the collection of elementary historical data and identification of current key indicators of specified areas of need. There has therefore also been a link with social class status, since the pay and working conditions for women in this kind of low-level work are deemed to be very different from the elite training and working conditions required for either detailed psychological analysis or medical diagnosis – or indeed for the managerial and higher administrative roles that are required in the larger organisations.

However, the importance and the difficulty of making good enough assessments of complex individual and micro-social situations has always been potentially obvious. In recent years, the question has been at the forefront of public discussion, notably in relation to child abuse scandals and mental health tragedies, and increasingly in relation to other groups who may be at risk, or in need, such as older people, or those who cause others to be at risk, such as offenders.

One question that needs to be answered is how far social science theory can be used to assist and justify the difficult decisions involved for professionals who have such responsibilities in these areas. A traditional academic stance has been to study the practices of professionals and other practitioners from a suitable distance – from the proverbial ivory tower – and to comment eruditely on the theoretical implications and adequacy of their performance. This has sometimes resulted in a seemingly elitist perspective on the work of female 'semi-professions' (Sibeon, 1990 and 1991). The aim here is to try to pull together useful theoretical contributions from the social sciences to provide a sound basis for assessment, drawing on practice experience in order to make that selection and evaluation. However,

I deliberately try to use the theoretical contributions of authors from non-elite social groups in order to positively value the work of women (especially) in this area, and to counterbalance and inform the limitations of my own past and current experience and knowledge. In this way, the intention is to further understanding of what good social assessment entails; to increase respect for those who have to do it in difficult circumstances; to increase awareness amongst practitioners of the methodological issues and the implications of these for practice, and to increase theoreticians' awareness of the complexity and intellectual challenge of practice and its interpretation. The following is therefore addressed both to those involved in practice and to those involved in theorising about practice, in the hope that it will make a contribution in both areas, and ultimately that it will have some benefit for those on the receiving end.

The key task which has not been met by previous discussions of assessment is the primary shortcoming identified in a recent discussion of holistic assessment: 'there is no conceptual framework which adequately embraces the range of assessment tasks' (Lloyd and Taylor, 1995, pp.692–3). The authors were addressing the fragmented range of types of assessment done in social work, where government concern and intervention has resulted in initiatives which have not succeeded in resolving issues. Problems arise particularly because of the multi-professional *and* multi-disciplinary nature of assessments in the health and social services – and also in other areas such as law and education, where the social aspect of assessment always intrudes. Problems also arise because of differences arising from values and perspectives that cross cultural, national and other social boundaries (Boushel, 1994). Published government guides to assessment (e.g. DoH, 1988; 1989a; 1990; 1991) concern both health and welfare services, but have not employed a theoretical framework which could evaluate and integrate the various professions, disciplines and perspectives which are involved. The aim of what follows is to contribute to that basis.

The concept of critical auto/biography

I am using the term 'critical auto/biography' to refer to a framework of related social research concepts concerned with understanding and intervention in individual lives. This area of interest is obviously central to social assessment, but it is surprising how little the social sciences have contributed to the complexities involved – until very recent times. The fact that the task of understanding individual people's lives and social relationships is not reducible to one discipline may be the reason why it has not received the kind of sustained, co-operative academic attention it deserves. However, female-dominated professions such as nursing and social work have also had low status in the academic world as well as in the rest of society, so (mainly male) academics and researchers have been less interested in studying their problems.

My interest has drawn on four main sources. Firstly, I have studied some of the academic perspectives that have been developing in the area of multi-disciplinary studies of micro-social situations, in the belief that they might have something to offer in terms of methodology and intellectual grounding. Secondly, I have studied the perspectives of dominated social groups in the belief that their insights are essential to both methodological and ethical adequacy of any approach that could possibly be useful to practitioners in these fields. Thirdly, I draw on the experience of working with social work colleagues and service users, and fourthly on researching assessment practice.

I use Liz Stanley's formulation of the term 'auto/biography' (with the slash separating 'auto' and 'biography') to denote the importance of the connection between understanding other lives in interaction with understanding your own, and vice versa (Stanley, 1992). The term thus includes both biography and autobiography, and various connections between them. I also follow her declaration about this field of study, and why it is of such innate interest – it is central to the study of the social sciences, as it raises many of the key questions which have concerned theorists and must also concern practitioners. Self-evidently, it raises issues concerning the relationship between micro-, mezzo- and macro-social levels of social life – from individual and small-group interactions, through organisational and community life to national and international relationships. It clearly raises the basic questions of human agency and structure, and the nature of structural and post-structural explanations: the extent to which the structural functional demands of social systems impinge on people's lives, explaining their behaviour, and/or can be resisted and changed by individual or group action. It also inevitably raises all the fundamental issues about values, perspectives, interpretation and identity, and provides a multi-disciplinary context in which the questions of inter-relationship between disciplines such as psychology, sociology, medicine and law cannot be avoided. It further raises issues about epistemology, ontology and ethics which bridge social science and philosophical fields of enquiry. Any methodology must have implications for these philosophical issues which deal with the conditions and nature of knowledge and being in the social world (Guba and Lincoln, 1994).

In Stanley's formulation, it also addresses concerns raised by postmodernist and post-structuralist ideas, such as diversity and discourse, which have also been influential in theorising the study of people's lives (Denzin, 1989).

However, given the context of her writing, key concepts such as deconstruction, difference, power and reflexivity are seen as already anticipated in feminist and other writings (Stanley and Wise, 1994). Similarly, postmodernism and post-structuralism are treated here as influential and contributory, rather than as 'foundational'. These theories have been well debated by feminists (e.g. Nicholson, 1990; Ferguson and Wicke, 1994), and some male academics regard the 'postmodernist' movement as past its peak (Marcus, 1994, p.563), but it is none the less useful to indicate these areas of overlap. The concern with representing lives and the methodological difficulties associated with this area of research is not confined to Stanley's writings but has been a major area of feminist investigation in recent times (and is reviewed in Marcus, 1995). A good example of an auto/biographical approach to research that has recently been published comprises the self-critical reflection and involvement a researcher studying the lives of people with learning difficulties (Atkinson, 1997).

I use the phrase '*critical* auto/biography' to indicate some development from Stanley's concept, with the emphasis on relevance to an applied context. I simply wish to stress the importance of practically *taking* a particular critical (and self-critical) stance on issues to do with values and action – a matter of central concern to people involved in action research, as well as workers in health and social welfare in general. Such workers assess and intervene in the lives of vulnerable people, and their own personal values, understanding and conduct are therefore important issues, and need to be the subject of critical reflection as well as commitment. The workers must of necessity simultaneously research, assess and construct the social world, with their own participation, histories and identities as crucial elements in the process.

There is also a (loose) connection with the 'critical theory' tradition of social criticism (Jay, 1973; Harvey, 1990; Kincheloe and McLaren, 1994), which also deliberately takes up an evaluative perspective critical of dominating ideologies and structures. The point here is to connect with social science traditions which have tried to view social life from a critical perspective, especially views from 'below', which express the interests and perspectives of dominated social groups generally, and more specifically the interests and perspectives of the user groups whose members are the subjects of professional assessment. I also value the link with other liberal and postmodern academic traditions concerning the *critical* evaluation and deconstruction of ideas – particularly dominant ones – which attempt to show: 'connections that are hidden ... to understand the world *and* to change it' (Humphries, 1996, p.iii).

Another feminist writer has already used the concept of 'critical autobiography' – although without the slash separating the 'auto' from the 'biography'. Morwenna Griffiths has been concerned with analysing the 'web of identity' that is constituted by the changing intersection of social difference in people's lives. Her interest is more focused on understanding the fragmented self, and she distinguishes between the simple individual narrative of traditional autobiography and a 'critical autobiography' which: '... makes use of individual experience, theory, and a process of reflection and re-thinking, which includes attention to politically situated perspectives' (Griffiths, 1995, p.70). Thus, although her attention is concentrated on the identity of the self, her approach is grounded on feminist concerns with experience, theory and situated perspectives and is therefore broadly compatible (though different from) the way I am using the different term 'critical auto/biography'.

Since the construction of the life-course is itself a negotiated and situated part of social reality, then it behoves any attempted account to examine the way the account is itself constituted (Gubrium, 1994). The conclusion drawn here is that there is therefore every justification in making clear to the reader the value basis for the proposed methodology: this could be regarded as a helpful deconstructive writing practice (Stanley, 1993). It does not entail a denial, but a recognition and admission that the writer (or assessor) belongs to an actual social world, and accounting for that in the approach taken. This is especially important for this particular author in attempting to develop a general theory of assessment, but unable, for example, to identify ontologically with Stanley's feminist auto/biography. Not having had the experience of being female, nor being part of other dominated social groups (e.g. black, gay or disabled) has specific implications for this author's ability to understand concepts drawn from outside his experience. I assume that any writer or practitioner must draw critically on the range of experiences they have had, and must use their intelligence and imagination for the rest (see 'Autobiographical notes and acknowledgements'). But the evidence is that people's intelligence and imagination are inevitably limited by their social location and experience.

The relevance of methodology?

At this point, we may ask is there really any relevance in discussion of the above complex methodology for many practitioners? The academic use of unnecessarily obscure concepts and neologisms, and the workload pressures desensitising practitioners to the importance of reflection and analysis would suggest not.

The answer comes in two parts, intellectual and practical. The first involves a clear issue of logic and consistency: the use of various methods to assess people and situations cannot adequately be justified on a casual, common-sense basis. Any number of fairly obvious objections can be raised, but principally the great variety of interpretations of what common-sense methods might be in this area, including what is taken as common sense in different professions. A distinction that needs to made, which may help to clarify the point, is that between a methodology – a justification or rationale for using certain methods – and the methods or procedures themselves. The two terms are related but different. The methodology is the rationale which is exemplified in the related methods, and the methods must be consistent with the methodology: 'The methodological question cannot be *reduced* to a question of methods; methods must be fitted to a ... methodology' (Guba and Lincoln, 1994, p.108; emphasis added). The difficulty lies in defining what kind of methodology is relevant to the sorts of methods that will help practitioners study micro-social circumstances. In this section, I concentrate on explaining the concepts of an appropriate methodology for social assessment. It is an argument that presents a particular kind of research methodology – critical auto/biography – as the most relevant and effective basis for this kind of task.

The second reason for discussing a complex methodology as a basis for a practical task such as assessment is itself a practical argument. It is that the status of the assessments done by women workers is linked to the status of the workers themselves, and they are therefore often undermined or ignored in various contexts where they should be more seriously considered. This happens especially in the court system, but also throughout the health and social services, where workers' assessments are under scrutiny by male-dominated managers and other interconnected elite groups. The advantage of developing a methodology which is informed by a significant use of social science theory is not only that it gives the use of various methods some consistency, and an improved degree of comparability, but also that it gives social assessment the status it deserves, as an exacting and intellectually justifiable, as well as a skilful, ethical procedure. The question here is how easily can workers make use of the methodology, however appropriate it might be? This will largely be dealt with in Part Two, but some general considerations will also be examined in Part One.

Assessment as research

It is surely not coincidental that the development of feminist theory in the social sciences has seen a re-evaluation of qualitative approaches to research, especially over the past fifteen years, and that much of this research has taken place within the context of health, welfare and educational settings. Prior to that, the social sciences had relatively little space for qualitative research methods, except in anthropology, and in participant-observer studies of groups. The study of individual lives was left largely to varieties of behavioural and cognitive psychology, which focused on the psychological rather than the social aspects of assessment, and outside most universities, to the psychodynamic therapists, and to literary biographers. It is well known that qualitative social research into individual lives thrived briefly in the 1930s, but declined thereafter. The situation now, of course, is very different. On the one hand there has been a flowering of qualitative research methodologies, often (but not exclusively) as a direct result of women's academic work. Associated with this has been the re-valuation of research into individual lives, to the extent that there is now an enormous list of terms relating to it, emanating from various disciplines, including: auto/biography, interpretive biography, life history, oral narrative, case study, oral history, personal narrative and life story (for others, see Hatch and Wiesnewski, 1995a, p.124).

The practical implication of this is that the work of social assessment, which has often suffered from a problem of low status, can and should now be justified in terms of a *research* methodology, drawing on the variety of available models. It is rightly becoming a common theme in social and health-related practice that there *is* a close relationship between practice and research, and that practice can utilise and justify itself in terms of research methodology. In social work, Sheppard and others have called attention to this development, focusing on the parallels between the processes of research and practice, especially in the area of assessment (Archer, 1990; Everitt *et al.*, 1992; Broad, 1994; Clifford and Cropper, 1997b; Hart and Bond, 1995; Sheppard, 1995).

Sheppard uses the model of analytic induction to drive his examination of how qualitative research methodology should be applied in social assessments. In practice, this means that he focuses on three basic features:

1   the progressive and comparative development of clear hypotheses;
2   the search for disconfirming data
3   the reformulation of the hypothesis or redefinition of the problem in the face of disconfirming evidence.

This enables workers to choose hypotheses which are least likely to be wrong, but depends on some practical application of routine scepticism about hypotheses, and engagement in discussion about them, particularly with more experienced workers (thus drawing on a wider fund of practice wisdom). It appears to draw on post-positivist methodological assumptions (Guba and Lincoln, 1994) which centre on the probability of truth, but without accounting for values or other factors in sufficient depth.

This approach, though useful in emphasising the parallels between the process of health and social work practice on the one hand and social research methods on the other, is not specific enough in describing a methodology that is particularly relevant to assessing people's lives. This seems unfortunate given the recent development of multiple research methodologies designed specifically for understanding lives. Nor does it help to generate or decide between different areas from which hypotheses may be drawn. The worker is assumed to have a storehouse of hypotheses which can be used whenever required. The research methodology comes into play only after one has been chosen. There is neither questioning nor direction as to the issue of which hypotheses should be chosen, and why, and who is doing the choosing – crucial issues when someone's welfare is at stake, as well as in relation to contemporary themes in the social sciences which emphasise the situated character of all research. This situated reality may also include legal or other mandates which are not conducive to the 'pure research' model of analytic induction. A methodology of research is needed which must be able to take more account of the constrained contexts of research in the social world.

The effect of a CA/B research methodology is to provide an informed place to start developing hypotheses, and a way of guiding that development which includes Sheppard's advice but goes beyond it. For example, it is an implication of this framework that (in addition to discussion with experienced colleagues) one of the places to both look for, develop and test out hypotheses is in the perspectives of both users of services and especially those who, users or not, have relevant experiences of oppression, and valuable insights that overturn prevailing concepts. This is essential in view of the ethical, legal and policy advice for assessing workers that they should work in partnership with those being assessed, the vast majority of whom lead lives circumscribed by various kinds of oppression. Secondly, the effect of this application of this methodology is that it directs the development of research and assessment procedures towards methodological considerations that are particularly relevant to assessing oppressed lives – that the approach taken needs to be multi-disciplinary, multi-method and multi-professional, and also that the approach has to be contextualised within an historical framework. A holistic understanding of the complexity of real lives has to begin by placing them within a real social and historical context within which various forms of domination structure the experiences that people have at that particular time. This again provides a specific direction to research and assessment that is lacking in Sheppard's approach.

Another area in which the latter fails to connect adequately with the needs of social assessment is in the relationship between research and practice. As indicated, Sheppard discusses the way in which practice wisdom is positively related to discourse within the professional team, but does not consider the relationship between assessment and the process of engagement and intervention in the lives of the people concerned. The methodology of action and partnership research has been recently featured in relation to health and welfare services, and the parallels between it and the process of assessment are highly relevant (Reason and Rowan, 1981; Reason, 1988 and 1994; Whitaker and Archer, 1994; Hart and Bond, 1995).

The activity of assessment is not easily assimilable to conventional research terms, where the researcher stands outside the social action considering alternative hypotheses. Assessment involves action – being a participant in interaction with the research subjects and others. The model for an assessment methodology therefore needs to draw on these kinds of research models. It especially needs to be aware that there is no distinction that can significantly be made between assessment and intervention. Assessment *is* a form of intervention; it *is* a series of actions and interactions which in itself is likely to have a 'therapeutic' effect, whether intended or not (Tantam, 1995, pp.16–17). It may instead have the opposite effect, of course, and be damaging to those involved. It is therefore essential that a methodology for assessment can account for the conscious, active involvement of the assessor, and draw on research methodologies that are able to elucidate this aspect. Critical auto/biography recognises the multiple, shifting nature of power relationships, and the importance of a realistic, reflexive analysis of the position of workers and professionals in relation to users, colleagues and managers. A key issue here is the importance of the nature and degree of the participation of the range of professional and non-professional people involved. The principles imply a critical approach to participation, taking into account the varying political and institutional positions of different workers and different users, assessing the potential for both abuse and empowerment amid the dilemmas of conflicting needs and interests.

Finally, the CA/B framework takes into account both the objective factors in people's lives, as far as these are ascertainable from documentary and witness evidence, but also includes the meaning of human action as understood by the participants, drawing on hermeneutic and ethnographic traditions. Sheppard's discussion of research methodology has been criticised for failing to be sufficiently inclusive in relation to these traditions and their important focus on human meaning and interpretation (White, 1997). CA/B is thus aware of the inevitability of the uncertainty inherent in research and assessment into social life (cf. Parton, 1998), and the 'selective representation' of reality that is the best that can be hoped for (White, 1997, p.742). However, it provides a constructive way of reflecting on the process and helps maintain a creative balance between 'the pitfalls of naive objectivism and the nihilism of anarchic relativism' (White, 1997, p.751).

The methodologies of research in various disciplines in the social sciences thus need to be explored for concepts relevant to the demands of the process of social assessment. The suggestion being made here is that a CA/B framework provides a specific research methodology that meets the needs of social and health workers who endeavour to understand and assess the lives of people belonging to very different social divisions, taking account of the power issues which divide all those concerned, including the assessors. It incorporates concepts drawn from different social science methodologies in a holistic, open-ended way that combines values and methodology, and is therefore primed for further development and criticism.

Foundations for critical auto/biographical methods

A basic premise is that the need for powerful and subtle tools of analysis lies in the existence of major social divisions which involve fundamental differences of experience and perception (Clifford, 1992–93 and 1994). A consequence of this is that the question of values in social science is centre stage, because of the necessarily situated, participant status of any possible knower. It is therefore rational and desirable that values are themselves also the subject of discussion, and are openly and intentionally locked into a methodological framework, rather than cast in the role of hidden underpinning.

The question of values is familiar territory in the social sciences, and the area of values is a fundamental place to begin the quest for basic principles for a methodology relevant to the applied social sciences. I have therefore tried to access the perspectives of people who are outside the dominant academic traditions – though I am restricted in the ways I can do this, because of my own limited experience and knowledge. This is to make simultaneously an ethical and methodological choice, the need for which can be justified in sociological terms as an indispensable strategy for adequately understanding the social world in view of the dominance of established interests and concepts over our perception and creation of 'reality' (Scambler, 1996).

I have investigated basic principles mainly in the writings of women belonging to differing social divisions, who themselves have access to perspectives drawn from their own experience. One early example has been the work of a black male anthropologist who has analysed black culture, and used his conversations with black interviewees as a way of sharing and checking the analysis (Gwaltney, 1980). Similarly, Patricia Hill Collins has attempted to elucidate basic principles of understanding in the social sciences, and has deliberately not only drawn on her own experience as a black woman, but has made a point of discussing her conclusions with other black women (Collins, 1990). Not only is this seen as a matter of ethical practice, it reflects a position which can be derived from their discussion of social science method. There are a number of perspectives emanating from 'black feminisms' (the phrase itself is an over-simplification – see Nain, 1991; Mirza, 1997b), but the contributions of people drawing on the experience of *other* oppressed groups also give access to those who are willing to listen to 'counterhegemonic' perspectives (Personal Narratives Group, 1989). This means, for example, listening to the perspectives of disabled people who are not only critical of disabling physical environments (Oliver, 1992b), but also critical of disabling social theories and methodologies (e.g. Oliver, 1992a; Morris, 1992b). I have also drawn on the efforts of others to understand the perspectives of oppressed groups to which they themselves do *not* belong (an issue pertinent to myself). For example, I have drawn on Fiona Williams's attempt to understand black perspectives in social policy as a white woman (Williams, 1989), and David Morgan's discussion of feminist principles of method (Morgan, 1992). I have also drawn on white feminists, including lesbian writers whose keen awareness of difference and reflexivity has been influential both in understanding the theory and in the choice of terminology in this book (Stanley, 1987; 1990; 1992; 1993; 1994; 1996; Stanley and Wise, 1983 and 1994).

My understanding of these authors produces some basic principles which overlap and have to be taken together. Each can be read differently depending on theory and interpretation: my aim here is not to argue for a closed (foundational or essentialist) system of concepts, but to contend that these principles can and should form the basis for a methodology in health and social welfare simply because it provides the best account currently available of how to understand and position oneself as a participant and observer in making a social assessment. (They may obviously have relevance to other issues.) I produce here a summary, each item of which I will further explain and discuss below.

Methodology and oppression

It is essential that the methods used to understand and assess people and social situations are self-critically linked to a relevant research methodology, in relation to their content, form, process and procedure, and that this methodology is informed by the perspectives of oppressed groups themselves. There is therefore an explicit relationship built into this framework with distinctive values on the one hand and (simultaneously) specific concepts of research methodology and social theory on the other.

Social difference

It is important to systematically analyse social differences that exist between the dominant and dominated social groups of all the major social divisions within society, usually identified as 'race', class, gender, sexual preference, disability and age. Differences can also be identified in relation to other social divisions, such as health status, religion and region.

Differences within and across the social divisions categories also have to be thoroughly taken into account. The complexity of oppression arises from their interconnections and overlaps, specific to particular circumstances, individuals and groups.

Reflexivity

The observer has to be understood as a participant within the theoretical and practical framework. The mutual involvement of the observer and the observed implies that their perceptions interact. The *values* and perspectives of both are therefore central to the process of assessment. However, this process can only be understood in the context of the power differentials between them. This personal interaction is thus understood not only in psychological terms, but also as a matter of sociology, history, ethics and politics.

Historical location in time and space

People's life experiences and events need to be specifically related to concrete times and places in the process of constructing historical and sociological accounts of their changing lives, rather than being viewed through the perspective of preconceptions developed from academic – or common-sense – theories.

Multi-disciplinary connections should be sought between individual, family, community and social histories. The life histories of individuals, including their medical and psychological histories, are thus given a real, concrete, geographical and historical context, focusing on the specific, rather than using abstract categories of either psychological or sociological analysis.

Interacting social systems

Personal biographies must be placed within the wider context of social structures. By taking account of the interactions of the different levels of social life, the individual's situation is viewed in relation to various social systems. This includes the family, peer groups, organisations, communities, and so on up to and including the international context. All these social systems will have a specific direct and/or indirect impact on individual biography, and conversely, the individual's actions themselves have a wider significance, both constituting and changing the systems in which they are involved.

It is *not* assumed that these systems function homeostatically (they do not always adjust themselves successfully when disturbed by internal or external changes), nor that they are autonomous, nor that their identification is incontestable. This means that causation may be internal or external to a system, and that the definition and continued functioning of a system cannot be assumed, but should be assessed within changing historical circumstances.

Power

It is also essential to analyse the distribution of material wealth and power, including the simultaneous impact of unequal power relationships in the present, and the historical accumulation of cultural and economic capital against which oppressed groups struggle.

Power issues in social relationships need to be considered at different levels: at the level of political, social and economic structures, *and* at the level of personal power arising from cultural, institutional and psychological factors. Power may be exercised over people tacitly or overtly, but may also be actively produced and wielded by people. The bottom line of analysis is the access of individuals, groups and agencies to physical and material resources, which help meet their needs and develop their strength and potential.

Explanation of Figure 1

1   The methodological framework of CA/B principles is summarised in the diagram, attempting to represent the basic principles visually. It uses lifelines which are situated in relation to each other in time and space. The use of single life lines is common in social work practice, and has begun to be used in feminist social research (Davies, 1996). In this diagram the life line is assumed to represent not only the 'objective' chronological aspects of a life history but also the 'subjective' meanings and perspectives of participants, as expressed in oral histories.

2   Historical location is given by the accurate historical dating required, and by the identification of place and changes of place over time. The history and sociology of the life-course thus contextualise lifespan psychological development.

3   Social difference is represented in two ways: firstly, by the inclusion of social divisions themselves – partial, fragmented social systems within

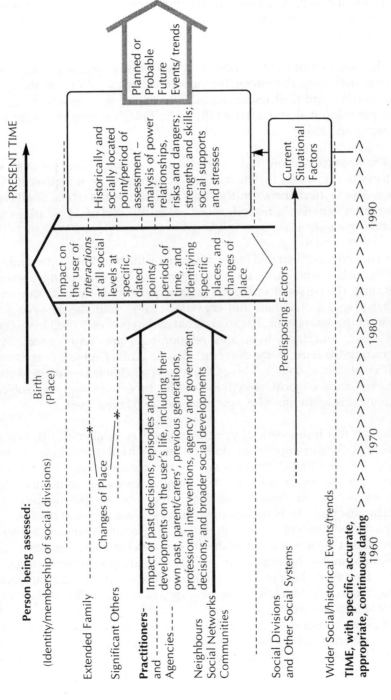

Oral histories/life stories of individuals are represented by life lines; their psychological development is contextualised by a life-course sociology focusing on the social divisions and assessed by an auto/biographically located practitioner.

Figure 1 A critical auto/biographical framework for social assessment

wider social history, and having differential impacts on any specific situation – and secondly, by the identification of specific individuals' membership of the social divisions, as far as appropriate and possible.

4   The fourth principle of power is represented (inadequately) by the arrows, indicating the interactive impact of causal factors on the lives of individuals – and their impact on other lives and systems – both vertically (at a point in time) and horizontally (over time), creating changing needs, strengths and risks.

5   The interconnection and interaction of personal and political social systems is illustrated by the vertical dimension, which represents social space. The vertical arrows in the diagram indicate the interaction between different system levels, from the personal micro-level of relationships to the political macro-level.

6   Reflexivity is illustrated in the diagram by the time lines representing the practitioner(s) who make the assessment and the employing agency (or agencies). The personal and professional experience of the assessing worker is thus placed individually and organisationally *within* the framework, and is part of the assessment. The stories told and hypotheses used by users and assessors about their lives and relationships are 'represented' by the interacting life lines, so the diagram takes account of subjective meaning as well as 'objective' data. However, there is an inevitable tension between the apparent chronological objectivity of the time lines and the subjective meaning and memories of people's life stories (Davis, 1996).

Although this framework of principles has been deliberately drawn from writers with anti-oppressive political and ethical commitments, it can readily be seen that it connects with many contemporary and traditional themes in the philosophy of the social sciences, in multi-disciplinary approaches to life history research, and also in postmodern, post-structuralist thought. However, there are also some points of tension.

The noted theorist of interpretative biography Norman Denzin has asserted that the recent return of the life story celebrates the importance of the individual under the conservative politics of late postmodernism (Denzin, 1992). However, the aim of this framework for critical auto/biographical research into individual lives is to provide a rationale for the study of micro-social situations sensitive to the experience of social oppressions, not for a justification of oppressive individual experiences by neglecting the wider social systems and histories which impinge on people's lives.

This framework is not presented simply as a symbolic interactionist life history approach, since the social and historical structuring of experience by the political economy is also taken into account, as well as the intersubjective negotiation of meaning within and between individual lives. These brief indications of the affinities that CA/B has with contemporary social theories will be revisited and expanded throughout Part One, and occasionally cited in Part Two.

First-principle implications

Methods and methodology

The implications of basing assessment practice in health and social welfare on a CA/B research methodology are numerous. The principle that methods used to understand and assess people and social situations should be linked to a relevant research methodology, and that this methodology is informed by the perspectives of oppressed groups themselves, immediately emphasises the connection between principles of method and principles of value. They are integrally connected, so that the values and ethics are *not* external, desirable extras, but are implicated in the nature of the methodology itself. For example, the principle of difference questions the assumptions and values of all participants in the light of the major cultural and social divisions. The principle of reflexivity directs critical attention to the role of the assessor as participant: the values of assessors' perspectives and the ethics and implications of their interactions with others. This research methodology is one in which the researchers are actors who must be reflexively aware of the nature of their values, and consciously make ethical and political choices.

The first implication of this first principle concerning methodology is therefore that it demands a thoroughly questioning and critical attitude towards the values of the assessor, with special reference to the relationship of the assessor to oppressed social groups in general. This view of values is consistent both with recent student texts in health and social welfare (e.g. Webb and Tossell, 1991; Thompson, 1993; Dalrymple and Burke, 1995) and with recent academic discussions of value issues in relation to social welfare (Hugman and Smith, 1995; Banks, 1995). However, it has been rightly pointed out that following criticism of the (partially) anti-discriminatory position of the Central Council for Education and Training in Social Work in its rules on training (CCETSW, 1989), the subsequent revision was not simply the result of a right-wing backlash. The danger of reducing feminist ideas on difference and diversity to an orthodoxy of discrete categories of oppression was also a relevant factor (Featherstone and Lancaster, 1997, p.57). There is also the opposite danger of reducing ideas of difference to relativistic concepts of individual circumstance which do not take experiences of personal and structural oppression seriously. It is proposed here that the combination of concepts presented above avoids either fallacy, and the issue will be discussed further in later chapters.

In addition, in the context of a specific situation, the values of the assessor and their particular range of social experience need to be interrogated in relation to the particular others with whom communications may take place. Part of that interrogation will not only be concerned with the individual(s) making the assessment, but also with the organisation for which they work, and whether the institutional arrangements for making assessments are structured in ways that ignore the implications of the methodology (and if they are, what that implies for the assessment). For example, by not employing black assessors, or by managing the organisation with predominantly middle-class males, or not providing disabled access, organisations can and do customarily have a fundamental influence on the nature of assessments.

Another basic implication of this first principle is that the methodology provides the basis for making judgements which should thoroughly permeate the assessment. This means that the principles form a theoretical framework which provides a kind of template with which all forms of assessment need to conform. This applies whether the information for the assessment is very sketchy or very detailed, whether the process is very short or long, and whether the information-gathering is pre-planned according to the categories of a pro forma or questionnaire, or whether the interview is semi-structured or open. The design and execution of interviews needs to take account of these principles in the planning stages, and the same principles need to be used in the review stages. There needs to be permeation of the process of investigation and assessment by the basic principles, but also a separate review check on the assessment based on the principles, before deciding about intervention. This may be necessary at more than one stage, depending on how complex the particular assessment is.

Both the reactions of the users to the assessment process *and* the changing perspectives of the professionals need to be scrutinised within this framework, so that the reactions of those being assessed can be understood as a specific response to a particular set of powerful relationships at a particular point in their lives, the life of the agency and its representatives, and wider family and social history. The methodology thus ensures continuity as well as comprehensiveness of assessment, facilitating an understanding of interventive assessment, where assessment and 'treatment' occur simultaneously over a period of time. The methodology should also provide the infrastructure for any further more specialised assessments. It is accepted that more specialised and detailed methods of assessment, drawing on different theoretical resources (Milner and O'Byrne, 1988), and assessment schedules focusing on specific problem areas will often be required, in addition to this basic conceptual framework. These methods will always need to be critically assessed so that their methods and procedures are consistent with the basic CA/B principles (see Figure 2).

The unifying role of the methodology in relation to the procedures and processes of assessment has implications in relation to the comprehensiveness of assessments (note that the principles overlap and interact as a methodological whole, and therefore need to be taken together). All assessments should at least have the potential of working towards being 'comprehensive' because of their relationship to the methodology, but workers have to make decisions about the degree of investigation which is appropriate for the purposes of that particular assessment, taking into account the ethical and legal issues, identifying any information shortfalls, the reasons for them, and any proposed action. However, it is also a crucial implication of this methodology that because of the processual nature of social assessment and the changing values and perspectives of worker and service user and multi-professional relationships, it is neither accurate nor helpful to assume that there is an identifiable stage when a 'comprehensive' assessment has been 'done', if this implies that fundamental issues do not need to be re-examined. Nor is it helpful to automatically assume that the more information which can be extracted and used, the better. The level and completeness of information has to be an ethical, political and professional decision, balancing the function and responsibilities of the agency and the interests and needs of users and other parties who may be directly or indirectly affected. The methodology provides some comprehensive 'cover': the assessor does not need to assume that a longer or more in-depth assessment is necessarily preferable, and should be able to justify the decision, having reviewed the basic principles for assessment.

Although in practice there may be many reasons why further information either cannot or should not be sought, there are (obviously) good research-methodological reasons why, generally speaking, further information is desirable, especially in understanding the complexities of micro-social situations, where various social sciences have emphasised the importance of 'rich, detailed data' (Charmaz, 1994), often drawing on anthropological approaches to the same issue of 'thick description' (Geertz, 1973). The principle of using the richness and specific detail of narrative to capture the many-layered complexities of the lives of black women (Etter-Lewis, 1991) also supports the health or social worker's detailed knowledge of the interconnected lives of others in relation to their own.

An interesting comparison with detailed professional assessments can be drawn by looking at the use of narrative in the non-fiction novel, as in Truman Capote's *In Cold Blood*, where a rich, detailed account is given of a

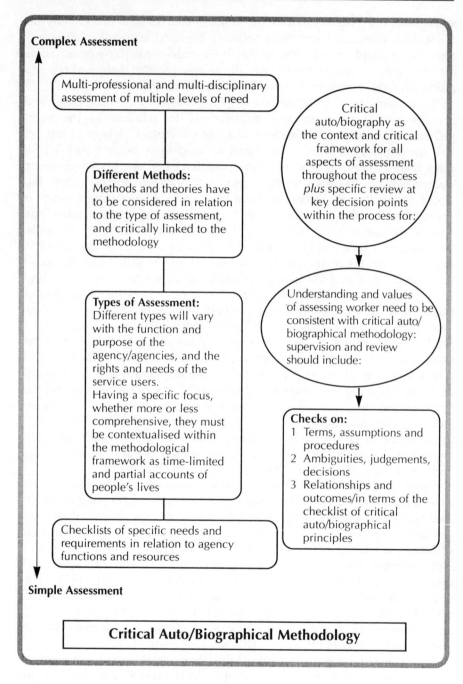

Complex Assessment

Multi-professional and multi-disciplinary assessment of multiple levels of need

Different Methods:
Methods and theories have to be considered in relation to the type of assessment, and critically linked to the methodology

Critical auto/biography as the context and critical framework for all aspects of assessment throughout the process *plus* specific review at key decision points within the process for:

Types of Assessment:
Different types will vary with the function and purpose of the agency/agencies, and the rights and needs of the service users.
Having a specific focus, whether more or less comprehensive, they must be contextualised within the methodological framework as time-limited and partial accounts of people's lives

Understanding and values of assessing worker need to be consistent with critical auto/biographical methodology: supervision and review should include:

Checks on:
1 Terms, assumptions and procedures
2 Ambiguities, judgements, decisions
3 Relationships and outcomes/in terms of the checklist of critical auto/biographical principles

Checklists of specific needs and requirements in relation to agency functions and resources

Simple Assessment

Critical Auto/Biographical Methodology

Figure 2   Applying a research methodology to assessment

real-life murder (Zeller, 1995). However, unlike the purpose of a literary work, or that of a conventional piece of research, CA/B methodology does not assume that it is necessarily appropriate in any given context to attempt always to extricate any particular level of detail from stories of people's lives. This has to be a negotiated decision: an *action*, for which both parties have degrees of ethical, legal and political accountability.

Finally, because critical auto/biography is being presented as a research methodology, and because of its emphasis on multiple perspectives generated (amongst other factors) by social divisions, it is doubly important for the assessors not only to generate hypotheses in an informed and critical way, but also to look for *disconfirmation* of their hypotheses in a similarly informed way, rather than search for confirmation of their own views (Strachan and Tallant, 1997, pp.21–3). Sheppard's view of the process of qualitative research fails to identify the importance of searching for different perspectives, hypotheses and disconfirming data from the sources where they are most likely to be found (Sheppard, 1995). The development of clear hypotheses and the availability of disconfirming information is likely to be assisted if the implications of critical auto/biography are followed: that rival perspectives, views and information are likely to be found by deliberately enquiring for them *across* the barriers of power and social division, as represented in specific circumstances by people, whether service users, colleagues or others in the community, who themselves belong to different social divisions and organisations, and have different experiences of social life.

Too often the emphasis is upon finding verifying rather than disconfirming evidence, but the point here is that accepting the Popperian stress on disconfirmation is not enough. You need to know where to look for it in the social world, *and* how to interpret it. Disconfirming evidence and rival perspectives need themselves to be 'read' within the CA/B framework, so that issues of self-interest, power and reflexivity can be assessed. To what extent are disconfirming perspectives or information adequately based on relevant social experience and knowledge, or on dominant ideas directly serving the interests of the powerful? This does not mean that the latter evidence can be dismissed, but it does raise the possibility that there might be explanations which could throw a significant light on the background conditions for those views and their limitations, or for the availability of that evidence.

More importantly, on the other hand, organisations and movements of dominated social groups are clearly places where alternative ideas might be found with great relevance for service users. This orientation to 'empirical' research goes beyond a simple concept of 'bias', and includes the inevitability of incorporating and representing values within research. However, this framework also questions the origins and application of the evaluative concepts upon which the research evidence is based, at the same time as it supports the search for disconfirming evidence, especially in relation to the researcher's own perspectives.

Recent debates about objectivity and bias in research have hinged on issues of epistemology and ethics. Hammersley has rejected the involvement of values (ethical or political) in research, arguing for a 'non-foundational' concept of avoiding bias, so that research is devoted primarily to the production of knowledge, where that end is ultimately judged by the research community (Hammersley, 1993; 1995; 1997; Hammersley and Gomm, 1997a and 1997b). It is significant that feminists have been quick to dispute this avoidance of values (Humphries, 1997; Romm, 1997). It is difficult to see how Hammersley can unequivocally defend academic research communities that have so often in the past represented dominant values in their methods and products as knowledge. The aim of an auto/biographical research methodology is to maximise the likelihood of the production of knowledge by alerting the researcher (and the reader of the research) to the social conditions of knowledge production, especially as they affect themselves (Stanley, 1996).

However, in both social research and social assessment, the aim of representation of reality is not an optional extra, and the production of 'knowledge' has to be the most serious ethical concern, particularly in the context of social assessment, where decisions are made about life and liberty. The dilemma is that values are both integral to the constructive production of knowledge about people's lives and must be included within the methodological framework. But values are also potentially subversive of knowledge-production, dissolving it into subjectivity and politics. The conclusion has to be that this dilemma is contained and held within the framework so that complex issues are grappled with: 'there are no easy ... answers to the real and complex ethical and epistemological issues which feminists have identified in relation to research referentiality, [and] ... these issues shouldn't be ignored' (Stanley, 1996, p.46).

The following summary is offered as a practical aid to assisting the process of questioning the methodological basis of social assessments, taking account of the involvement of values and the need to be able to make the assessment refer to the realities of people's lives (see also Chapters 2 and 3).

A Questionnaire/Summary of the general practical implications

1   How far have the hypotheses utilised in this assessment been sourced from (a) users' perspectives, and (b) the perspectives of relevant oppressed

groups? How clear are they to you as the assessor, or to other experienced colleagues involved? To what extent does this reflect shared or conflicting values and social divisions?

2 To what extent does the recruitment and service policy of the employing agency reflect critical, anti-oppressive values? How much does it reflect dominant forces external to the agency? To what extent is power concentrated in the hands of any particular social group(s) within the agency? Is there a complaints procedures to which users have easy access? Is there a harassment and grievance procedure to which staff have access? How far do ethical principles permeate assessment methods at institutional levels? What are the implications for your assessment?

3 To what extent do the principles of CA/B method permeate the details of the content and process of the assessment? Are there review points in the assessment which permit these principles to be checked through before decisions are taken?

4 To what extent has information been sought from documentary and third-person witness evidence? How far has this conflicted with the user's perspectives, and has any conflict been resolved as consistently as possible with CA/B principles? To what extent have the contributions of different disciplines and professions been brought together in the assessment process? How far and how critically have multiple perspectives been used? How comprehensive is the assessment in relation to the methodological requirements? How comprehensive *should* it be in this case, or how focused?

5 How far have you sought information which could *disconfirm* the working hypotheses which you have been using? Who disagrees with them, and why? How far does conflicting information and argument reflect different perspectives, values and positions of relative power? What further evidence would help to answer these issues? How far have the original hypotheses been reformulated? Have alternative views from relevant organisations of oppressed social groups been considered or involved anywhere in the process?

6 How far can you demonstrate that you are able (assuming it is appropriate) to offer a detailed, 'thick' description of current and past circumstances, drawing on multiple observations, (cf. White, 1997, p.750), social history interviews, documentary evidence and differing perspectives? (Note: Social workers and other low status health and welfare workers (and users or carers) sometimes have detailed knowledge which is not given proper credit.)

This approach provides guidance to the kind of hypotheses which it will be useful to examine, and how to progress this micro-research. It simultaneously provides some indication of the ethical and political questions that will be encountered, as well as the intellectual scepticism that is required in the search for practice wisdom. This is not the only research method that is relevant to assessment in health and welfare work (and it is not intended to rule out other traditional methods such as behavioural or psychodynamic assessment), but it is particularly appropriate to the task of social assessment of people's lives, and provides a multi-professional and multi-disciplinary framework which alerts the worker to issues of power and difference which affect themselves and their assessments. It contextualises other kinds of assessment – in health, education, psychology or law. It is a comprehensive basis for social assessment.

2 Taking social difference seriously

Introduction

This chapter examines social difference in relation to assessment, and argues that major social divisions should be taken seriously. However, the problem is *how* to do this when the theory is contentious and practice is even more so. It is essential to try to encompass the infinite variability of social differences at the individual level, and to try to grasp the broader-structured, changing relationships at group and societal levels. In order to do this effectively in the practical context of social assessment, the major social differences have to be considered systematically, both separately and together, and integrated into a complex analysis which is capable of encompassing the subtle, micro-social as well as the gross qualitative and quantitative differences between different social situations.

This chapter examines problems of differing perspectives, concepts and values, and some of the strategies that have been proposed for coping theoretically and in practice. It discusses briefly each of the major social divisions and their internal divisions, their inter-relationships, similarities and differences, and considers some of the implications for research and assessment of social differences in micro-social situations.

Social difference and assessment

It is important to thoroughly analyse social differences in social assessment because it is these differences that conceptually, politically and socially engender many of the problems which lead to the referral for assessment.

Conceptually, the difficulty of interpreting human behaviour arises not just from the sheer multiplicity of differences between people, but because the major social divisions are indicative of fundamental differences of experience and perspective which make it difficult for people to understand the 'other'. Socially and politically, the difficulties of assessment arise from the multiple oppressions and disadvantages that are caused by the existence of social divisions, and because the practical problem is to do with assessing precisely those who belong to the dominated social divisions, and who have suffered discrimination and oppression.

Therefore, analysis in social assessment has to take account of the relationship that exists between the dominant and dominated social groups of all the major social divisions. These are often but not universally identified as: 'race', class, gender, gays and lesbians, disability and age (including at least two major subgroups – children and young people, and older people). Differences can also be identified in relation to other significant social divisions, for example: health status, including mental health status, HIV and AIDS status, religion, culture, region and nationality. Quantitative and qualitative differences *within* the social divisions categories also have to be taken into account.

The overall picture is thus one of multiple and fractured interconnection and overlap between varying social divisions, specific to particular social and historical circumstances. However, there are commonalities as well as differences, and some of the multiple connections have reinforcing rather than splintering effects. This can be true of dominated groups where, for instance, poverty and low social class status often accompany membership of other groups, such as being disabled, older, black or female. Conversely, the dominant divisions also often overlap in the shape of white, able-bodied, middle-class men.

The aim here will be to set out a view of social division which broadly reflects some of the major concerns of dominated groups themselves, but also informed by contemporary social theory (particularly in its relation to research methodology). This should produce a concept of social difference which has utility in understanding and assessing the lives of people who frequently have experience of one or more of the various oppressions.

Background: Different concepts and values

Long before postmodern and post-structural theories were popularised, it was clear to many working within moral, social and political philosophy that social and political concepts were always debated because they reflected basic differences in values and perspectives which were linked to differing linguistic communities and social discourses. The early arguments of Winch about the complexities involved in the idea of a social science drew on Wittgenstein's views about the nature of ordinary 'language games' (Wittgenstein, 1963). The importance of seeing the meaning of concepts as defined by their actual use in particular social discourses rather than given in some 'essential' way by reference to external realities had important implications for social science (Winch, 1965). The concepts used in social science were drawn from ordinary discourse, and were the continual subject of dispute between differing groups and individuals with differing values and ideas about society. There could therefore be no 'essential' meaning to these concepts. Social concepts have thus long been regarded as 'essentially contested' (Gallie, 1964; MacIntyre, 1973) because of persistently conflicting and changing values and perspectives between social groups, which consequently provide major challenges to interpretation and application, especially in areas of applied social science such as social assessment.

Social work in particular has also been well aware for a long time of the connections between contested values, concepts and differing social groups and communities. Historically, the difficulty of understanding and using concepts across differing cultures in social work practice led to the device of distinguishing between 'primary' and 'secondary' values. The first represented basic ethical values, and the second reflected the perspectives of differing cultures in different times and places within and between societies (Konopka, 1958). This was a worthy, if insufficient, attempt to cope with the issues. The basic primary values were then elaborated by academic moral philosophers in the 1970s and 1980s as a foundation for making moral and conceptual judgements in both health and welfare services, based on Kantian ethics and Mill's Utilitarianism (Plant, 1970; Timms and Watson, 1976 and 1979; Downie, 1977; Downie and Telfer, 1980; Downie and Calman, 1987). This universalistic moral position came under attack at the time from those who questioned the validity of assuming that individualistic liberal ethics were necessarily a universal or primary basis for values and the evaluation of social situations (Simpkin, 1979; Clifford, 1982), and has since been increasingly called into question by feminist and postmodernist moral and cultural critiques. Social workers and social work academics have appreciated the significance of these critiques, and have produced numerous studies of the complexities of values and social concepts over the past decade, influenced by feminist and postmodernist thought (Rojek, Peacock and Collins, 1988 and 1989; Rodger, 1991; Sands and Nuccio, 1992; Stenson, 1993; Saleeby, 1994; Parton, 1994a and 1994b; Featherstone and Fawcett, 1995b; Katz, 1995; V. White, 1995).

Postmodernism and social difference

The trend of postmodernist social theory in recent years has been in the direction of the recognition of ever greater subtleties of concepts of difference (Barrett, 1989), with increasing criticism of any attempt to identify either an overarching theoretical framework or to prioritise any particular social difference as having greater explanatory value than any other.

A common theme of accounts of the rise of postmodernism and post-structuralism in social theory is the identification of major social divisions as sites of misconceived theoretical constructions. Monolithic or totalising attempts to explain society solely in terms of either social class or gender differences have been attacked, and have given way to an awareness of the multiple, shifting nature of social relationships, which cannot be caught in one explanatory scheme. In addition, the great theme of postmodern thought is how explanations are themselves part of discourse. Indeed, the fashion has been to challenge the whole concept of reference to reality: discourse is understood as self-referring and self-contained. The real world is 'extra-discursive', and cannot be directly 'grasped' by language.

There are thus considerable barriers to understanding the real social world, precisely because of the multiple social and cultural differences exemplified in the differing constructions and discourses which are used to describe and create it. This can be understood as a challenge to conservative ways of thinking, of whatever political colour, but can also be interpreted as radically liberal or nihilistic and apolitical.

Attempts to relate these theories of social difference to child protection, and to older people, describe the relevance of recent academic debate in terms of its rejection of grand theory, of fixed categories of group and individual identity, and of binary oppositions between them. Instead, authors advocate: 'multi-factor explorations which are specifically located, self critical and which recognise that people shift and change ... retaining a suspicion of coherent theories which purport to tell the truth about the world as it is' (Featherstone and Fawcett, 1995a, p.76). A number of implications for child protection are proposed: for example, that generalisations about abusive men, peaceful women and powerless children are inaccurate and unhelpful, as gender and age should not be used as fixed categories. Similarly, older people are not to be located in terms of a fixed view of the life-course, indeed: 'time, ageing and the historical past are not entirely real' (Phillips, 1996, p.144). The conclusion of some applications of postmodernism to understanding social situations seems to be to reposition theory in favour of individual psychology and subjective meaning, and away from sociology. There is a: '"turn" to psychoanalytic perspectives by many who espouse postmodern/poststructuralist perspectives'

(Featherstone and Fawcett, 1995a, p.65). This seems questionable in so far as it tends to cede the basis of assessing social situations to one particular expert discipline, ignoring economic, political, legal and social structures.

There are some strengths to this account of social difference, notably the insistence on the complexity and specificity of the categories, issues which are certainly germane to assessing social situations. However, some contemporary feminists and some black writers are critical of aspects of postmodernism's origins and potential in relation to social difference. It has been argued that its origins lie partly in the backlash against feminist writing in the 1970s, which in any case had anticipated many of the most useful aspects of these white, male academic theories (Stanley and Wise, 1994, Postscript). These are judgements which are heatedly disputed amongst feminists, (e.g. Hoff 1994a; 1994b; 1996; Kent, 1996; Ramazanoglou, 1996). However, it is certainly the case that although there are good grounds for taking the 'anti-foundationalism' of post modernism seriously, the critique of rational explanatory theory is not new, and has been part of traditional conservative political thought for a long time, (cf. Oakeshott, 1933 and 1962). It is not surprising therefore that some versions of postmodernism are treated with suspicion by many feminists because of their apparent apolitical reductionism.

An understanding of social divisions which can be reduced to infinite subjective variation is of little use either to those social groups which have struggled against oppression, or to researchers or health and welfare workers trying to make sense in their assessments of the social conditions affecting individual and group situations. Similarly, although the social and linguistic construction of social relations is a fundamental feature of any contemporary social theory, there is little to be gained by overemphasising the construction of reality by language to the point where there appears to be no extra-discursive reality, and where non-linguistic factors assume an ever diminishing role in social explanation. However, much depends on exactly how the concepts of the various postmodernist and post-structuralist thinkers are interpreted. Clearly, some have found them useful and stimulating in the ways indicated, and they are used by many to demonstrate the importance of social difference. Others, however, caution against an overly fragmented view of social relationships, especially in view of evidence of increasing polarisation in the 1980s and 1990s, advising that: 'contemporary societies are both fragmented *and* subjected to polarizing and unifying tendencies' (Bradley, 1996, p.210). An understanding of the concepts and perspectives which flow from social difference thus needs to take account of the 'persisting nature of social hierarchies, as well as the interplay of relationships which gives rise to ... fractured identities' (Bradley, 1996, p.214).

Social difference: Perspectives of the oppressed

Some of the most valuable contributions towards interpreting and deploying the concepts of social theory in ways that positively contribute to an understanding of the various social oppressions are made by writers consciously drawing on their perspectives and experience as members of dominated groups themselves. Attending to these perspectives therefore acknowledges from the beginning judgements of value, and does not pretend to bypass the socio-cultural construction of concepts. It *does* imply that some strategies for dealing with these complexities are more fruitful, adequate, effective and ethical than others. The reality of major social divisions is central to this book, and whilst the uniqueness of individual experience is fully appreciated, the most useful tactic is to return repeatedly both to the broad, interconnected structuring effects of dominant social groups on the one hand, and on the other, to the distinctive generative practices and peculiarities of ordinary individual lives. Both ends of this spectrum have to be contextualised by the mezzo-social world of groups, communities and organisations where structural and personal factors interact – where social assessment takes place.

The dichotomy between overarching theory on the one hand and anti-foundationalism on the other is itself a binary opposition, as Stanley and Wise have pointed out in the Postscript to the second edition of their study of feminist research methodology (Stanley and Wise, 1994). Stanley's auto/biographical theory therefore rests on the kind of 'fractured foundationalism' which, whilst accepting the postmodernist critique of monolithic grand theories, insists that the related binary opposition between women and men, fundamental to any feminist theory, is *not* to be rejected: 'Without this a distinctively feminist philosophy and praxis would no longer exist, would be dissolved into an apparently ungendered deconstructionist position' (Stanley and Wise, 1994, p.205). The same kind of consideration arises in relation to the other major social divisions, and the complexity and specificity of social assessment arises from the interconnecting and overlapping of a number of fractured binary oppositions – not from a reduction of these complex and related social practices to the unmediated chaos of individual psychology and personal circumstance.

The theoretical arguments discussed here are intended to convey the importance of social divisions, their complexity and interconnectedness, and the relationship between understanding and experiencing social difference and oppression. Experience itself is rightly not accepted as an absolute category by many writers, but it remains an important concept for members of social divisions concerned by the experience of oppression. The concept underlies many feminist writings, and it is the complexity of personal experience in relation to the social divisions that has produced significant work in social research methodology that is directly relevant to social assessment. For example, the views of Stanley and Wise referred to above were developed from their original perceptions about their own lesbian feminist experience and its implications for research methodology, leading to the rejection of totalising theories which ignored their own specific experience and understanding of social life (Stanley and Wise, 1983).

Similarly, many black women have contributed to an understanding of social difference that centres on both the pivotal importance and multiplicity of social divisions in their own lives. Over the past fifteen years, black women have made a substantial contribution to understanding social division, which from the beginning was characterised by an awareness of the complex interconnection of social differences in their own experience. The earlier black feminists focused particularly on 'race', class and gender, criticising black men, and Marxist and feminist theorists when black issues relating to women were marginalised or ignored (Carby, 1982; Davis, 1982; hooks, 1982 and 1984; Amos et al., 1984; Lorde, 1984a; Bryan, Dadzie and Scarfe, 1985; Bhavnani, 1986). A growing self-confidence and awareness of the value of their theoretical contribution in the social sciences was marked by a further body of academic publications which nevertheless still drew on their varied experiences of oppression (e.g. Collins, 1990; Phoenix, 1990; Parmar, 1990; Bhavnani, 1990 and 1993; Anthias and Yuval-Davis, 1990 and 1992; hooks, 1991 and 1994; James and Busia, 1993).

An important development in black feminist thought has been an increasing awareness of the problems associated with the term 'black', arising from the earlier focus on its use as a political expression highlighting the oppression of non-white women in white-dominated societies. Although always keenly aware of differences of ethnicity, culture, skin colour and nationality between 'black' women, there is even greater sensitivity to the range of women who may suffer racism but do not accept this term (e.g. Nain, 1991), and those who have a 'mixed parentage' or 'dual heritage', and do not lay claim to an undifferentiated original 'black' identity, and who thus exist on the margins of the margins (Ifekwunigwe, 1997; Ahmed, 1997; Ang-Lygate, 1997; Rassool, 1997).

In addition to these black women's contributions, white feminists, black men, gays, lesbians and disabled writers have made numerous contributions to understanding the importance of social difference in recent years, many of them having been influenced by black feminist writings. Recent white feminists especially have responded to the challenge of black perspectives positively, developing further their conception of social difference, sometimes also influenced by postmodern and post-structural ideas about difference in theory (Ramazanoglou, 1989; Nicholson, 1990; Fergueson and Wicke, 1994), research practice (Opie, 1993; Maynard, 1994a and 1994b) and health and welfare policy and practice (e.g. Williams, 1989; Holland, 1990; Humphries, 1996a). However, there have been continuing reservations by white and black feminists and others about the postmodern disapproval of 'fixed categories', and about the appropriateness of holding on to concepts of social division.

The position of Stanley and Wise referred to above in relation to auto/biography is reflected in the position of black feminists who, whilst insisting on the importance of recognising the complex and shifting nature of social differences and deconstructing their own use of the term 'black', remain committed to the view that the binary opposition between 'fixed categories' of black and white should not be entirely rejected. As Mirza indicates in her discussion of the outlook of contemporary British black women: 'In spite of postmodernism, little has changed for the majority of black women, globally and nationally. For them power is not diffuse, localised and particular. Power is as centralized and secure as it always has been' (Mirza, 1997b, p.20). She advocates vigilance against the appropriation of black feminist experience by 'masculinist postmodern discourse', and asserts that: 'you can have difference (polyvocality) within a conscious construction of sameness (i.e. black feminism)' (Mirza, 1997b, p.21).

The idea of a 'fractured foundationalist' position which insists on the importance of binary oppositions between male and female, black and white, and all the other dualisms of social division seems essential for the realities of conflict and oppression to be fully appreciated. Yet this position equally acknowledges the importance of deconstructing these categories, and continually reassessing the changing, fractured relationships and constructions that are involved. The critical auto/biographical method aims to achieve this in relation to the study of micro-social situations by its emphasis upon time and place, on the complexity and interconnection of social divisions, and the reflexive positioning of the participant-observers.

Social difference and research methodology

The different social divisions, when considered separately or in various combinations, have produced a variety of insights relevant to social research methodology and therefore to social assessment. There is only space here to mention some of them, and there will inevitably be gaps which arise because of the writer's ignorance and inability to share all the different perspectives of the wide range of interconnected oppressions. The following is therefore only a partial review of the wealth of insights and ideas about research that have been generated in recent times which can inform the development of a sound theoretical base for social assessment. (A summary of the implications for assessment practice is appended in the form of questions for social assessors at the end of this chapter.) Some of these contributions are discussed in more detail elsewhere in the first part of this book.

My contention is that various writers, drawing productively and consciously on the perspectives of the dominated groups to which they belong, have made proposals for understanding and researching their own situations and experiences which are broadly consistent with the CA/B framework suggested here. It is not being suggested that there is a single identifiable position, but that there are some common enough themes that appear to be significant.

Some of the most decisive contributions of white and black feminists have been discussed or referred to above, but the range of feminist ideas about research is extensive (Campbell, 1995). The general implications for social research must include a systematic investigation of the broad categories of social division, as well as an equally methodical consideration of the interconnections, overlaps and specificity of social difference as it appears in the whole process of social research and assessment. It must include sensitivity to the conceptualisation and terminology of the research project, but also to the realities of changing balances of power and control arising from membership of different social divisions internally within the research process, and externally in the institutions and organisations which provide the funding, the political and economic framework. Black and white feminist research methodologies have been a particularly important source in the search for a theoretical basis for assessment, and are repeatedly cited in the following chapters.

There is a recurrent appeal in both black and white feminist discussions of social theory and research method about the need to listen to and understand the life stories of black and white women. This is discussed further in Chapter 4 in relation to historical location, where the feminist use of oral history and the relevance of life-course sociology is examined. Both black and white feminists have placed considerable emphasis on the importance of recovering the voices of women in history, and an understanding of women's lives that does not attend to these demands appears to be inadequate. Equally, they have both emphasised the importance of the connections between women – the sociality and collective aspects of women's lives – as a fundamental part of social research methodology. This is also discussed in Chapter 5 in the context of interacting social systems. They also place particular stress on issues of reflexivity and power, which are again discussed in detail in subsequent chapters. The point here is that the dominated groups have specific value perspectives which have implications for any social research methodology, and especially for the interpretation of lives.

Lesbian and gay contributions to social theory and research methodology have been developing in recent years, and amongst other issues, they have emphasised the importance of localised social practices, in which power is exercised and resisted. They have usefully drawn on both their own experience and on social theory to demonstrate the significance of practices of power in their lives. The post-structuralist Foucault, as a gay male, is seen by some gays as an icon in this regard (Halperin, 1995), but lesbian writers also make impressive critical use of his theories (Cooper, 1995). Lesbian writers have also made significant contributions in the area of understanding changing identities (Lorde, 1984b; Martin, 1988; Fuentes, 1995), and both gay and lesbian writers have made stimulating contributions to oral history writing (e.g. Cant and Hemmings, 1988; Lesbian History Group, 1989; Lesbian Oral History Group, 1989; Gay Men's Oral History Group, 1989). As already noted above, Stanley and Wise write from an explicitly lesbian as well as a feminist position, and Stanley's auto/biographical theory has been important in writing this book.

Disabled writers have made some notable contributions to social theory and social research methodology in the past decade, and their work will be discussed in some detail in Part Two. They have particularly questioned the assumptions and values of able-bodied research and professional assessment that has delved into the lives of disabled people. By comparison, the traditions of working-class, socialist and Marxist social theory are very long-standing, but have been eclipsed by national and international political events in recent years. They have also been overtaken by developments in social theory itself, having been the principal target of postmodernists and post-structuralists, especially in the form of Althusserian Marxism, which appears to have amply met the criteria for a totalising theoretical structuralism based on the interests of one section of society (Althusser, 1969 and 1971).

Humanist variants of Marxism and humanist socialism had previously been critically attacked by structuralists such as Althusser for placing the human subject at the centre of history. However, despite the decline of class-based social theory, a recent discussion of social class in Britain suggests that a degree of theoretical convergence between neo-Weberian and neo-Marxist sociologists currently exists, focusing on the *persistence* of class differentials between: 'a dominant class based on the ownership of capital; an intermediate class based on the acquisition of educational and/or organisational assets, and a subordinate class based on the possession of physical labour' (Edgell, 1993, p.81). There are thus also continuities as well as disruptions in theorising social class, and despite trenchant feminist and postmodernist criticism of Marxist theories, there is still some relevance of radical, class-oriented issues for research methodology (Harvey, 1990). These continuities are also sometimes evident in black feminist discussions. For example, Mirza recently refers to a Marxist critique of postmodernist concepts of power (Callinicos, 1989) precisely because of the persisting reality of self-legitimising economic and political power structures which are imposed on the lives of poor black women from the centre, rather than simply being produced by local social practices (Mirza, 1997b, p.20).

The social division of age is itself often subdivided crudely into children and young people on the one hand, and older people on the other. Contemporary social theories lay emphasis on the variable social construction of age differences (Pilcher, 1995), so this identification of subdivisions is itself always questionable. The existence of ageism is widely recognised (Bytheway, 1995; Thompson, 1996), but the term is commonly used to refer to discrimination against older people. There will be a discussion of social theory and research method in relation to the assessment of older people in Part Two. The use of life history work, especially oral history and reminiscence, has been an important contribution of workers in this field to the theory and practice of assessment. The theoretical issues involved in researching and assessing children and younger people will also be discussed in Part Two. Health and welfare workers with this group have also made a significant contribution to assessment theory and practice, and the social construction of younger age groups, and their position as oppressed social groups is increasingly recognised, as are the implications of this for research (Scraton, 1997).

Conclusion

A recent survey of social division and inequality provided by a woman sociologist reaches the kind of conclusion that appears consistent with the perspective presented here (apart from its regrettable omission of disability from consideration as a major social division). She refers to the: '*double and contradictory* nature of the dynamics of inequality, at once unifying and dividing' (Bradley, 1996, p.211). Whilst inequalities and identities have fragmented, repeatedly dividing and subdividing, as postmodernists and post-structuralists have demonstrated, there have equally been polarising tendencies in modern societies in which continuing commonalities of oppression are evident. She therefore ends her account of social division and difference by suggesting that: 'A reworked version of modernist analysis, benefitting from the critical insights of postmodern and post-structuralist thought, offers the best hope for an adequate understanding of ... the nature of contemporary society, both fragmenting and polarising' (Bradley, 1996, p.214). It is therefore important to analyse *both* the differences and the commonalities in any process of research or assessment.

The conclusion of this discussion of social difference is therefore to recognise that the impact of social divisions has serious effects at the various levels of social practice, including the personal and structural parameters of people's lives. They therefore need to be methodically considered by professionals making social assessments. However, in addition, the social divisions also help to generate alternative perspectives which are reflected in differing values and theories.

The professional social assessment cannot avoid taking up an evaluative position in regard to these differing discourses (if only by default), and the position presented here is that recent theorising by black and white feminists and others taking up a deliberately critical stance offers an approach which is theoretically adequate (for example in relation to Bradley's discussion), and ethically acceptable. It implies the recognition of differing values and concepts across and within differing communities and cultures, but also continuing, changing, structural commonalities. It also implies appreciating the unavoidably reflexive involvement of the professional researcher and/or assessor in owning their own values and assumptions, without the comfort of there being some overarching 'primary' and indisputably moral framework to justify their judgement. It suggests both a continual effort of awareness, and the persistent espousal of a considered evaluative position which is based on the recognition of the theoretical significance, but also the diversity and historical location of the insights, values and perspectives of oppressed groups.

Practical questions for social assessors

Note: These questions must be considered in conjunction with other questions that are appended to the discussion of the other main principles in Part One. The questions can be used with case examples to discuss the application of principles to practice situations.

1   What is the social division membership of all the individuals involved in this assessment, as far as it is possible to tell?

2   Sometimes it is not possible to know the above because they are hidden, or unclear (e.g. some ethnicities, some disabilities, gay or lesbian status). In any particular case, how important/appropriate is it to try to find out, or to bear these in mind?

3   Have you considered *all* the major social divisions systematically?

4   What differences are there *within* each social divisions category (e.g. what

precise kind of disability, ethnicity, age group, etc.) that are relevant to this particular person?

5 What interconnections are there between social divisions in individuals' lives, and what *qualitative* difference does this make (e.g. does a particular person have multiple membership of oppressed social groups, or of powerful groups, or a mixture of both, and how is this interconnection related to the specific kinds of social divisions involved?)

6 What other social differences might apply to the particular person(s) concerned (e.g. mental health status, HIV and AIDS status, religion, culture, region and nationality)?

7 What perspectives and understanding does this person have in relation to their own membership of social divisions, and what social networks (if any) connect them to others in positions similar to theirs, including organisations and movements relevant to their particular oppressions?

8 What commonalities are there between the apparent differences, and how far do social differences reinforce each other in this particular situation?

9 How are concepts of social difference being constructed in the interactions between people (including yourself) involved in this assessment process?

3 Reflexivity: Personal involvement and responsibility

This chapter discusses the implications of reflexivity for social research and assessment. It examines the idea of the assessor as a participant in the social world, the ways in which there is mutual interaction – direct and indirect – between the person assessing a social situation and the persons being assessed, and what the implications of this are for social assessment. It considers the ethics and politics of their structured situations, especially the ways in which service users are, or should be, involved in assessment, and the interaction between this and the responsibility for assessment outcomes, in view of the specific differences, biographies, social systems and powers which constrain and enable them.

Concepts of reflexivity are now common in the social sciences, and especially in contemporary qualitative research methodology (Steier, 1991; Fine, 1994). In the social sciences, theories are said to be reflexive when they refer to themselves: the sociology of knowledge is the classic case of a discipline which must necessarily explain itself within its own theory. In contemporary social science, the concept is of considerable importance to recent theories, including ethnomethodology, structuration theory, feminism and postmodernism. The fundamental reason for this is the trend away from positivist approaches to the social sciences. The researcher is now usually seen as a participant within the social world, and even contemporary 'postpositivist' positions tend to adopt a critical attitude towards the complicating issues of observer involvement – if only because they are also now widely acknowledged in the natural sciences (Guba and Lincoln, 1994).

Reflexivity and modern society

It is worth referring first to the broader concept of reflexivity as used by sociologists to describe contemporary society (Giddens, 1991), because this provides a significant context for issues of reflexivity for individual social researchers and assessors. Scambler asserts that: 'the importance of the concept of reflexivity as defined by Giddens is now widely acknowledged by sociologists' (Scambler, 1996, p.577). Gidden's structuration theory includes a concept of reflexivity in which: 'social practices are constantly examined in the light of incoming information about those practices, thus constitutively altering their character' (Scambler, 1996, p.577). This means that there is no certainty about established institutions and forms of knowledge, leading to the concept of the 'risk society' (Beck, 1992). This view of contemporary social relations is important because it links the concepts of reflexivity and risk, providing the setting for the difficult role of social assessment, a connection which has already had an impact in areas of health and welfare where risk – and risky – assessments have to be made (Parton, 1996a and 1996b; Parton, Thorpe and Wattam, 1997). There appear to be connections between reflexivity and riskiness as an inherent part of assessing social situations, of which assessors are themselves aware, being subjected to changing feedback from agency and government research, as well as within the interactions of an assessment process itself. In addition, the culture of individual risk and blame inclines assessors themselves to find individual faults, and to avoid being found to be at fault themselves.

The implications are about the ways in which the general social climate of reflexive uncertainty has an impact at institutional and individual levels: the 'reflexive monitoring of risk is intrinsic to institutionalised risk systems' (Giddens, 1991, p.119, quoted in Parton, Thorpe and Wattam, 1997, p.237). Explicit in this analysis of contemporary society is the uncertain role played by morals and values in disputable judgements. The dominant value of risk avoidance is an example of a negative concept of harm prevention – a value that is consistent with the more culturally individualised Western societies of the late twentieth century (Douglas, 1986 and 1992). However, this masks ambivalence about positive values: 'Moral standards are not asserted openly, but in quantitative, theoretical and causal forms' (Parton, Thorpe and Wattam, 1997, p.237).

Moreover, this value-based linking of reflexivity and risk in contemporary social practices makes social assessment even more difficult than it need be, as long as these issues are masked and not explicitly accounted for. Ironically, the danger is that the issue of individual reflexive awareness may be used to constrain rather than raise awareness, and Giddens has been criticised for over-emphasising it as a feature of the 'late modern' era. Rather, it is argued: 'Risk and uncertainty are the consequences of pressures to adopt individualistic perspectives in a society characterised by interdependency' (Furlong and Cartmel, 1997, p.113). The aim of a CA/B social research methodology is to provide a basis for social assessment which takes reflexive factors explicitly into account, but within a theoretical framework which offers a context for evaluating both individual perspectives and risk.

Reflexivity and participation

Giddens also uses a closely related concept: the 'double hermeneutic', which is particularly important to understanding the narrower concept of reflexivity in research methodology. It simply means firstly that the social researcher studies 'phenomena which are already constituted as meaningful' (Giddens, 1984, p.284), and enters the social world as a participant in order to study it (as contrasted with the traditional view of science as external observation). Further, the observations and concepts that the social researcher develops are themselves part of the social world, and may influence it. In qualitative research, reflexivity involves the consideration that any researcher in the social sciences is a participant in the interactions involved in research relationships, and the outcome of the research activity is a significant product of who the researcher is, and the whole interactive situation in which that person is doing the research.

This general point can be unpacked in a number of ways, and has been especially important to feminist research methods in recent years. It is not simply that the researcher may have a bias or interest in finding specific evidence to support research outcomes to which they have some prior intellectual, financial or other commitment (though this is important enough as an issue). It is also a matter of the research *method* itself being an issue of evaluative intellectual and ethical judgement, closely related to the specific researcher's understanding of the social world. It is also concerned with the *subject* of research, and why that has been chosen by the researcher as a matter of interest. It is also an issue of the *process* and context of research. Who, or what institution has underwritten and legitimised the research, and what impact does that have on the researcher's conduct? What relationships are developed in the course of research, and how does the interaction between the researched and the researcher affect the availability, collection and analysis of data, and the dissemination of outcomes? It is generally concerned with the ways in which the researcher constitutes and produces the knowledge, rather than simply observing and recording an objective reality outside the self.

There are many issues, of which the above are some of the most obvious and important. It should be clear that the concept of reflexivity relates closely to issues concerning ethics and values in research, and is central to the concept of critical auto/biography. It should also be noted that there are close connections between these research issues and the practice of social assessment. This is one of many areas of overlap between social assessment and research practice: both have to take account of issues of reflexivity and ethics. It is also important to note that the concept of reflexivity is not undisputed, and is interpreted differently, depending on the theoretical assumptions employed.

Reflexivity, postmodernism and critical auto/biography

A postmodernist view of research puts much emphasis upon the specific, reflexive, local and particular nature of any research, and its construction of partial texts and stories (Oleson, 1994). It is famously against grand narratives that purport to explain the world: according to this account, we use the concepts of a research programme not to investigate reality, but to construct reality. It is a theory which has been made use of by feminists and anti-racists, but has also been criticised by both these groups for the dangers of conceding too much to a position which undermines any critical edge. It *is* important to be aware of the partial and situated nature of any research, and the reflexive involvement of the researcher within a particular range of discourses – this is how feminists and black and other oppressed social groups came to recognise that what passed as objective research was in fact closely connected to particular elite contexts and values. But the recognition of reflexivity in research should not ignore the structural aspects of social division that simultaneously create illusions of objectivity and construct the social world.

The concept of reflexivity contained in auto/biography is partially related to postmodernist ideas, but Stanley and Wise argue that related concepts developed first from feminist discussions of research method and epistemology, not to mention other, earlier intellectual traditions (Stanley and Wise, 1994, pp.189–90). Certainly, the idea of reflexivity has been central to critical as well as constructivist theory in the social sciences (Guba and Lincoln, 1994). A key issue in feminist discussions has been how to interpret and value the research done by women, and part of that debate has for a long time been about the person of the researcher (Stanley and Wise, 1983; Stanley, 1987), how a woman researcher's position gives her a *different* access to the social world, and what that implies for interviewing and analysis. This is sometimes associated with feminist standpoint theory (Haraway, 1988), and is consistent with an emphasis on the specific importance of the woman as researcher (Roberts, 1981). However, Stanley's auto/biographical position takes account of the complexities of overlapping social divisions, and the existence of *plural* standpoints, asserting the importance of the: 'Proclamation of the reflexivity of feminist research processes; acknowledgement of the contextual specificity of feminist as of all other knowledge; recognition of who a researcher is, in terms of their sex, race, class, and sexuality, affects what they "find" in research' (Stanley and Wise, 1994, p.228).

The argument clearly applies to other social divisions, where, for example, a disabled person as researcher may have a different understanding, access to, and impact upon the social world compared to a non-disabled person (Oliver, 1992a; Morris, 1992b). It is not simply a matter of the researcher as a person by themselves, but obviously and simultaneously also an issue of who they are in relation to who they are researching (see Stanley, 1987 for an account of her changing perspectives on historical biographies which altered with changes in her own life and understanding). Someone whose experience of the social world separates them from those being researched will have a different perspective on the social circumstances of the subject of research – or of assessment. These differences of perception affect the capacity of the researcher or assessor to understand the shifting nature of a reality which is socially constructed and changing.

However, some feminist and black social critics caution against postmodernist reductionism in research, which tends towards the position that: 'Any social process can have a multiplicity of meanings, since meaning depends on context, and context is different for every human subject' (Malik, 1996, p.191), reducing research knowledge to particular subjective perspectives. Stanley and Wise's argument in favour of a 'feminist fractured foundationalist epistemology' (Stanley and Wise, 1994, p.230) means that reflexivity is combined with an awareness of fractured social collectivities involving gender, class and so on, which form the context and being of individual researchers. A key issue for feminist reflexivity therefore is awareness not only of the specific local factors affecting individual consciousness, but also the wider structural factors such as the major social divisions.

The identities of the 'researcher' and the 'other'

The much-debated issue of identity also needs to be understood in this context, as part of a 'fractured foundationalist' view of identity. The postmodernist emphasis on the fragmentary, changing nature of a person's identity (whether the researcher's or the subject's) tends to undercut the whole enterprise of understanding a life. Denzin's discussion of Derrida concludes that: 'there can only be multiple versions of a biography or an auto/biography' (Denzin, 1989, p.47). However, Stanley's auto/biographical method is characterised not only by the uncertainty and particularity of a specific social and historical location, but also by situating both writer and subject in relation to the major social divisions. She accepts the 'fictive element' in the creation of identities (and thus life histories), but denies that this means there are no points of connection with material realities.

It is simply the case that the inter-relationship between interpretation and creation of identities and life stories and the material world is *complex* (Stanley, 1992, p.253). A good example of this would appear to be the way in which British black women have recently discussed their own self-creation of the multiple dimensions of their identities, yet simultaneously make connections to the concrete material realities of being 'black', British and female (Mirza, 1997a). The identity of the researcher changes through time and space, and conditions the whole nature of the research. But this makes it more rather than less important to clarify and own that identity as much as possible.

Understanding the complex ways that social divisions impinge on the identity of the self implicitly raises parallel issues about the possibility of understanding and representing the 'other', especially where that 'other' belongs to different social divisions. This is obviously a crucial issue in social assessment and research. As with the identity of the self, there are similar complex considerations which have been thoroughly reviewed in recent work by feminists (e.g. Wilkinson and Kitzinger, 1996). The position of Stanley with reference to the ability of research to represent and refer to the 'other' is again that they are 'complex ethical and epistemological issues' (Stanley, 1996, p.48). In order to deal with them, she advocates the importance of intellectual autobiography for all researchers as a means of displaying the analytical issues involved, and thus 'helping the reader to engage with the resultant knowledge-claims' (Stanley, 1996, p.48). The 'Autobiographical notes and acknowledgements' at the beginning of this book are intended to serve that function here.

Reflexivity and dialogue

In addition, it is important to note that feminist and black writers have urged the view that research involves a social *dialogue* which 'requires that not all voices are equal', and there should be 'a willingness to engage in critical debate and accept that some views are more equal than others' (Malik, 1996, p.236), otherwise there seems little point in doing research aimed at improving our understanding of the world. Other black and feminist writers also pay close attention to the need to engage in critical dialogue with the researched, (e.g. Gwaltney, 1980; Lather, 1988; Collins, 1990; Skeggs, 1994), and especially with the individuals who are oppressed both by the nature of research and by their membership of dominated social divisions. Such considerations in social research methodology are also vital to social assessment, as are the evaluative consequences of such a position, and are well grounded.

Arguments about critical dialogue are found in many other theorists. Based on Habermas, Scambler has argued that the concept of communicative speech action has important implications for sociologists in general. The use of language is said to *presuppose* a commitment to intersubjectivity, equal accessibility and reason, and therefore the principal commitment of sociology should be towards engaged, participative analysis of social action. Because of the fundamentally reflexive nature of modern society, and of sociology within it, sociologists need to act: 'consciously through alliances of interest ... most notably [with] the new social movements' (Scambler, 1996, p.579). Conversely, there needs to be an examination of the allegiance of sociology to the needs of the state: by accepting research contracts to evaluate the progress of government initiatives, the questions of research are displaced onto the agenda of the dominant systems, rather than being focused on the longer-term and more critical issues that are raised by dialogue with the powerless. Friere also advocates dialogue with the oppressed, but in different terms (Friere, 1972). He is often quoted as the exemplar of a dialogic process of consciousness-raising in research and education, providing 'a classic model for how consciousness raising forges links between personal empowerment and the social dimension of people's circumstances' (Adams, 1996, p.55).

Reflexivity and narrative

The notions of *reflexive* listening to the stories of service users and the linking of biography and autobiography are not new in health and social work. In social work education, it has been argued that helping trainee social workers to 'discover how they got the way they are' helps to provide them with: 'the key to the experience of others' (Miller, 1981, p.347). Similarly, Timms drew on literary sources to justify a conception of counselling in health and social services as essentially based on mutual story-telling, since narrative is central to understanding human identity (Timms, 1986). More recently, and partly in response to postmodern influences, the idea of narrative as the basis of the attempt to share meanings in relationships between workers and users has again been emphasised, especially with respect to issues of empowerment and the intersection of meanings and perspectives (Saleeby, 1994).

In research methodology, the development of narrative methods has increasingly been of importance. Recent studies of qualitative research methods emphasise the importance of using approaches to narrative in exploring personal experience (Clandinin and Connolly, 1994) and life history (Hatch and Wisniewski, 1995b). The method is seen as essential to any research which will succeed in exploring interior social worlds, yet the crucial issue of reflexivity means that in telling a story, the researcher has always to deal with the complex issues of voice, and whose voice is eventually reflected in the text that is produced: problems which arise from an 'embodied reflexive awareness' (Soderqvist, 1991, p.158). The postmodern interpretations of this issue are considered by Maynard from a feminist perspective. She contends that reflexivity has been one of the features of a feminist approach to research method. However, issues about the rigour of the methods used must include their relationship to a clear theoretical framework which raises questions about oppression, encouraging reflection and awareness. Reflexivity in research is therefore a mutual sharing of stories, but one in which there must be: 'an interpretative and synthesising process which connects experience to understanding' (Maynard, 1994b, p.24).

Summary of reflexive concepts

The idea of dialogue and negotiation within a clear theoretical framework as part of the reflexive research relationship is ethically and politically central within a CA/B methodology. It clearly identifies the following points.

There are unavoidable moral, epistemological and political issues that have to be faced in researching someone's life (including the impact of life review on the emotions). The researcher/assessor has to acknowledge their own evaluative interpretive position, but also to be open to listening (to the user's story and perspectives) and to discussion and negotiation. The degree to which the researcher's involvement helps to change the subject's perspective on their own life is itself partly a matter for ethical, political and 'therapeutic' judgement. However, it is also possible that the impact on the researcher may be significant in unforeseeable ways, both theoretically and therapeutically: the experience of researching and assessing lives is potentially disturbing and life-changing on both sides of the equation (Marshall, 1994; Clifford and Cropper, 1994). The researcher/assessor needs to be prepared for the possibility that either the subject or the worker may need emotional support or more structured help as a result of this intimate process.

Imbalances of power and knowledge can be very complex (Bhavnani, 1990). The researcher's cross-cutting membership of social divisions is unlikely to be exactly the same as the subject's. If it were, that would also be highly significant. Quite possibly, membership of certain social divisions will not be apparent, may be uncertain, or may gradually (or suddenly) be revealed – by either party. The knowledge of the experience of social division that subject and researcher are able to utilise is a key factor which affects the negotiation and production of knowledge. The researcher needs to be as aware of this potential as possible, and alive to the ethical and political implications. In addition, whilst the ostensible object of research – the subject's life – makes them the expert, the researcher is able to draw on social science knowledge which qualifies and contextualises the subject's understanding of their own life. This also, together with the institutional and social position of the researcher, emphasises the importance of the moral and political obligations of the researcher to seriously consider the development of the consciousness of both the subject and themselves in the process of research. The implication is towards a concept of empowerment in the process of CA/B research, but clearly the notion of empowerment envisaged here is politically complex and ethically multi-dimensional.

Implications of reflexivity for practice

In view of the above, there is no justification for ignoring the issues of reflexivity in research, and every reason to take seriously the auto/biographical and ethical and political issues that arise in the study of lives in particular. It is especially pertinent to social assessment research, but there are 'no easy solutions' (Gallagher, Creighton and Gibbons, 1995). On the contrary, there are serious implications for ethics when this perspective is understood and applied:

> The contention that values lie at the heart of the validation process implies that the ethical issues of research and assessment cannot be seen as subsidiary or technical matters which can be well or badly resolved: they are constitutive of the knowledge that is produced, and as such require that the primary actors – the researcher and/or social worker – *must* consider their own commitments. (Clifford and Cropper, 1994, p.51; cf. Harrison and Lyon, 1993)

Part of the requirements which must be met on this account is that there must be a systematic examination of the multiple, varied and changing relationships between the people involved in research. There needs to be an awareness on the part of the researcher of all the dimensions of CA/B method and the values that have been discussed above, and various strategies need to be developed at different levels to take account of the issues involved. For example:

> there are a range of actions that can be taken ... These include deconstructive textual practices (Opie, 1993, p.57); sharing perspectives in participatory dialogue with living subjects; acknowledging deficits of experience and consulting with colleagues who have relevant knowledge and experience; collaborative research which includes people with radically different life experiences; making community links with groups whose experiences offer significantly different insights and monitoring recruitment and selection policies of students, researchers, and staff, to maximise the range of experience within a department or agency. All these proposed strategies have to be carefully analysed in terms of the political/power issues, in order to avoid or at least minimise, the exploitation of the various people concerned. (Clifford and Cropper, 1994, p.52)

Deconstructive practices in writing research are relevant, in that the author tries to allow the reader to actively engage with the discourse involved. This can be done in various ways, including being open about the researcher's biography and membership of the social divisions, and the values that have informed the research, so that the reader can make a judgement about where the research is coming from, rather than the research being presented as something objective and authoritative (Stanley, 1996). Another such move is to make clear to the reader the messy process of the research, rather than pretend it was all carried out exactly as planned. Another important method is to be exceptionally clear about alternative hypotheses and anomalous pieces of evidence which do *not* fit in with the line that you yourself are taking, or with the values that you hold. This can be read as form of falsificationism (Popper, 1963), but it follows equally from a principled reflexivity which helps the reader assess what is *not* supporting the assertions of the writer. It is a particularly important strategy in health and welfare services, where it is essential to the spirit of partnership that the research and/or assessment is open to challenge from the user's or carer's perspective – or from the perspective of a related profession.

Again, the implication is that reflexivity in CA/B research must entail the enaction of a principled reflective practice, involving self-review and discussion with colleagues and users. This is consistent with the development of concepts of reflective learning practice in education, management and social work, based on the work of Schon (Schon, 1983). This has been used recently in connection with concepts of empowerment in social services (Gould and Taylor, 1996; Adams, 1996). However, the CA/B perception of reflexivity in research and assessment practice, especially when taken in the context of the other CA/B methodological principles, offers a broad approach to an understanding of the complex issues involved.

Reflexivity: Some practical questions for assessors

Note: These questions must be considered in conjunction with other questions that are appended to the discussion of the other main principles in Part One. These questions can be used with case examples to discuss the application of principles to practice situations.

1   What membership of the various social divisions do you yourself have? What legal and organisational power/responsibility and what knowledge do you possess in relation to the people that you are researching/assessing?

2   What are the implications of your answer to question 1 in relation to this particular person or persons (and in relation to colleagues and other professionals)? How far do you share similar experiences of social divisions, and how far are your experiences of life very different?

3   What are the constraints and possibilities of working in partnership with this (these) person(s), given the above differences, commonalities and positions? How far do they understand the power and functions of your organisation? How do they see it (and you) in relation to themselves?

4   How far can you facilitate the telling of the service user's story, create a dialogue, construct a shared narrative, and take into account both their and your rights, responsibilities and perspectives? How do they see you as a person and as a professional? How aware are you of muted as well as dominant voices in listening to the user's stories? What kind of support do they need in relation to you? How far can you understand and respect their values – and vice versa?

5   How can you further your own self-assessment and review of the situation: what kind of critical supervision and support do you need? How aware are you of your own and others' changing perspectives during the process of assessment, and is it possible to keep a reflective record of those changes?

6   How far can you and colleagues and the service users critically assess the policy, law and practice which your agency is responsible for enacting in the light of (these) particular circumstances?

4 Historical location

This chapter studies the important issue of understanding people in specific historical times and places, and draws on the insights of a number of disciplines in order to do this. In particular, it draws on history and oral history, life-course sociology and life history research methods, and lifespan developmental psychology. There are significant connections between recent developments in all of these areas and some of the central concerns of anti-oppressive writers in relation to the principle of historical location. Collins, as a black feminist attempting to analyse black feminist thought, compares her 'holistic' methodology with C. Wright Mills's 'sociological imagination', and describes both as: 'a way of knowing that enables individuals to grasp the relations between history and biography within society' (Collins, 1990, p.230).

Ignoring the historical location of individual action is a potentially oppressive, pathologising strategy, which fails to take account of the dynamics of social change in which individuals participate. This stress on connecting individuals, groups and communities within the context of social history is a key component of a critical approach to research and assessment methodology which seeks to understand the meaning of human action. Its full significance can be elaborated further by an evaluation of the disciplinary areas already identified.

Oral history

The importance of oral history in social assessment has already been documented elsewhere (Clifford, 1994 and 1995; Martin, 1995), and feminist approaches to oral history have made significant contributions to an understanding of the importance of the life story and its historical context (Gluck and Patai, 1991). Social assessment as a form of biographical research needs to incorporate principles of historical scholarship: awareness of interpretative issues, the complexity of historical situations, and the search for and questioning of historical evidence (Tuchman, 1994). Contemporary historians fiercely debate the canons of appropriate interpretation, and whilst traditional views of the historians' skills (Marwick, 1989) are still influential and important, various postmodernist critiques (H. White, 1995; Jenkins, 1991 and 1995) have raised crucial issues about the nature of history, some of which are central to CA/B method, and will be discussed further below.

Historians themselves are well aware of the importance of studying biography and group biographies (or 'prosopography' – Stone, 1981). Especially important for assessment is the combination of understanding the changing perspective of the person telling their life story at the point in their lives at which it is being told, whilst at the same time reserving judgement as to the possibility of rival interpretations of the evidence as given, especially in the light of further evidence which may be acquired from other oral or documentary sources.

In principle, a social assessment must aim at an adequacy that can subsume the story-teller's perspective within a wider brief, attempting to develop the story with the user as far as that is possible. This means that CA/B method, and social assessment, must be a user's oral history *plus* the use of other historical sources and methods, such as oral histories of other witnesses, historical documents, including references and agency records, as well as evidence drawn from direct observation by the interviewer (Kofodinos, 1990).

It is only within the last two decades that oral history has established itself with a relatively firm footing as a recognised branch of history, basing itself around new journals devoted to this method (Thompson, 1984), developing an impressive range of illuminating work (for example, Perks and Thompson, 1998). The movement has its origins in a concern with the lives of ordinary people who have not in the past featured in established historical texts. There was therefore from the beginning a commitment and interest in the lives and the knowledge of working people who did not belong to the dominating social groups, and their perspectives and experiences. The method has been able to draw on historical roots such as African traditions of oral transmission of historical knowledge, and has continued to develop its methods and theory in recent years (Tonkin, 1992; Stuart, 1994; Stanley, 1994; Yow, 1994)

The ability of oral history techniques to illuminate the lives of people who belong to the dominated groups within our society has much to offer an anti-oppressive approach to social research. The connections have become particularly striking with the publication of books and papers which present oral history as a feminist practice (Personal Narratives Group, 1989; Gluck and Patai, 1991; Sangster, 1994), as well as others with a keen interest in black oral history (Etter-Lewis, 1993; Martin, 1995), gay and lesbian oral histories (e.g. Lesbian Oral History Group, 1989; Gay Men's Oral History Group, 1989; Davis and Kennedy, 1991) and the oral witness of disabled (e.g. Walmsley, 1995; Goodley, 1996) and working-class people (Seabrook, 1982), and certainly older people (Bornat, 1989 and 1994). They explicitly prioritise the task of setting lives into a specific historical context which is interrogated for its particular social difference, and also examine the processes of oral history interviewing in ways that are directly relevant to the process of anti-oppressive social research. They are consistent in their appreciation of the role of oral history in contributing to the dialogical understanding and self-awareness of people from dominated social divisions as well as to the structural issues of social power and the specificity of time and place.

Some of the issues presented by oral historians from this perspective are as follows. Firstly, in some circumstances there is the liberating nature of the method itself, and its 'inherent' compatibility with ethical, anti-oppressive values: 'the telling of the story can be empowering, validating the importance of the speaker's life experience' (Gluck and Patai, 1991, p.2). A black woman specialist in linguistics claims that: 'It is oral narrative that is ideally suited to revealing the "multi-layered texture of black women's lives"' (Etter-Lewis, 1991, p.43). It has also been argued that: 'Within the human sciences, oral history – both the method and the discipline – has often been cited as the exemplar of how social research can be empowering' (Bhavnani, 1990, p.145). However, as Bhavnani warns, there is no automatic guarantee of any research method being empowering – any method can be used to mask power inequalities, and this leads to the second area of interest for CA/B method: that feminist oral historians are critically aware of the power issues that arise in the process, content and context of their work.

There is an explicit commitment to the investigation of power in the content of the work, linking broad patterns of inequality: 'as an explanatory framework for a life experience, gender … [is] inextricably bound to class and ethnicity' (Olsen and Shopes, 1991, p.193). There is also an examination of the power inequalities in the process of the research, which 'places research subjects at grave risk of manipulation and betrayal', and in the 'dissonance' between the collaborative fieldwork interview and the research product, over which the interviewee has little or no control' (Stacey, 1991, pp.113–14). There is a keen awareness of the context of research, its material inequalities and the social and political environment which determines that context, together with a determination that: 'By doing work where we have personal commitments, our academic contributions are more likely to come out of a personal, creative, politically engaged self, one that has a social – and not just an academic – purpose' (Olsen and Shopes, 1991, p.201).

The latter point is connected with a third issue raised explicitly by the practice of feminist oral history – the focus on reflexivity and values. A number of authors emphasise the point that what is happening is not the telling of one story, but two stories. The life history of the interviewee as told from their perspective is one story, whilst its reception and reinterpretation by the interviewer is another (Borland, 1991; Mbilinyi, 1989). This aspect of oral history is mirrored in Stanley's comments on how powerfully biography and autobiography are intermingled in the process of studying the history of someone else's life: 'this person with this particular personal and intellectual history in this time and place who understands in now this light, and now that, first one then more facets of this other person' (Stanley, 1987, p.22). In other words, the principles of historical and social specificity apply both to the researcher and the subject, and to the relationship that develops over time between them. This inevitably makes the oral history ethical and political in its implications.

Thus oral history is a method of understanding which successfully places people's lives in specific changing historical contexts of social divisions – making the connections between biography, history and social structure through changing times in ways that make sense to both subjects and researchers. The detailed historical record of complex interactions undermines simplistic categories and generalisations. This is an important point forcefully made by women researching into the lives of working-class women: 'as a person narrates a life story, and the account wends its way through the accumulated details of a life, social categories are exploded: the subject becomes an actor in simultaneous, multiple roles that do not conform to easy generalisations' (Olsen and Shopes, 1991, p.193). As a discipline, oral history makes a vital contribution to understanding the complex detail and interconnecting layers of meaning and influence in people's lives, and is therefore an essential component of CA/B method.

The focus of history is upon the exploration of human pasts, interpreting human documents and human testimony in the context of these multiple details, and of the wider historical patterns and influences which bear upon particular lives. However, feminist historians (oral and otherwise) have also clearly been aware of themes familiar to postmodern and post-structural theorists, such as the view that people's lives should not be reduced to simple linear terms, nor be simplistically represented as 'reality' unmediated by the auto/biographical and oral/textual processes (e.g. Tonkin, 1992; Stuart, 1994).

However, some feminists and anti-racists take the view that history needs preserving from too much postmodern criticism (e.g. Stanley, 1990; Caine, 1994; Hoff, 1994a; Sangster, 1994; Ramazanoglu, 1996). Malik criticises the inability of postmodernists to treat history seriously (Malik, 1996, pp.247–8), whilst Hoff argues that postmodernism is not 'history-friendly', because it is hostile to the material reality of the historical world of time and causation (Hoff, 1994a). The latter paper led to a contentious exchange (Kent, 1996; Hoff, 1996), but Sangster argues in a less hostile way for: 'a feminist oral history ... enlightened by post-structuralist insights, but firmly grounded in a materialist feminist context' (Sangster, 1994). The importance of Stanley's feminist concept of auto/biography is that it tackles these issues squarely, but retains a commitment to both 'materiality *and* meaning' (Bradley, 1996, p.10, my emphasis) in the context of sociological approaches to life history research method. This will be discussed further in the next section.

Sociology, life histories and the life-course

It is surprising that the life history approach to research in sociology has not been utilised much more as a basis for social welfare practice (Anderson and Brown, 1980). The life history approach largely disappeared after its initial popularity in the 1930s, but there has been a revival of interest in it (Plummer, 1983), particularly in recent years (Smith, 1994). 'Life-course sociology' has also only relatively recently become the preferred term for the study of what was previously examined under the heading of 'life cycle' and 'family life cycle', and represents a theoretical move forward in the attempt to link biography and history (Morgan, 1985). However, there has recently been a great interest in sociology around concepts of life history and biographical research, as a result of feminist, phenomenological and postmodernist concerns with narrative and personal experience. Feminist approaches to research in sociology have strongly argued that since the personal and political are closely connected, the detailed qualitative investigation of the personal is equally important as research into wider and more public aspects of social life, and is crucially inter-related with these wider aspects (see Stanley, 1990).

The essence of the life history method is that it should be: 'a horizontal and vertical reading of the biography and the social system; back and forth from biography to social system, and from social system to biography' (Bertaux, 1981, p.21). It is this complex effort to relate the individual to social systems within a temporal framework which is of great relevance to social work, and which can be easily related to black feminists' perspectives, as it is essentially anti-reductionist, specifically historical and reflexive, and potentially relates to the material differences between the social divisions. The method can be used in an individualistic and humanist way, but the approach being suggested here is explicitly linked to the ways in which individual lives are connected to the social structure, and especially the social divisions.

Bertaux distinguishes between a life story method based on interviewing a subject about their perceptions of their own history, compared to a life history method, which relies principally upon documents (Bertaux, 1982, note 4, pp.7–9). This distinction raises issues about the validity of evidence about a subject's personal history versus its meaning for them and their perception of it. This is a central issue, concerning the interpretation of that evidence and the priority of the actor's interpretation over that of the researcher. In social assessment, both aspects are important since the meaning of accounts of participants is important, but so is third-party and documentary evidence about what has happened in the past, when issues of life and liberty are at stake. This also links up directly with black and feminist and neo-Marxist concerns about understanding people's lives, and taking account of ideologies – looking at both objective and subjective factors at personal and social levels.

The tradition of life history research has always placed emphasis upon the nature of the research interview as a dialogue, in a sense, between cultures – closely related to anthropologists' concerns about the same issue. When social divisions are taken fully into account, it is *not* simply a question of 'a good life story' being 'one in which the interviewee takes over control of the interview situation and talks freely' (Bertaux, 1981, p.39): it is much more complex. The relevant concept of 'dialogue' is one which Friere used some years ago to indicate the *mutual* effort required to come to some appreciation of the perspectives and lives of the different other (Friere, 1972). Feminist sociologists have developed this interplay of biography and autobiography within the changing historical context considerably in recent years (Stanley, 1987; 1990; 1992; 1993; 1994). Auto/biographical sociology is now one of a number of developments that are especially relevant to *professional* tasks involving the assessment of people's lives (Clifford and Cropper, 1994). The existence of a journal and a subgroup of the British Sociological Association which specialises in auto/biographical research and theory indicates its current importance. It continues the tradition of sociological research into life histories, but with much greater and more critical sophistication.

Feminist sociologists have interacted with recent phenomenological, literary and other postmodern influences in theorising the study of lives (Smith, 1994). The noted sociologist and theorist of interpretative biography, Norman Denzin, uses Derrida to justify the view that 'A life is a social text, a fictional narrative production' (Denzin, 1989, p.9). His own work on biography has restricted the connection with history because of the view that both biography and auto/biography 'present fictions about "thought" selves, "thought" experiences, events, and their meanings' (Denzin, 1989, p.24). This has the consequence that 'students of the biographical method must learn how to use the strategies and techniques of literary interpretation and criticism' (Denzin, 1989, p.25) rather than any notion of conventional historical scholarship.

Stanley's feminist conception of auto/biography is a development of life history sociological method which on the one hand is explicitly based on a view of multiple social oppressions, and on the other is able to take account of postmodern, post-structural objections to foundationalism in the social sciences. She argues that the importance of a number of features of good auto/biography (judged by feminist standards), such as the concept of the fractured identity of the self in auto/biographical writing, and the inter-connectedness of the self with others, are matters of feminist writing that pre-date postmodernism (Stanley, 1992, p.15). She presents feminist auto/biography as founded upon four main elements, which provide a 'focus and a set of tools' (Stanley, 1992, p.244) for the study of lives:

1 'attention to social location and contextualisation and in particular to subject's position within ... their social networks ... socialising biography decentres the subject and ... shows both subjects to share much with their peers, and also that everyone is in some sense unique' – she describes this as an 'anti-spotlight' approach to individual lives (Stanley, 1992, p.250);
2 authors should identify themselves as being from: '... particular socio-political milieux', and in acknowledging these conditions of production of the auto/biography, the author facilitates 'active readership' by 'providing alternative evidences and points of view' (Stanley, 1992, p.251);
3 a qualified anti-realism which views the telling or writing of a life story as: 'a fictive truth reliant on cultural convention'; this emphasises the problems of selection, memory and narrative conventions, but 'does not mean that such writings have no points of connection with the material realities of everyday life: it rather emphasises how complex the relationship is and that neither realism nor a total rejection of it will do' (Stanley, 1992, p.243);
4 an 'a priori insistence that auto/biography should be treated as composed by ... ideological practices, and analytically engaged with as such' (Stanley 1992, p.253); this relates to the conviction that 'feminist *experience* is of different and disagreeing interpretations of the world, founded upon the often profoundly different material and experiential positions of differently located groups of women' (Stanley, 1992, p.243).

This effectively means that the ideas and values which the author brings to the writing of a life should always be questioned in relation to the social divisions and discourses which they bring to it.

This conception of a feminist auto/biography raises the question of how men and members of other dominant groups can relate to these methodological tenets. This is particularly apposite in view of the present author's gender. It seems that anyone *may* understand and attempt to use these ideas, but, as Stanley points out, feminism is not just about methods, but also ontology, and this is the sense in which anyone's understanding, but particularly that of members of dominant qroups, is circumscribed (Stanley, 1992, p.253). Their particular existence and being in the world limits and conditions the contingencies which they will experience. It must therefore place limitations on the possibility of, for example, any male being able to explore the interconnected worlds and experiences of women. The existence of vast amounts of literature in the social sciences and elsewhere written by feminists who have felt the need to elaborate these connections in the context of male-dominated disciplines surely supports this view. I presume that it does not prevent but encourages members of dominant groups to take note of the different experience of others whilst at the same time learning as much as possible from their methods. It means taking an evaluative position, whilst recognising the limitations of knowledge and experience. The same logic must also apply to other major social divisions, and suggests that awareness of one's own social location and limited experience should lead to a degree of modesty for everyone in making knowledge claims.

The related field of life-course sociology appears to be of growing importance for understanding personal and family history. As a field of study, it can use both the life history method and other methods of research in order to understand the interactions between personal and family life-courses and social history. Morgan drew attention to its significance a few years ago when he noted that: 'The "life course" approach, to date, seems to be the main area where the meeting between history and sociology has made some kind of theoretical contribution' (Morgan, 1985, p.176). A life-course approach to understanding people's lives should be an integral part of CA/B method, and recent feminist sociology has drawn on it, especially in Scandinavia, using a 'life line' method (Davies, 1996).

The essence of life-course sociology is that it places change and development at the centre of the analysis of personal and family lives, and makes connections between 'family time', 'individual time' and 'historical time'. It is to do with: 'complex relationships over time between ageing, between family, education and work careers, and between historical experiences' (Morgan, 1985, p.177). It is a theoretical improvement over the common approach to family and developmental histories of using 'stages' or 'family cycles' as concepts around which any given family analysis must be organised, and it is in a better position to make connections between biological and psychological time on the one hand, and sociological and historical time on the other. For instance, life-course sociologists have been more appreciative of differences and variation, and concerned with linking historical time with individual biography, rather than the tendency of the life cycle approach which interprets family life through the lens of the stereotypical stages of parenthood, 'treating less frequent cases as marginal or deviant' (Morgan, 1985, p.178). The latter approach has obviously negative implications for understanding gay or lesbian, step-parent, extended households or one-parent 'families'.

Some important aspects of life-course sociology concern the variety of connections that can be made between the different elements. First, there is the issue of the timing and synchronization of life transitions between the various individuals, and between the family and its sub groups, with an interactive impact of one on another when individual and 'family' transitions do or do not coincide. Second, there is the impact of historical processes such as war or unemployment on the timing of personal and family transitions. This is sometimes accessed by studying comparative cohorts born at different points in time, and can also take in the differential impact of such events and processes on social divisions as they affect the life-course (Harevan, 1978). Third, the concept of 'transition' as used in life-course sociology is broader than that of 'stage', including the idea that any transition has dynamic implications for wider social networks and institutional change. Fourth, the 'family unit' is unpacked as 'a set of contingent career lines which vary in synchronization and problems of resource management' (Elder, 1978, pp.55–6), whilst retaining the concept of the 'family' as a social system which also has transitions which reciprocally impact on individuals. Fifth, a life-course analysis can focus on either the individual or the 'family', or on other social groups, institutions or informal networks, so it therefore has considerable flexibility and analytical power. For instance, it facilitates the study of *both* the particular life-course of a woman, with its distinctive patterns and transitions, and the same life-course as part of the life-course of a 'family' group and its 'systemic' relationships through time.

Morgan's conclusion makes a point that explicitly links life-course sociology and the concerns of this book with anti-oppressive social research values: 'this historical approach to the family may show us the interplay between home and work and between the public and the private spheres, thus providing us with some useful linkages with some feminist concerns' (Morgan, 1985, p.179). Indeed, the concept has been put into good use by feminists to illuminate the changing life-courses of women, and how significantly different they are from those of men (Burgoyne, 1987; Allat, 1987). A CA/B perspective is about understanding relations between history and biography in society in a way that takes account of power structures and social divisions, and therefore the contribution of life history and auto/biography, and of life-course sociology, is of considerable potential significance in contributing to this end.

Lifespan developmental psychology

Historically, there has been medical, psychological and psychiatric dominance of social history-taking as a form of assessment in health and social services with regard to its intellectual justification. It is not always appreciated within these disciplines that social research requires a distinctive methodology from the theoretical perspectives of medicine or psychology. However, the development within psychology in recent times of an awareness of its own inadequacies as a stand-alone expert discipline is to be welcomed (Smith, Harre and Van Langenhove, 1995a and 1995b; Fox and Prilleltensky, 1997). This has been partly due to the influence of postmodernist criticism of its foundationalist assumptions (Potter and Wetherall, 1995; Richardson and Fowers, 1997), but much more as a result of feminist critiques of its asocial, 'malestream' assumptions (see, amongst others, Sherif, 1987; Squire, 1989; Nicholson, 1995; Wilkinson, 1997). These developments need to be seen in the context of a critical history of psychology itself (Harris, 1997).

However, an anti-oppressive biographical approach to assessment cannot err in the opposite direction and ignore psychological issues. The stress placed above on the sociology and history involved in assessing lives does *not* mean that cognitive and behavioural psychological explanations are irrelevant – they have an important role to play, but need to be seen within these wider contexts, and may also need to be critically evaluated where they involve social concepts.

Developmental and lifespan psychologies are sub-disciplines within psychology specially relevant to understanding and assessing lives (Runyan, 1982; Parkes, Stevenson-Hinde and Marris, 1991; Howe, 1995), but need to be used within a CA/B theoretical framework. This ensures integration with a perspective on psychological and psychiatric developments in individual lives which does not cede pre-eminence to the status of medical and psychological explanations. This has both intellectual and practical significance in view of the position of women within the health and welfare services, as workers and users (see Chapter 1). This is a strategy which questions the adequacy of any psychological approach to social research which is not explicitly and theoretically integrated with appropriate sociological and historical factors of interpretation, nor connected with anti-oppressive values.

Developmental psychology has itself been changing for many years, and has always involved varying theoretical perspectives, from the biological and cognitive to psychodynamic and psychoanalytical. The influential application of psycho-dynamic theories to the whole lifespan is particularly associated with Erikson (Erikson, 1958; 1975; 1977), whose influential works not only founded the discipline of lifespan developmental psychology, but also signalled the start of the modern period of the cognate field of psycho-history (Runyan, 1988, pp.12–14). Developmental psychology has not always been associated with a lifespan perspective, but it is significant that attachment theorists have published an updating of their approach from this angle (Parkes, Stevenson-Hinde and Marris, 1991). Cognitive and psychoanalytical contributions have concentrated on the earlier years of development.

The field as a whole has obvious relevance to the study of lives. However, the discipline has been heavily criticised recently in ways that are parallel to the concerns of CA/B method. Burman attacks the 'oppressive consequences of developmental psychology's unwillingness to own up to its culturally situated, partial claims to truth' (Burman, 1997, p.136). Development is focused on the individual organism which undergoes a natural, universal process, unaffected by its social milieu. The child is seen in abstract terms unrelated to the socio-historical environment, or the structures of power – something that is an 'irony', since the whole discipline is 'structured around the asymmetrical relationships between adults and children ... [and] researcher and researched' (Burman, 1997, p.146). Collaboration between psychologists and life-course historians is beginning to show them the importance of the changing 'matrix of ecological systems' (Elder, Modell and Park, 1995b, p.246) within which development occurs.

Lifespan developmental psychology emphasises the complex interconnection between childhood and later stages in life, and needs to include the individual within the changing social context: 'The argument is not that early childhood experiences have no effect, but that the effects of such experiences are mediated by intervening experiences and contingencies, and that personality and behaviour are continually shaped throughout the life cycle' (Runyan, 1988, p.226). There is a clearer understanding that the relevance of social circumstances not only means putting behaviour in the context of individual and family history, but also placing it within the context of wider structures: 'Particular life-course patterns depend not only on the individual's distinctive interactional styles, but also on the structure of the environment in any given historical period' (Caspi, 1990, p.32). Burman contends that: 'The recent resurgence of "lifespan" developmental psychology is a corrective to the individual, child-focussed orientation that has pre-occupied the mainstream' of developmental psychology (Burman, 1997, p.135). Lifespan developmental psychology should therefore be viewed as making a potential contribution to an anti-oppressive perspective on social research, but necessarily one which needs to be reinterpreted systematically in the light of specific historically structured contexts relating to the social divisions.

An example of this is provided by Gilligan's discussion of Erikson's eight stages of psycho-social development (Gilligan, 1987). Her critique is that this remains a conception that is based on the achievement of separation, with female connectedness and attachments being regarded as developmental impediments. Feminists and others have since been critical of Gilligan's focus on gender alone, and have indicated the applicability of this kind of critique to other social divisions (Larrabee, 1993). However, the use of developmental psychology in social and health work remains of great influence (Fahlberg, 1988; Gibson, 1991; Howe, 1995), and the point here is to indicate the importance of using it *critically*, within a CA/B framework, for the purposes of social assessment.

A further contribution which lifespan developmental psychology can make towards an anti-oppressive and black feminist framework for social assessment is in the area of understanding the process of recalling and recounting personal and family life histories and events. Firstly, there is the way that autobiographical memory changes across the life-course, and associated with this, the issue of the construction and validity of personal memory. Secondly, there is the significance of the narrative form as the structure of autobiographical recall and recounting. Thirdly, there is the function of autobiographical memory as an integrating factor for personal identity.

It is not surprising to find that the story a person tells about their own life does not remain static, but changes over time, and clearly this must be taken into account whenever someone is being interviewed about it: 'At any one point in the life course the personal narrative represents a particular interpretation experienced as internally consistent, of currently experienced memories' (Cohler, 1982, p.212). Time itself is experienced differently across the life-course, and lifespan developmental psychology helps to examine these changes. For Cohler (1982), the overall picture is that the 'developmental organisers of childhood are principally determined by maturation', whilst 'developmental shifts across adulthood are more likely due to socially determined factors' and 'take place in a particular historical context and must be understood as multi-directional' (Cohler, 1982, pp.220–1). In old age there is an increase in reminiscence activity related to the need to reflect upon and integrate perceptions of the past.

However, both historians and psychologists agree that even where mythical elements play a part in the construction of autobiographical memory, that does not reduce the importance of the account. From a historical perspective, the mythical elements 'need to be seen both as evidence of the past, and as a continuing historical force in the present' (Samuel and Thompson, 1990, p.20), whilst for the psychologist, 'a defining feature of autobiographical memories was that they inherently represent personal meanings for a specific individual' (Conway, 1990, p.186), and are therefore an important part of that person's identity. Neither is it necessary to dichotomise myth and reality: 'Oral memory offers a double validity in understanding a past in which, as still today, myth was embedded in real experience: both growing from it, and helping to shape its perception' (Samuel and Thompson, 1990, p.6). This approach is well exemplified by the black lesbian autobiography of Audre Lorde, which she specifically describes as a 'bio-mythography' in order to stress the point that her writing about herself consciously combines myth and reality in the struggle to be true to her present self and her past (Lorde, 1984b).

Lifespan developmental psychology and some related areas such as psycho-history and the psychology of memory can thus be used to complement the concept of a CA/B approach to social research by giving it the possibility of a psychological dimension which is compatible with anti-oppressive values (cf. Hopton, 1997). However, these disciplines clearly need to be contextualised within the sociological and historical frameworks already discussed for it to be consistent with a CA/B methodology. The principle of historical location establishes a multi-disciplinary perspective as a basis for this methodology, and expresses an anti-oppressive value commitment in its attention to the specifics, rather than the stereotypes, of human situations. It also helps to curb the individualising and pathologising effect of conventional psychology and psychiatry.

Practical questions for assessors

Note: These questions must be considered in conjunction with other questions that are appended to the discussion of the other main principles in Part One. These questions can be used with case examples to discuss the application of principles to practice situations.

1   What is the current date, and/or the date when the intervention or assessment being considered is taking place, and how does that affect this particular person, given their age and stage of life? What implications does this historical location also have for you?

2   What is the timing of key social transitions and events within their life, and what was happening *at that time* in related social systems: their families, local communities, peer groups, and nationally? In particular, what is the history of their relationship with this (and/or other agencies), and how has the agency changed over that period of time?

3   How does the history of their personal psychological development and their medical history inter-relate with these sociological and historical

developments? What kind of personal life trajectory do they appear to have to you, and how do *they* perceive and talk about their life stories?

4   What geographical place do they currently occupy, and what changes have they experienced over the years? What was the timing of these changes, and how far does it coincide and interact with other personal, family or related systems changes at local and socio-cultural levels?

5   To what other historical evidence do you have access (agency records, personal records and documents, third-party life stories and witness evidence, reports and communications from other professionals)? How far does the user have equal access, and how far can the information be shared? What differences of perspective and interpretation arise from considering these different sources? Have you taken into account the socio-historical location of these sources of information in your attempt to interpret their significance?

6   What dominant stereotypical and generalised explanations and concepts need to be avoided when considering this particular person and their changing specific social/historical location?

7   How much information about the histories of the people in this situation are you able to access? How appropriate is this amount of information to enable you to: (1) understand the lives of these users and/or carers, and (2) negotiate and resolve the professional task? What ethical and/or political issues arise from trying to elicit more information, either directly or indirectly? How far can you demonstrate that you are able to offer a detailed knowledge of life histories, drawing on multiple interviews, documentary evidence and differing perspectives?

5 Interacting social systems: The personal and the structural

Introduction

This chapter discusses interaction across the range of social systems, from the most intimate level of individual relationships to the broadest level of international relations, and the various ways in which this dimension of the social world impinges on the possibilities for social assessment. After situating the main theoretical issues within the debate about (social) structure and agency (individual action and intention), it will look at the use of systemic approaches to social assessment, and compare them with black and white feminist and other arguments concerning the nature and interconnection of the personal and the political. In the light of this, it will examine the relationship between social systems at different levels, their location in time and space, social difference, reflexivity, and power in the processes of social assessment.

Social systems, social theory and oppression

CA/B method raises fundamental issues about the relationship between micro-systems and macro-systems, and between structure and action in sociology. These are central questions in sociology which are continually debated and cannot be dealt with adequately in a brief space. The purpose of this chapter will be to suggest some ways in which a CA/B approach connects with current social theory on the one hand, but also with the interests of oppressed and user groups on the other. The intended effect of this is to indicate the possibility of a theoretical framework which can support a CA/B approach to social assessment in relation to this specific issue of interacting social systems which appears to be so vital to the perspectives of dominated social groups.

It has long been obvious that different kinds of oppression are perceived by dominated groups as operating at various 'levels' of society, including, but going beyond, the individual. The feminist slogan that 'the personal is political' was usually intended to convey the meaning that intimate social relationships between men and women were not simply a matter of individual psychology, but were conditioned by wider social factors affecting all women, and that they were (re)constituted by power relationships which 'reflected' and were connected to wider social structures of patriarchy. This sometimes encouraged a view of women as (to a degree) victims of processes of socialisation and structures of power over which they had little control: 'Girls are socialised to see women as providing service and pleasure for men' (Abbott and Wallace, 1979, p.224). It implied that they were entrapped in various social systems, from the micro-systems of home, family, neighbourhood and local organisations to macro-systems such as segregated labour markets, education, social security, legal, political and cultural systems. This view has been developed in recent years to allow for various degrees of choice, resistance and manipulation by women and girls (Abbott and Wallace, 1979, p.125). It is difficult to imagine a version of feminism which does not involve some appreciation of the ways in which social systems interact powerfully – to the detriment of some, and the benefit of others. However, the view that the 'personal is political' *always* equally implied that the social systems which influence women's lives are not conceived as completely deterministic: the second point about the personal also being political is to recognise the possibility of resistance to the exercise of power, and the responsibility of awareness and choice in individual lives.

Other dominated groups have similar concerns, and a similar pattern of argument emerges in relation to disability, for example, about the significance of the social systems which provide the disabling environment which oppresses the dominated groups. The contrast is often drawn between a medical or pathological view of individual behaviour and circumstances of the disabled versus a sociological view of social oppression which sees individual behaviour as constrained and subordinated to social system imperatives that fulfil the interests of the able-bodied. All the different forms of oppression lead to these kinds of claims, in opposition to dominant views which sometimes deny the importance of systemic social factors, and place responsibility for any kind of disadvantage on either natural biological, or individual psychological factors (or both). Other dominated groups are equally concerned about the possibilities of resistance, and individual and group strategies for change. Given the variety of forms of oppression, there is also the issue of the relationship between differing systems of domination, including interconnections and overlaps which generate commonalities as well as qualitative and quantitative differences.

However, views which stress the importance of social systems are not confined to critical theories of society which reflect the interests of dominated groups. There have been strong proponents of variants of systems theory right across the political spectrum, and the inter-related concepts of system, structure and function have been central to sociological debate from the earliest period. In the middle of the twentieth century, the influence of conservative Parsonian and General Systems Theory strongly affected health and welfare assessment, whilst at the other end of the political spectrum Althusser and other Marxists also had a major impact for a period. In the former theories, assumptions were made about shared values and self-adjusting systems. In the latter, the opposite view predominated: systems existed, but were based on the suppression of fundamentally conflicting interests and values. However, in recent decades the notion of overarching systems determining the lives of individuals has given way to more complex conceptualisations of the relationship between individuals and society, and between micro- and macro-sociology. Various micro-sociologies, especially phenomenology and ethnomethodology, have tended to emphasise the ways in which the social is created in human interaction, in conversation and routine behaviours which are daily re-enacted. The relationship between the actions of individuals and the influence of systems therefore remains a major area of debate in social theory.

Early uses of the concept of system in health and welfare

The American sociologist Talcott Parsons influenced a generation of health and welfare workers to comprehend society in terms of a system based on broad consensual values (Parsons et al., 1951; Parsons, 1952). His view of the social system meant that the behaviour of individuals needed to be seen in the broader context of the social system as a whole, which in turn meant that alternative (and superior) explanations and understandings of behaviour were available. Health and welfare workers had to understand these social system dimensions if they were to play their own systemic role adequately – as part of the system's equilibrium mechanisms, functioning to maintain the value consensus, controlling and educating deviants – the 'fixers' of the system (Howe, 1989, p.52).

Although Parsons described his theory as an action system, it appeared as though the social system itself was the main actor: individuals play their allotted roles well or badly, as constrained by system variables. However, the strengths of his concept of system were evident in the way it was used by other social scientists from the 1950s to the 1970s, such as in political science, where it had a major impact (Easton, 1953 and 1965). Its intellectual attraction lies in its ability to explain how individuals sometimes behave to meet systemic needs despite their conscious intentions to do otherwise. For example, health and welfare workers may wish to make significant changes to oppressive social policies, but their role actually cushions the impact of oppressive social policies, deflecting the forces of change, and preserving the very system they wish to transform.

However, the development of systems theory in the post-war period had a significant connection to the general cultural emphasis upon empirical science at that time. The concept of system was seen by many social scientists as offering a route through the social which would potentially lead to the construction of a truly scientific analysis of society, with the implication that such an analysis would be universally valid.

The concepts of General Systems Theory and unified science were intended to assert the concept of system as a fundamental concept which could be applied equally in social as in natural science, underpinning both, regardless of subject matter (Von Bertalannfy, 1968). The substantive differences between the natural and human sciences were thought to complicate but not override this common basic conceptual scheme. This also appealed to health and welfare professionals searching for a scientific knowledge base for their interventions in social situations.

A number of publications using systems concepts (Pincus and Minahan, 1973; Goldstein, 1973; Siporin, 1975; Specht and Vickery, 1977) influenced social workers in particular, with the American emphasis on the scientificity of the concept being watered down in its British version. In the USA, there were high hopes for a scientific account of 'planned intervention and change activities in regard to personality and social systems' (Siporin, 1975, p.95). In Britain, a more modest aim was to 'integrate' social work methods in order to develop a unitary concept of social work that would match the unitary Social Services Departments that were created in 1974, thus controlling social interventions in health and welfare from one organisational and theoretical base. What should be remembered about the influence of systems theory on health and welfare workers is that having previously been largely dominated by psychological and medical models of assessment, the social system concepts were important in providing a theoretical basis for *social* assessment. In addition, systems assessment was used in combination with other more psycho-dynamic and psycho-social methods, as workers tried to get a rounded understanding of the person in their social situation, continuing and developing existing traditions of enquiry. This no doubt partly explains the persistence of systems theory in health and welfare, even into recent times (Roberts, 1989; Preston-Shoot and Agass, 1990; Souflee, 1993; Hanson, 1995).

A range of criticisms have been levelled at the application of the concept of system to social phenomena in general, and to health and welfare issues in particular (Langan, 1985). The use of an overarching scientific theoretical framework to explain the working of all social systems has now been radically undermined by postmodern and post-structuralist criticisms of social theory. Parts of this critique are connected with (now) widely accepted views concerning the nature of consciousness and society that go back a long way, to phenomenology (Schutz, 1967) and other European interpretative traditions. In recent sociology, Giddens emphasises the observer's interpretation of human action and meaning as itself part of the world it analyses, and thus plays a role in changing what it also observes (Giddens, 1991). However, the Parsonian and General Systems Theory approach to social science presents the social system as an object in the real world that can be known by the impartial social scientist. From a contemporary perspective, the authors seem blissfully ignorant of the extent to which their vision of an empirical social science and a homeostatic social system reflect American and British values in the post-war era. These assumptions included an over-optimistic assessment of degrees of consensus about values, a lack of attention to the dynamics of historical change, and a limited awareness of oppression and the operation of power.

The same criticisms could hardly be levelled at Marxist uses of concepts such as 'structure' and 'system'. There is a tradition of radical social work which has drawn on Marxist thought in order to emphasise the role of the capitalist social system in structuring the lives of ordinary working people (Galper, 1975 and 1980; Jones, 1983). However, although there is a much greater awareness of power structures and conflicts of values, and certainly a far greater commitment to understanding the changing place of social systems in history, there remains in some versions a 'scientific' view of the social system as a determining structure, in a parallel way to the Parsonian model, but it centres on one form of oppression – social class. As with Parsons, the 'structuralist' model has retained some influence (Davis, 1992; Mullaly, 1993), partly because it is used in combination with other methods of understanding which also focus on the personal (in Davis's case, with feminism). However, the radical structuralist approach has been the target of post-structural criticism, especially when drawing on Althusser's structuralist interpretation of Marx, but also in its humanist forms, when it assumes human nature to be the subject of history.

The assumptions made about the concept of system do not in these latter forms always involve a commitment to the total determination of the individual or group by the overarching social system. There have often been Marxist interpretations of systems as 'contradictory', in which working people have actively resisted system imperatives, and achieved change (Rojek, Peacock and Collins, 1988). A more complex approach to concepts of system which can include contradiction and action appears more promising from a CA/B perspective, especially if its focus on one form of oppression is widened to include equally other oppressive dimensions.

Developing systems concepts in health and welfare

Variants of systems theories continue to influence health and welfare workers. Ecological models of social interaction originating in the USA have attempted to extend systems theory along more developmental lines (Germain, 1979; Hartmann, 1979; Germain and Gitterman, 1980). Treating the person on the analogy of an organism within a natural environment, it is able to take more account of historical development of people living within communities, linking personal and community development. With a greater awareness of social change, it is able to incorporate some elements of resistance within the system. However, it remains subject to some of the criticisms of systemic approaches already considered, and its concept of the 'life model' remains linked to assumptions about basic shared values which have been sharply criticised (Gould, 1987), and does not meet the requirements of CA/B principles. It still sees the social system as a naturally evolving ecological environment which can be naturalistically studied.

The most important legacy of systems theory for health and welfare workers is its bearing on assessment and intervention in family systems. Family therapy has developed as a major therapeutic resource for a range of health and welfare professionals, with multi-disciplinary and multi-national contributions leading to a variety of schools. Systemic family therapy has been one of the most important of these (Skynner, 1976; Treacher and Carpenter, 1984), but most versions of family therapy pay some attention to systemic aspects of family life.

In addition, the routine use of attachment theory by psychiatrists and psychologists connects easily to a systemic view of family life (Reder and Lucey, 1995). Indeed, the concept of an evolving set of attachments within a biological group is also very compatible with ecological theories of social systems. Theories of family therapy, whether officially 'systemic' or not, have therefore made great use of the concept of system. The key implications are that behaviour is interpreted as functional for the family system, rather than being caused by individual or external factors: emphasis is laid upon circular rather than linear causation. Earlier versions of the theory were open to some of the objections made against general social systems theory: assumptions about shared values, homeostasis, lack of awareness of reflexive, historical and power dimensions. However, feminists have criticised some of these aspects (Goldner, 1991), and family therapy is now 'asking practitioners to scrutinise and reassess their own value bases, family scripts and gender attitudes as an important prerequisite to challenging inequalities in families and society' (Preston-Shoot and Agass, 1990, p.98).

The concept of the family as an overarching system influencing the behaviour of individuals is therefore considerably attenuated. It is evident that historical power structures operating outside the family have to be accounted for, and interpretations of meaningful family behaviour must be understood within historical and social contexts, and made with awareness of the reflexivity affecting all individual participants (including workers). The system of the family does not determine its behaviour: the nature of the system itself and its relationship with other systems and individuals is called into question. However, the issue of how far the changing family structures and behaviours can be understood as intermediate, fragmentary 'systems' remains very much alive. Recent collaborative work by developmental psychologists and life-course sociologists has emphasised the 'changing matrix of ecological systems', and the 'importance of analyzing relationships between the child and a variety of environmental systems, as well as relationships between these systems' (Elder, Modell and Park, 1995a, p.246). The implications for women are equally important: 'Much more attention needs to be paid to the dynamic nature of household units ... and women's lives also need to be situated in a wider array of situations and contexts' (Katz and Monk, 1993, p.18). Thus different individuals within a family group relate in different ways to different systems within and outside the family.

Recent sociologies and interacting social systems

Within sociology, the development of micro-sociologies such as ethnomethodology, phenomenology, discourse and conversation analysis, and the advent of postmodern and post-structuralist thinking has generally militated against the concept of system as an overarching determining structure. Indeed, the strength of these micro-sociologies and the post-structuralist critique has called into question the nature of macro-sociological theory and the relationship between actor and social system: 'micro-social research ... challenges any conception which takes individuals or individually motivated action to be unproblematic units of which social phenomena are somehow composed' (Knorr-Cetina, 1981, p.24). It is argued that the complexity of social relationships at the micro-level cannot be subsumed at the macro-level, and no simplistic concept of system will do at either level. The debate about the relationship between micro-, mezzo- and macro-social systems, the relation between the actor and the structure, and the nature of social structure is interpreted now in many different ways.

One discussion of how to apply such concepts in health and social welfare identifies and rejects two kinds of reductionism: both that which explains the social in terms of individual action, and that which reduces individual action to affects of the system (Sibeon, 1990 and 1991). Sibeon assumes that both Marxist and feminist analyses fall under the latter heading, as inevitably committed to reducing all individual behaviour to affects of an oppressive system, and regards middle-level systems, such as institutions and organisations whose decision-making interactions are often recorded and can be examined, as the most appropriate for sociological study. However, as Dominelli notes, this: 'denies patterns of structured inequality which affect women as a group at macrolevels of abstraction but which can be further subdivided into more definitively differentiated groups at microlevels of abstraction to reveal the complex multiplicity of oppressions' (Dominelli, 1997, p.32). It is clear that the CA/B approach to research and assessment needs to be able to encompass the macro-level structures of inequality across the social divisions, as well as mezzo- and micro-level systems which interact with each other to help to constitute and reconstitute the macro-systems, but at the same time have the potential to resist and change behaviours and consciousness. Human agents are thus seen as inherently social beings, but not as predetermined by social systems which are themselves characterised by contradiction, change and interconnection.

Dominelli refers to Giddens's 'structuration theory' (Giddens, 1984) as having 'much in common with anti-racist feminist theory' (Dominelli, 1997, p.81). Likewise, other feminists see Giddens's view of agency and structure as usefully 'avoiding both determinism and voluntarism' (Apter and Garnsey, 1994, p.30), without either rejecting macro-structural inequalities or the interactions of individuals which enact or resist inequalities at the micro- and mezzo-levels. Giddens makes it clear that: 'the structural properties of social systems are both the medium and the outcome of the practices that constitute those systems' (Cassell, 1993, p.122). He describes this as the 'duality of structure', and distinguishes this position from the systematic relationship between parts and wholes in functionalist theories (Juckes and Baresi, 1993). In the latter case, the system functions 'independently' of the intentions or knowledge of the agents.

In Giddens's view, social systems exist simultaneously at micro- and macro-levels, since it is through the (re-)enactment of structural rules and the (re)appropriation of existing conditions and resources that the structures persist: 'The constitution of agency and structure are not two independently given sets of phenomena, a dualism, but represent a duality' (Giddens, 1984, p.25). Human actors have some limited knowledge of their position in various overlapping social circumstances, but they are not able to know all the outcomes of their actions, and they act within existing social systems, whose specific powerful 'structural properties' – their rules and resources – are already given. Giddens approves of Marx's view that men (*sic*) make history, but 'not under conditions of their own choosing' (Giddens, 1976, p157). He cites a famous study of working-class boys in school whose intentions and actions are presented as rational reactions to specific circumstances which yet inherently function as part of a wider system of distributing working-class boys to low-paid, working-class jobs (Willis, 1977).

On this account, social systems are complex phenomena that fundamentally exist through time and space, partly as a result of the unintended consequences of individual action. The functionalist bracketing of time is rejected, as the patterning of social relationships occurs fundamentally through time as well as space. The functionalist objectification of systems is rejected, since the system is regarded as being continually (re)produced by actors in specific circumstances, not as an object that exists without any connection with agents' knowledge and intentions. The postmodern view of social practice as the site of both power and resistance is thus affirmed, but not at the cost of totally denying the validity of structured inequalities of power encapsulated in continuing social systems of domination and oppression. The existence of overlapping and changing systems at various levels of micro- to macro-social practice is also a strong feature of Giddens's social theory. On this account, social systems are not part of some given (background) environment, but are implicated in all human action and interaction. The interaction of social systems within and between individuals and groups needs to be conceptualised on this non-biological, social basis in order to have an adequate basis for understanding the personal and political aspects of oppression. This contemporary conception of social systems is certainly relevant to CA/B research and assessment, and makes sense in terms of the complexities of health and welfare practice.

However, it is worth noting that Giddens's view of agency and structure has also been criticised because it concedes too much to the agency of individual actors. Hay argues that Giddens's work: 'certainly reflects the rich texture of social (inter-) action, but this is achieved by detaching the micro-practices of everyday life from their broader social and political context' (Hay, 1995, p.198). He points out that other contemporary theorists who acknowledge the dialectical relationship between agency and structure also offer a more definite account of the roles of systems and structures in people's lives, and thus are able to provide a more complete account of the way oppression and resistance to it occur. He argues that 'critical realists' (Bhaskar, 1986; Jessop, 1990) posit: '*layers* of structure which condition agency and ... define the range of potential strategies that might be deployed by agents (whether individual or collective)' (Hay, 1995, p.199; emphasis added). These layers of structures and systems, ranging across the micro-, mezzo- and macro-levels of social life, have complex sloping contours which favour certain actors and strategies over others, thus accounting for the struggles and oppressions which simultaneously mark the experience of dominated social groups. This dynamic approach is highly consistent with the CA/B framework, and provides a more subtle version of the significance of systems concepts in health and social welfare. Structure and agency are seen as completely interwoven facets of social phenomena.

Hay concludes that it is therefore crucial that two interlocked issues be addressed when considering social processes: firstly, that 'We must always ask ourselves constantly how processes *external* to the immediate unfolding of the events we are interested in have an impact (often in ways that are not immediately obvious) upon the context and the strategies, intentions and actions of the agents *directly* involved' (Hay, 1995, p.205), and secondly, to examine the strategic ways in which social structures at every level both enable and constrain – but in ways which empower some but not others.

It is important to eschew accounts of either social systems or individual agency which ignore the complexities of the dialectical relationship between them, and to take into account the full range of systems and structures which contextualise action. As a basis for social assessment of micro-level individual and family circumstances, the CA/B framework can usefully draw on these theoretical resources. It means that neither systems nor individuals should be seen as irreducible social 'realities', but their enmeshed, changing, flawed character requires careful examination of the complex enabling and constraining of individual and collective strategies at multiple levels.

Practical questions for assessors

Note: These questions must be considered in conjunction with other questions that are appended to the discussion of the other main principles in Part One. These questions can be used in conjunction with case examples to discuss the application of principles to practice situations.

1   Looking at the different *levels* of social life that impinge on the life of this person – at micro-, mezzo- and macro-systems – can you identify the range of social systems that are particularly important in this case (for example, systems and sub-systems of family, neighbourhood, your agency, the law)? Which systems have direct (versus indirect) relevance to this situation, and

what interconnections and interactions between various systems appear to be particularly significant for understanding this specific situation?

2   Given your identification of the various systems in this case, how have these systems been changing? Can you identify any directions of change, and what consequences there have been (or might be) for other systems as a result of the changes you have identified?

3   What are the perspectives of the other participants in relation to the social systems which bear on this situation – especially (but not only) the views of the user(s)? What systems do *they* identify, and how do they orient themselves towards them? How far are these perspectives on interacting social systems similar to or different from your own? What knowledge, rules and resources do they have access to in relation to these systems?

4   To what extent can the different systems be seen as closely related (i.e. that one is a sub-system or supra-system to another)? To what extent do they have boundaries which clearly distinguish them? To what extent is one system either vulnerable or supportive in relation to another? What interconnections, overlaps and interactions between various systems have particularly affected and/or continue to affect the life of this person?

5   Which systems are affected *by* the user (and user 'systems', including dependents, carers, family and/or cohabitees)? What impact has/does this person had/have on various systems – what positive *or* negative contributions have they made to family systems, peer groups, neighbourhoods, health and welfare agencies, and other social systems? What needs do they meet, what powers do they resist, or what threats or risks have they constituted in relation to these systems?

6   To what extent are behaviours and circumstances known to you understandable as a product of internal interactive 'functioning' of identifiable, relatively bounded systems? Alternatively, to what extent are they attributable to linear causes, and a product of either current or historical factors, within the system, or from other overlapping systems?

6 Power

Introduction

Given the aims of critical auto/biography to provide a theoretical framework to explore the circumstances of oppressive social systems in individual lives, there is clearly a need for a broad and inclusive concept of power which can articulate the varied situations and aspects of oppression. The definition of power is an evaluative one which needs to be justified – something for which there is not sufficient space here.

However, there are key aspects to the dimensions of a relevant concept of power, which will be indicated, together with some of the sources which can be used to help justify this approach. There must be sufficient flexibility in the concept of power to enable it to deal with the complex interactions which characterise individual experiences of power, and which will be most relevant to the micro-situations in which social assessment take place. The principle of taking power issues into account in a systematic way will then be useful as a basic principle for social assessment.

Power is classically a central concept of political philosophy, political sociology and political science, and in the 1950s the dominant views included the Weberian concept of power as consisting of the ability to make decisions in situations of conflict. This appealed to Western political scientists who could try to identify 'who gets what, when and where' as a result of those decisions (e.g. Dahl, 1970). However, Parsons developed a version of power which related it to cultural consensus rather than conflict – the ability to secure common goals (Parsons et al., 1951) – and which avoided the zero-sum concept of power (i.e. power possessed by one group to the degree that it is not possessed by another), which he judged to be a fault in Wright Mills's view of social power structures and social conflict (Wright Mills, 1956).

Inevitably, Marxists have emphasised structural aspects of power in circumstances of conflict, where power is exercised against the interests of the working class, sometimes without the suggestion of intention or agency on the part of either dominant or dominated groups (Poulantzas, 1973). However, other Marxist theorists attribute considerable importance to power as an expression of conflict which involves both agency and structure, action and language. The concept of power as 'hegemony' in Gramsci meant that the ruling classes were able to rely on the relationship between social practices and ideas to maintain their power with less need for individual acts of power: the threat of force was only a backstop for 'freely' given consent. The Frankfurt School and later critical theory also place much emphasis on the generation of unequal power relations through material and cultural social practices which produce ideology and manufacture consent (Marcuse, 1964).

Power and postmodernism

It is against this historical backdrop that recent discussions of power have taken place. Contemporary post-structural and postmodern theorists have influenced discussions in health and social welfare, where references to Foucault's concept of power seem to have become compulsory (Humphries, 1994; 1996a; 1996b; 1997; Featherstone and Fawcett, 1995a; 1995b; Fawcett, 1996; Holloway, 1996; Pini, 1997). This is undoubtedly because his views on power have attracted considerable attention from feminist theorists (amongst others, Fraser, 1989; Hartsock, 1990; Ramazanoglou, 1992; Sawicki, 1991a and 1991b; McNay, 1992; Cooper, 1995; Hekman, 1996). Although their views are divided, I shall argue that there are *some* characteristic patterns to a feminist and anti-oppressive concept of power which are important to help frame a CA/B methodology.

Power is omnipresent, according to Foucault, and should not be viewed merely as a negative exercise in decision-making by the powerful against the powerless. His view of the modern age is that it constituted a new regime of power: 'a regime of its exercise *within* the social body, rather than *from above* it' (Foucault, 1980, p.39). It has many sites, and inheres in many discourses at local and national levels – it is not just wielded by those usually recognised as powerful. This view is supported by writers who welcome the postmodernist denial of polar opposites and zero-sum approaches to power, finding it helpful to recognise that, for example, women and children also have power, and should not be represented as the innocent recipients of the exercise of adult male power (Featherstone and Fawcett, 1995a). An important part of this conception of power is the recognition by Foucault and others of the connection between knowledge and power: those who define the concepts which are used in a particular discourse empower themselves in relation to the 'other'.

This view is significant in relation to social assessment – including biographically informed methods of assessment – because it is precisely the use of language to describe, define and evaluate others that is central to the whole process: 'the practice of biography ... typically operates as a means of normalisation, and thus as an instrument of disciplinary control' (Halperin, 1995, p.130). This use of language is transcribed into various texts such as organisational records or court reports, and its various audiences reinterpret its significance, and take further action (or not) in the context of their official and unofficial powers. Assessment is therefore one of the many sites where power is exercised in society to transform individuals into the citizens of the state, and the professional use of expertise in assessment is one of the techniques of power in social practice (Johnson, 1993). This has implications for the use of any expert knowledge, including the social assessment methods being presented here, and requires considerations of ethical and political self-awareness that were discussed in Chapter 3 on reflexivity.

Power is also seen as a productive force in Foucault, not simply as a preventive or repressive force. This is also welcome to health and welfare theorists who appreciate the need to have a conception of power which can be positive and used in the various forms of 'resistance ... in local struggles ... at the everyday level of social relations' (Humphries, 1994, p.187).

The whole issue of *empowerment* in the process of research, assessment and social action requires a subtle concept of power which some feminist theorists have consciously drawn from Foucault (Cooper, 1995; Humphries, 1994 and 1996b). Burman's balanced view of Foucault's contribution highlights the value of his 'politics of subjectivity' which 'is empowering in so far as it avoids positioning women as passive victims', and provides a framework to theorise about power relations (Burman, 1990b, p.209). Cooper is more enthusiastic about the 'polysemic' concept of power she derives from Foucault, able to incorporate both an understanding of power as oppressive, entailing domination, and as creatively resistant, using new forms of knowledge and discipline (Cooper, 1995, p.26).

Critiques of postmodernist concepts of power

Even Cooper would agree that her understanding of Foucault's view of power is a reinterpretation informed by specifically feminist values. Ramazanoglou has summarised a feminist position on power succinctly:

First, women's experiences suggest that men can *have* power, and their power is in some sense a form of domination, backed by force. Secondly, this domination cannot be seen simply as a product of discourse, because it must also be understood as 'extra-discursive' or relating to wider realities than those of discourse. (Ramazanoglou, 1992, p.22)

Numerous feminists have therefore had reservations about the degree to which Foucault's concept of power is compatible with any explicit political position, given its 'deliberate distancing and "deconstruction" of any progressive political programme' (Burman, 1990b, p.211). Stanley and Wise are clear that understanding the relationship between knowledge and power is not new, and has 'rightly been the watchword of radical movements since the eighteenth century' (Stanley and Wise, 1994, p.192), and as noted above, has been a central feature of critical theory in the twentieth century, as well as a theme of recent feminism. However, they are also critical of the over-emphasis on discourse and the absence of politics in Foucault, concluding that: 'the "linguistic turn" of post-structuralism is not a sufficient basis for feminist praxis' (Stanley and Wise, 1994, p.198). All this signifies that the analysis of power should not be reduced to the study of the different uses of language, regarding this as constituting 'reality'. Power has to be researched in ways which, whilst including the role of concepts, discourse and language, *also* get to grips with the range and structure of powers which exist in the material world.

Similarly, some black writers committed to opposing racism may use the celebration of difference in post-structuralism as a means to open up the power infrastructures of discourse, and the relativity of knowledge: 'Each group speaks from its own standpoint and shares its own partial situated knowledge' (Collins, 1990, p.236). However, they are *also* insistent on the importance of a critical dialogue to search for commonalities of oppression, and disparaging of the Foucauldian assumption that power is best understood as the 'war of all [individuals] against all' (Malik, 1996, p.236). The omnipresence of power does not on this account reduce discourses to a level of undistinguishable competition, nor restrict considerations of power solely to issues of discursive practice.

The new sociologies of ethnicities 'have not turned away from the study of material disadvantage and power disparities: they do not celebrate diversity at the expense of ignoring inequality' (Bradley, 1996, p.143). Historically, black writers have been very conscious of both the personal and institutional aspects of power exercised against them, and their need to use and develop their own individual and community power (e.g. Carmichael and Hamilton, 1969), and the most recent writings of black women do not suggest any change in this direction: 'In spite of postmodernism, little has changed for the majority of black women, globally and nationally. For them power is not diffuse, localised and particular. Power is as centralised and secure as it always has been' (Mirza, 1997a, p.20).

A recent sociological study of Foucault's concept of power makes the point effectively and amusingly in relation to the health service. Porter's comparison of the power of soldiers and nurses to engage in the Foucauldian activity of surveillance concludes, on the basis of an empirical investigation, that there is no competition: soldiers, unsurprisingly, are much more able to extract information from private citizens than nurses. Porter's participatory research led to him being assaulted by British soldiers in Northern Ireland who had no difficulty in removing personal information from his wallet – ironically, even including a written note and reference number concerning an M. Foucault, taken to be a possible IRA connection! Therefore, Porter argues, contra Foucault, that power does not originate primarily in its exercise – the capacity to exercise power is possessed latently by certain groups, by virtue of their relationship to existing structures of power – and that to reduce all social processes to the exercise of power relations obviates the possibility of comparative analysis. In many instances, therefore, power *does* come from above (Porter, 1996, p.67). This also needs to be taken into account in social assessment – *in addition* to the construction of power in the practice of social assessment itself: that is, professionals making assessments need to examine the operation of power not only in their own exercise of it in their 'expert practice' and construction of user's lives, but also *through* the differing relationship of individual workers, agencies and professional groups to various structures of power, such as administrative, political, financial and social power, at local and national levels.

Power and empowerment

A critical issue for people making social assessments is to understand and try to take account of the way in which power is exercised both by and through them – both positively and negatively. They are agents of organisations which carry out government policy at the local level, and their own active use of expertise, discourse and resources helps to constitute the social relations that they assess (Johnson, 1993). However, their own productive exercise of power is significantly constrained by the power which is exercised through them by central authorities whose directions are enshrined in law and policy. It is especially important to be clear about the fundamental power of the law in health and welfare, which has increased in recent times. Never before has there been so much centralised direction of training, practice and administration of health and social welfare in Britain, following the community care and childcare legislation drawn up in the late 1980s. Law and policy always need to be interpreted and applied, but detailed guidance about making assessments is now compulsory reading for workers, and the financial and administrative framework ensures that the guidelines are broadly followed, limiting workers' power of manoeuvre. A social policy academic has commented critically on the limitations of postmodernist concepts of power in relation to the economy, the law and the state. The postmodern emphasis on diversity and choice fails to take account of the fact that: 'the grip of industrial capitalism on everyday life is as vigorous as ever, and the capacity of national governments to ... use increasingly sophisticated methods of social control is also evident' (Taylor-Gooby, 1994, p.402).

In the limited space that workers have to use their power, how far can or should professional assessment try to (re)conceptualise relations of power in order to understand and intervene effectively and ethically – even to 'empower' the user? Some of the implications were raised some time ago in Benton's 'paradox of emancipation': 'if the autonomy of subordinate groups is to be respected, then emancipation is out of the question; whereas if emancipation is to be brought about, it cannot be self-emancipation' (Benton, 1981, p.164). There cannot be self-emancipation because the subordinate group is not aware of its need for emancipation because it has internalised dominant concepts. It cannot be emancipated otherwise without disregarding its right to self-determination.

At an individual level relevant to social assessment, if a person does not recognise that their 'objective' needs are not being met because they have internalised their oppression, how do you justify the claim that there is an abuse of power from which that person should be freed (especially when no one person can be held responsible for exercising power over them)? For example, a woman may accept her role as a housewife, and has no option but to care for her children if neither the state nor her employer offers childcare (and no one else offers help), and the ideology requires that the woman cares for the child, house and partner (if male). If she agrees with the ideology, how is it possible to say that power is being used against her? Benton's answer (Benton, 1981, pp.181–2) is about cross-cutting social locations of different groups of people, when people become aware of alternative possibilities: for example, when some women may become involved in a women's group. But how do you conceptualise and deal with the nature of power in social circumstances where a particular woman is *not* involved in a women's group, unaware of and unwilling to consider other alternatives, and not able to recognise an account of her life which is based on an appreciation of social difference and power structures? This is a common situation faced by people making social assessments, and the use of concepts drawn from outside the service user's experience typically leads to allegations that the assessor has used their power inappropriately, imported their own political agenda, and themself acted oppressively.

One consideration is that a person's wants and needs are often contradictory, and closer examination and dialogue with the person might well produce more complex views about whether needs were being fairly met. The importance of skilled listening and analysis of dialogue is emphasised in feminist oral history (Anderson and Jack, 1991), where dominant ideas are sometimes subverted by contradictory themes arising from the direct experience of oppression. In interviewing women, Anderson and Jack argue that a discussion may combine 'two separate often conflicting perspectives: one framed in concepts and values that reflect men's dominant position in the culture, and one informed by the more immediate realities of a women's personal experience' (Anderson and Jack, 1991, p.32). This clash of perspectives applies to all the social divisions: clearly, there are a range of dominant concepts drawn from differing social divisions which are frequently in conflict with personal experience. Their interconnection and relevance to a specific situation will depend on the unique combination of social difference in their lives and in the life of the interviewer.

A related key issue is whether there is information actually or potentially available which could have led them to different conclusions, or information actually or potentially available to the power-holders which could have led them to initiate action rather than 'make' a non-decision (Lukes, 1974). Withholding information about the availability of childcare, or failure to take equal responsibility for childcare needs, would illustrate an abuse of power by a male partner without him having to actually *do* anything. Failure to take any initiative on childcare issues on the part of the government or an employer would also exemplify the abuse of power in omitting to meet the needs of this woman and others like her, again without them having to actually *do* anything. Nor would they have to justify non-decisions, since they could rely on the internalised oppressive values to justify their inaction as entirely natural. It is this kind of complex relationship between discourse, power and practice which has led some to object (perhaps too strongly) that: 'a postmodern analysis does nothing to illustrate the nature of social work policy or practice and ... it obscures significant issues of power politics and ideology' (Smith and White, 1997, p.294).

One aspect of Benton's argument is the implication of the importance of dialogue with a person in an oppressed social position, so that they can be informed about possible options, and about different values and ideas. Their consciousness of available courses of action may then be altered, and their awareness and opposition to the use or abuse of power may then be applied. They may then be said to have been 'empowered' – made aware of the structures of power which affect the meeting of their needs, and enabled to consider ideas and actions which might make a difference (Friere, 1972). They are then using their own limited power in a positive way to counteract the dominant powers ranged against them. Needless to say, this is a simplified model of power which does not take into account complications arising from cross-cutting membership of dominant and oppressed groups. Thus, in using her power positively to meet her own needs against a man who oppresses both herself and their children, the woman in the above example may or may not be meeting the needs of the children – for instance, in relation to their ethnicity if their father is black and she is not. As in most situations, there are often cross-cutting issues of power which can cause difficult ethical and political dilemmas.

Another issue is that of the assessor as both a power-holder on the one hand, but also a subject of power on the other, who is seeking ways of understanding the situation in which s/he is also a participant. The assessor investigates historical and social relationships, based on whatever information is available, but s/he also has to select, evaluate and construct an assessment that inevitably reflects a (relatively) powerful position and the views about it that s/he holds. This will include an evaluative judgement about the extent to which the service user can be drawn into a dialogue about alternative perspectives and concepts, where there is the possibility that the assessor may learn from the user, as well as vice versa. And all of this takes place in a legal, organisational and social context in which ways of understanding are variously described and prescribed, for the user and the assessor. The resources of language, law, finance and therapy can all be seen as variations of the (Foucauldian) technologies of social practice which help to construct the social world. In other words, part of the answer to Benton's paradox (as applied to assessment practice) is *conscious* reflexivity: there is no alternative but for any professional assessment to make evaluative judgements about how to understand and act within the social world in relation to the power issues. The systematic study of power and oppression – including the assessor's own role in negotiations with users, and the power of the 'protection' systems themselves – is therefore essential in training and practice (Doyle, 1997).

In terms of CA/B method, the existence of unequal power differentials in the research relationship has to be understood in the context of the above discussion. Foucault has stimulated existing currents of thought about the micro-processes of power, but it seems a common theme is that 'his account of power is insufficiently structural' (Allen, 1996), and that he 'refuses to link power to any account of structural inequalities' (Bradley, 1996, p.104). Power is a complex and fluid variable that has to be considered from a number of different angles, and the process of CA/B research and social assessment necessarily raises evaluative issues of empowerment and disempowerment which the researcher has to consider. It does *not* entail a naive allegiance to current discourses of empowerment, which have recently been effectively criticised as embodying 'containment and collusion, a depoliticising of action for change, and must be viewed with scepticism' (Humphries, 1996, p.14). The wider aspects of power also bear upon the auto/biographical situation, and an understanding of 'why a discourse of empowerment is so dominant in global society at this historical moment' (Humphries, 1996a, p.2) needs to be part of the analysis of power relationships at the micro-level also, where empowerment is such a buzz word. In addition, the power of the researcher or assessor and their own individual (and their profession's, and their agency's) self-interest has to be part of the equation. The helping professions especially have a vested interest in presenting themselves as empowering others, when they are simultaneously empowering themselves, both individually and collectively (Baistow, 1994/5).

Recent feminist research practices attempt to grapple with these issues, and generally give an open, reflexive account of their efforts to take account of power issues in a positive way, yet with an awareness of the contradictions and subtleties involved (Wise, 1987; Bhavnani, 1990; Shakespeare et al., 1993; Maynard and Purvis, 1994), and these need to be read in tandem with current proponents of empowerment in health and welfare (Ahmad, 1990; Braye and Preston-Shoot, 1995; Adams, 1990 and 1996). Power and liberation are traditional themes of critical theory which continually need to be re-examined (Maclaren and Lankshear, 1994), and their application at a particular historical point in time in particular circumstances requires careful analysis. One of the aims of the CA/B framework is to contribute to this effort in relation to assessment practice.

Dimensions of power

A final qualifying perspective on the nature of power which is relevant to assessment practice can be drawn from recent sociologists who have drawn attention to different dimensions of power. Scott differentiates between three main kinds of power situation, deriving his ideas from Weber, Marx and Pareto, associating them with class, status and command. Class situations are defined very broadly as: 'situations that derive from the differentials of power that are inherent in sheer possession and market relations' (Scott, 1996, p.45). Status situations are positions of honour that 'give rise to domination by prestige', and command situations arise from the 'exercise of rulership and administration, and establish domination by virtue of authority' (Scott, 1996, p.45). In assessment situations, all three kinds of power can be considered separately, even though in reality they will often overlap.

Similarly, Giddens offers a multi-dimensional view of power that has been made use of by feminists (Davis, Leijenaar and Oldersma, 1991; Bradley, 1996). Whilst Giddens proposes a concept of power as broadly defined as Foucault's, in that it inheres in all social action, he is critical of the absence in the latter's theory of 'an account of the state' (Giddens, 1982, p.223), and argues for a conceptualisation of power that relates it to various social resources, including the administrative and military power of the state, as well as economic and cultural resources.

Bradley observes that Giddens does not apply his theory of power to gender, and it is significant that she elaborates his approach further to include other spheres of power – especially in the domestic arena. She suggests, following Giddens, but expanding his approach, that: 'it is possible to identify a number of dimensions of power in terms of access and control of different resources' (Bradley, 1996, p.105). Her first three categories correspond broadly to Scott's trio of power situations: '*economic resources* (property, wealth and money); *positional resources* (access to various positions of authority in both the public and private sphere); *symbolic resources* (including language, the various media of communication)' (Bradley, 1996, p.105). The latter resources provide the prestige that underpins status differences. However, she also suggests three further categories of resources that are particularly relevant to assessing micro-social situations and to CA/B method: '*domestic resources* (control over the provision of subsistence needs in the household); *sexual resources* (the giving and withholding of sexual pleasure); *personal resources* (use of individual character and qualities to exercise control) (Bradley, 1996, p.105). It is obvious that these resources are often interwoven in practice. However, it is useful for the purposes of a theory of assessment that the fullest possible account of power in social relationships be deployed (Doyle, 1997, pp.9–15).

Bradley gives an example of how male power operates at different levels, each interlocked and mutually reinforcing, from the individual use of physical power to positional and political power, and through to economic power (Bradley, 1996, pp.9–10). Her multi-dimensional categorisation provides a rich resource for thinking systematically about the operation of power in and through the workers, users, carers and other protagonists in the process of a social assessment, taking account of both productive micro-processes and structural aspects at mezzo- and macro-levels of social organisation. This kind of theoretical principle thus forms a basic component for a CA/B methodology for social assessment.

Conclusion

In the light of the above discussion, and for the purposes of CA/B assessment, power has to be understood as a social concept which is relevant to both the public and private spheres of life, especially in relation to inequalities in power, and the potential moral and/or political and legal issues that are thus implicated.

Power issues in social relationships need to be examined at different levels: at the level of political, social and economic structures, and at the level of personal power arising from the physical, cultural and psychological factors of social practice.

The bottom line of analysis is the access of individuals, groups and agencies to physical and material resources. Power is therefore seen as constituting, causing and reflecting real material differences between individuals, organisations and social groups, at the same time as it is inherent in, and relative to, ideas, languages, practices and cultures.

It is important to contextualise power in historical time and space, both in relation to the person making an assessment and in relation to whoever else is involved, either directly or indirectly through mezzo- and macro-social systems.

Power is also something which can be positive or negative – or contradictory – in its effects: positive when it is helping to secure constructive outcomes such as equalising the meeting of needs or resisting the operation of dominant forces. It can also be negative when it is used to prevent needs being met or (worse) to increase inequalities of need, or when it *fails* to be used to meet need. The existence of social divisions implies that power is more frequently experienced by the oppressed as coming negatively from above. This does not obviate the other aspects of power, but does provide a significant perspective within which to evaluate those complexities.

Power is thus a complex issue in terms of its daily production, use and ubiquitous influence in micro-social situations, and therefore needs to be thoroughly analysed in social assessments.

Power: Some practical implications

Note: These questions must be considered in conjunction with other questions that are appended to the discussion of the other main principles in Part One. These questions can be used with case examples to discuss the application of principles to practice situations.

1   What political and economic power – or powerlessness – does an individual have, arising from structural social divisions? That is, in the light of the available identification of social differences, what political and economic (dis)advantages does a person have, simply arising from their specific membership of multiple social divisions?

2   What physical, material and financial resources are actually or potentially available to this particular individual, either in their own immediate possession (including physical (dis)ability), or through specific social groups and organisations to which they have access?

3   What are the cultural and psychological strengths and weaknesses of this particular person? (Note that this needs to be answered not only in a general sense, but also in relation to specific others, including the researcher/ assessor.)

4   In the light of answers to the above questions, who is potentially vulnerable to this person? Who is potentially a danger to this person? Who may benefit from their strengths? This matter should be considered in relation to all those personally involved with them, including the assessor or researcher.

5   What is the wider context of organisational and social power in which the assessment is being made? What other sources of power could be brought to bear negatively or positively on either the subject of assessment or the assessor, and what effect might that have?

6   In the light of answers to the above questions what moral and political issues arise in relation to 'empowering' strategies in relation to this person? How far do vulnerable others need to be protected from their (or your) power?

7   Have you thoroughly reviewed the different levels of power involved in this situation, and their changing relative values during the process of your involvement?

Part Two

Critical auto/biography: Developing methods and dialogues in practice

Part Two is *not* intended simply as the application of a preconceived methodology. The practice wisdom of professionals – especially women and other low-status workers in the caring professions – and the perspectives of oppressed groups have been used as touchstones for developing the theory in Part One.

To a degree, therefore, the exploration of practice implications of the methodology is an examination and clarification of what experienced workers in discussion with oppressed users and groups have already been attempting, rather than a set of directives which dictate to them a radically different approach.

However, the art of good anti-oppressive practice is to be theoretically informed, critically aware of practice wisdom and open to the inevitable need for change in response to current developments in practice and theory, broadening the understanding of the details and the parameters of practice, and always working towards less oppressive methods in changing circumstances.

The aim of Part Two will be to illustrate how the theory of Part One explains what workers are doing, and to help to conceptualise it clearly, so that:

1   different methods in current practice can be consistently applied and contextualised in relation to each other;

2   any specific method can be used in relation to a broader theoretical framework to provide an adequate basis for evaluation of the method and for decisions to be made in practice;

3   new methods for practice can be developed either from ideas suggested from the theory, or from other sources but in correlation with the basic theoretical requirements;

4   old methods can be reviewed and criticised in terms of the developing theoretical framework.

5   methods of assessment used in different professions and different disciplines can be evaluated against the specific benchmark of social assessment, their differing perspectives recognised more clearly, and their inter-relationships be better understood and taken into account.

Methods of assessment used in practice will therefore be questioned in terms of the CA/B theory developed in Part One.

This part begins by tackling some intractable issues about the relationship between psychological, psychiatric and social assessment, because there are both theoretical and very practical issues which cut across all service user groups. Chapter 7 deals with issues of risk and need, which are also common aspects of the practice of assessment, showing how CA/B method helps to provide a standard framework. The following chapters study four major areas of social assessment, showing how assessment practice and theory in each can be usefully based on and illuminated by CA/B method.

Case study

This case study will be discussed briefly at the ends of Chapters 9–12, with the aim of giving some broad indications of the way a specific case in these areas would need to be analysed using CA/B methods. The case is intentionally short on information (as is often the reality in the initial stages), and the discussion deliberately does not aim to be exhaustive, but suggests *some* of the issues in this hypothetical case: the reader can consider what other issues might be relevant if it were a real case (and what other information it might be appropriate to seek) by consulting the practice questions arising from CA/B principles which are listed at the end of most of the chapters in Part One.

The case study could be used as a training exercise by taking the information given in Figure 3, and assessing the implication of the different principles in Part One for the different people identified in the case study, and also attempting to consider the practice implications for different user groups, and comparing any suggested answers with the brief discussion I have appended to Chapters 9–12 (without assuming that I have necessarily provided the 'right' answers). Figure 3 summarises the case within a skeletal, diagrammatic CA/B framework, and subsequent figures will further illustrate this dimension.

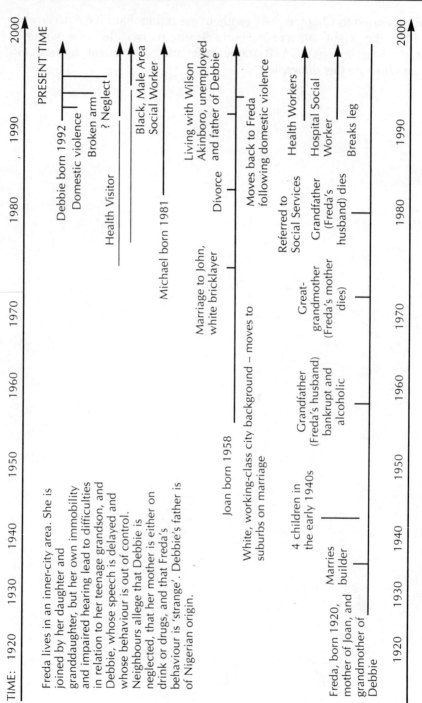

TIME: 1920   1930   1940   1950   1960   1970   1980   1990   2000

PRESENT TIME

Freda lives in an inner-city area. She is joined by her daughter and granddaughter, but her own immobility and impaired hearing lead to difficulties in relation to her teenage grandson, and Debbie, whose speech is delayed and whose behaviour is out of control. Neighbours allege that Debbie is neglected, that her mother is either on drink or drugs, and that Freda's behaviour is 'strange'. Debbie's father is of Nigerian origin.

Debbie born 1992
Domestic violence
Broken arm
? Neglect
Health Visitor
Black, Male Area Social Worker
Living with Wilson Akinboro, unemployed and father of Debbie
Michael born 1981
Divorce
Moves back to Freda following domestic violence
Marriage to John, white bricklayer
Referred to Social Services
Health Workers
Hospital Social Worker
Joan born 1958
White, working-class city background – moves to suburbs on marriage
Great-grandmother (Freda's mother dies)
Grandfather (Freda's husband) dies
Grandfather (Freda's husband) bankrupt and alcoholic
Breaks leg
4 children in the early 1940s
Marries builder
Freda, born 1920, mother of Joan, and grandmother of Debbie

1920   1930   1940   1950   1960   1970   1980   1990   2000

Figure 3   Case study: The 'A' family

7 Social assessment and multi-professional practice

Psychology, psychiatry and social assessment

In examining practices of assessment in different areas of multi-professional practice, it is difficult to categorise methods neatly in relation to disciplines and professions. There is much overlap and crossing of boundaries. The disciplines of psychology and psychiatry are used both theoretically and in various practical ways in all of the different user groups that are identifiable, particularly in health and welfare services. The domination of assessment by psychiatric and psychological models in all these fields, and especially in the legal arena, and the social status of the related professions that have characteristically used them mean that it is important to identify clearly what the difference is between social assessment and assessment based on psychological and psychiatric theoretical models. The foundations of the following comments have already been laid in the discussion of historical location in Chapter 4.

The purpose of this chapter is firstly, to distinguish psychological and psychiatric assessments from social assessment based on CA/B; secondly, to review social work assessment in relation to CA/B methods, and thirdly, to examine issues of multi-professional practice. It is argued that the CA/B framework provides a basis for a distinctive theoretical approach to *social* assessment, which is a compelling requirement for workers and users contending with the overwhelming status of the medical, psychiatric, psychological and legal establishments. Workers making such assessments may be part of the mental health system or may be outside it, since issues pertaining to psychology and psychiatry are not confined to persons labelled as 'mentally ill'. For example, mental distress, whether reactive or endogenous, is manifestly prevalent throughout the user groups that are assessed in health and social welfare. Therefore, there are frequently psychological aspects of assessment that need to be considered.

Psychology and psychiatry

CA/B's reliance on qualitative research methods aimed at understanding individual lives stands in some contrast to both psychology and psychiatry. It has often been noted that the rival traditions of psychoanalysis and psychology are both based on assumptions concerning the importance of scientific method: in this respect, 'Freud was brother under the skin to ... B.F. Skinner' (Sherif, 1987, p.43). Equally, in the area of attachment theory, one of Bowlby's original concerns was the need to ground an understanding of psychological development more firmly on an objective, scientific framework (Bretherton, 1991, p.10). In a final paper written just before his death, he claims, as a 'scientist': 'Once we postulate the presence within the organism of an attachment behavioural system ... many of the puzzles ... are found to be soluble' (Bowlby, 1991, p.293).

CA/B's engagement with time and place, and with social values, is not conducive to approaches which propose reductionist scientific explanations for human behaviour. However, the cost of ignoring the social and historical context of explanations of human psychology is high, and has been well documented, especially by feminist and black psychologists (e.g. Burman, 1990a; Burman et al., 1995; Robinson, 1995) in terms of the pathologising of oppressed groups. The discipline of psychology is the one that has been most criticised by feminists and others for its failure to place itself within social and historical contexts generally, and specifically for its historic inability to come to terms with power and gender issues (Sherif, 1987; Harris, 1997).

A related issue concerns the boundaries of psychological and psychiatric science and medicine, and is especially relevant to the question of assessment: that *social* assessment should be made in the light of socially and historically specific relations of power and dominance, and *psychological* (and psychiatric) assessments should be placed within this context, and not presented as part of a self-contained 'expert' discipline to which other workers must unquestioningly defer. For example, a study of researching psychotherapeutic relationships reaches the conclusion that an understanding of the 'synchronic and diachronic' (historical) features of that relationship's social context must be pursued, drawing upon bodies of knowledge 'outside of psychology' (Pilgrim, 1990, p.183). Squire also argues for the importance of the 'power relations which ... traditional psychology neglects' (Squire, 1989, p.111), and specifically highlights the work of black and Third World women as clear exemplars of 'associative feminist challenges to psychology's disciplinary boundaries' (Squire, 1989, pp.116–17). The converse of this is exactly what Sherif describes as the recipe for traditionally oppressive bias in psychology – *narrowing* the space and time perspective so that psychologists view 'as "scientific" the conduct of research on human individuals about whose past, personal loyalties and social ties, they knew next to nothing' (Sherif, 1987, p.44; cf. Harris, 1997).

The implications of the CA/B methodology thus relates both to internal critiques of psychology and psychiatry that have been discussed in recent times, and to the positioning of a form of social assessment that should have equal status with, and form a contextualising framework for (and a potential critique of) any psychological or psychiatric assessment. The internal debate continues at a methodological level in ways that connect with CA/B method. For instance, recent re-evaluations of psychology and psychological research methods place far more emphasis upon a grasp of the social context (Smith, Harre and Van Langenhove, 1995a), and include the use of life history sociological research methods supported by CA/B (e.g. Plummer, 1995). In psychiatry, there have also been re-evaluations of the various traditions, placing much more emphasis on the social divisions, with feminists and postmodernists especially trying to reinterpret and re-contextualise psychodynamic theories in the light of social and cultural factors (Sayers, 1986; Benjamin, 1990). The development of a 'critical psychology' tradition (Fox and Prilleltensky, 1997) also supports a position that is compatible with CA/B methodology. Assessment of mental health and distress, both within the mental health system and outside it, needs to be multi-professional, and professions need to have some appreciation of cross-disciplinary issues, therefore the awareness of some psychologists and psychiatrists of the relevance of sociology and history is to be welcomed. However, the contention here is that there is also a place for *social* assessment that should be relatively autonomous of either psychology, psychiatry or medicine, and that CA/B method should be the basis for it.

Psychological assessment

There are numerous variations in the theoretical loyalties of professional psychologists, with many operating in an eclectic fashion, but there is often an academic tendency towards behavioural and cognitive approaches. The following is a brief critique of a current approach to assessment from a specific professional perspective that draws on equally specific disciplinary methodologies. This example is chosen firstly because it is an excellent example of its type, involving the work of the leading psychologists in their field in the UK. Secondly, it assesses the behaviour of people with which other professionals are certain to have contact, thus requiring consideration of multi-professional and multi-disciplinary issues. Thirdly, it is about a matter of considerable topical importance in relation to the assessment of potentially dangerous people before their release into the community.

Psychologists have established themselves as experts in the context of secure settings, and their professional training is usually oriented towards behavioural and cognitive methods – a theoretical framework which has support in health and social welfare generally, for example in childcare social work (Sheldon and MacDonald, 1992–93). Social workers and health visitors often have to work with clinical psychologists in the assessment of risky childcare situations, and as with psychiatrists and doctors, the lower social status of social workers and nurses lends credibility to the recommendations that clinical psychologists make. It is thus important to examine the adequacy of theoretical frameworks emerging from this field from the perspective of CA/B method.

An impressive recent study (McMurren and Hodge, 1994) explicitly sets out a behaviourist methodology for assessing various kinds of criminal behaviour in the context of secure settings, drawing on four contemporary schools of behaviour therapy: the neo-behaviourist mediational stimulus-response model; social learning theory; cognitive behaviour modification, and applied behaviour analysis. The authors contend that a broadly behavioural perspective has considerable utility in working with offenders, and that in particular, it has been found in several meta-analyses that: 'programmes are more likely to be effective if they are explicitly based on a theoretical principle' (McMurren and Hodge, 1994, p.2). It is therefore important to have a clear understanding of the theoretical principle on which assessment is based. This is an important finding which applies generally across the social sciences, and is just as relevant to the need for a firm basis for social assessment as it is for behavioural psychology. The confusion that surrounds the subject stems partly from the lack of agreement on a theoretical and evaluative basis.

However, whilst their broadly behavioural approach to assessment does have much to offer, it is not sufficiently comprehensive or subtle to encompass all the complex requirements of assessment in human situations. The first criticism is simply that their approach is specific to a particular discipline – behavioural psychology. However, they are assessing sociological as well as psychological matters, which have social, political and ethical components. A multi-disciplinary approach is methodologically essential from a CA/B perspective, and a specifically sociological understanding of assessing an individual life needs to underpin, complement and critique the psychology. Secondly, their approach is similar to other behavioural perspectives in that it explicitly devalues social history, in their case on the basis of a rejection of personality theory. They explicitly place a greater emphasis on current rather than historical determinants of behaviour (McMurren and Hodge, 1994, p.14). This no doubt helps to differentiate their approach from psycho-dynamic psychologies, but it ignores the time-bound social structural determinants of behaviour, and an adequate socio-historical understanding of individual lives. Thirdly, the behavioural approach is based on a traditional scientific methodology which places the observer outside the theoretical framework. Contemporary research in the social sciences has become well aware of the importance of the concept of reflexivity, and this is a basic component of CA/B; an assessment which does not have this concept at its centre will be inadequate as a social assessment where a more complex view of the nature of research and assessment is required. A related issue is the final point to be made here: that values are at the heart of assessment. The values of the researcher/ assessor (and the social environments within which s/he works) should not be relegated to the position of an addendum, but should be central to the framework. CA/B highlights the values which complement these theoretical considerations – anti-oppressive values which link individual lives (including those of the assessors) to social structures based on the use and abuse of power.

This brief critique is only intended to indicate the main areas of difference, and does not preclude the use of behavioural methods as a means of assessment. It *does* militate against the use of behavioural assessment in isolation from a social assessment. The practical implications for assessment are therefore that such a psychologically oriented and focused assessment would need to be supplemented by a social assessment for purposes that would be relevant for the future management of the person(s) involved. A CA/B understanding of the person's situation and the place of the psychological assessment in their life would provide the social context within which to more fully evaluate the psychological evidence (Fox, 1997).

Psychiatric assessment

The practical implications of a social assessment based on CA/B in relation to psychiatry are clearly very different from the situation in behavioural and cognitive psychology. The concern of psychodynamic psychiatrists with social histories, and the interest of more medically oriented psychiatrists with medical and social histories, means that there is a much greater awareness of the element of time and development in a person's life. This obviously relates to the history of these disciplines, the interest of Freud and Bowlby in early childhood experiences, and of Erikson on development through the whole life. Equally, the medical model of the maturing biological organism and its structured unfolding connects well with attachment theory as well as Piagetian concepts of development. Clearly, there are different views of psychiatry and how it should draw on these differing inputs for the purposes of assessment. Rather than discussing these concepts in the abstract, a recent study of assessment by psychiatrists will be examined.

The psychiatric assessment of parenting is chosen because, again, there is a strong multi-disciplinary and multi-professional component. Reder and associate psychiatrists and psychologists have made a major contribution to the subject of assessing and intervening in the abuse of children by adults in recent years (Reder and Lucey, 1991; Reder, Duncan and Gray, 1993a and 1993b; Reder and Lucey, 1995), so this assessment encompasses work with both adults and children, whereas the previous discussion was about adults being assessed by psychologists before discharge into the community. However, the underlying principles of their respective theoretical frameworks each apply to both spheres of work, as both professions work with both children and adults.

Reder and Lucey make it clear, as did the behavioural psychologists (see above), that a theoretical framework is essential to their assessment. Indeed, they comment bluntly that in contrast with their own clear theoretical framework, the problem with social work assessment based on the 1988 Orange Book (DoH, 1988) is that: 'it contains an extensive list of recommended questions but provides no theoretical framework to help ... make sense of the answers' (Reder and Lucey, 1995, p.5). Key factors in *their* theoretical framework are:

1   It is interactional, where this refers primarily to personal and familial interactions, and Winnicott's view of the development of interactional sequences over time between child and parent is cited (Winnicott, 1960).
2   It is based on psychological history of both the relationship itself and the preceding relationships of parents with *their* parents. This is based on Bowlby's attachment theory, in which everyone is deemed to have 'an innate biological ability to parent, which a child evokes, but the detailed form that this takes hinges on individual experience' (Reder and Lucey, 1995, p.5). The evolution of patterns of attachment continue over the life-course, and influence adult as well as infant behaviour (Parkes, Stevenson-Hinde and Marris, 1991).
3   The intrapsychic issues of personality and identity of the individuals involved are thus an essential part of the interactive process.
4   It is also related to 'external stressors', which can include a variety of factors, such as poverty, poor housing and ill health.

The general approach is summarised in a concluding chapter as having a common basis in the view that what they are assessing is: 'the manifestation of a relationship which is sensitive to processes at intrapsychic, interpersonal and social/cultural levels' (Reder and Lucey, 1995, p.266), and that factors from all three levels therefore have to be integrated into the assessment. They identify attachment theory as a crucial element of their thinking, but stress that it is 'the nature of the relationship leading to, and surrounding, the particular family structure that is more relevant to outcome' (Reder and Lucey, 1995, p.269) rather than specific diagnoses of the parents such as psychiatric disorder or learning disability. They also insist on the importance of *not* relying on high-risk checklists, but considering each case in its own right, making assessment of the unique characteristics of the relationships involved. They are clear that what they are constructing is in the nature of an 'expert opinion' that is often subsequently offered to a court, and part of the justification for this is the view that what is offered is an 'independent' assessment – an overview of the multi-agency involvement with a family (Reder and Lucey, 1995, p.13).

There are inevitably both connections and contrasts with CA/B methodology, which is designed to provide a theoretical basis for social assessment rather than 'expert' psychological or psychiatric assessment. However, the points of comparison have implications for the internal construction of their framework of assessment as well as for the position of social assessment in relation to psychiatry and psychology.

The first point concerns the CA/B principle of specific social and historical location. Clearly, the use of attachment theory as a developmental principle over the life-course, connects with this part of CA/B method. Bowlby explicitly asserts that: 'starting during his first months in his relations with his mother figure ... [the child] builds up working models of how attachment figures are likely to behave ... and on those models are based all his expectations, and therefore all his plans for the rest of his life' (Bowlby, 1978, p.418). Assessment of attachment in both adults and children is therefore fundamental to this psychiatric approach – 'Development of the attachment dynamic is particularly significant' (Reder and Lucey, 1995, p.6) – and although no single factor is seen as 'causing' abusive behaviour, it is critically the absence of normal attachment ties which render an adult vulnerable to external stressors in relationships with children or adults. This emphasis on the importance of the mother–infant bond corresponds to Bowlby's thesis that a *biologically based system* of relationships maturing over time significantly determines the psychological predispositions of individuals. Other social factors are seen as *external* – contributory to the system's functioning, rather than constitutive of it. The psychological attachment system (however adequate or faulty) appears as the significant endogenous domain upon which external stressors impinge.

In contrast, CA/B methodology takes the sociological components of the developing child and family unit as *equally* constitutive as the psychological and biological factors. The psychology of the child and its carers is seen as part of other social systems, not regarded as background noise which may or may not interfere with endogenous developmental processes. This criticism relates to the conceptualisation of psychological attachment processes in relation to the social, and is partly a matter for discussion *within* psychology and psychiatry (see below). However, the main point to stress here is that the sociology of the life-course of particular children and families provides the ground for life history research using CA/B methods. The psychiatrists, like the psychologists, are impinging on sociological as well as psychological matters, therefore a specifically sociological understanding of assessing an individual life needs to underpin, complement and critique the psychiatry.

Secondly, although psychiatry (especially psycho-dynamic psychiatry, but not behavioural psychology) values the historical dimension, its focus on historical development is (understandably) primarily at the intrapersonal and the interpersonal levels. Thus it is not only the case that the sociology of interpersonal relationships needs to be added to a psychiatric account, it also needs to be set into the context of a specific social *history*, where the latter is *not* understood in traditional psychiatric terms as primarily a history of intrafamilial and personal events, focusing on psychological developments, but as an account of the historical specificity of a particular person having a fluctuating social identity within distinctive social groups within a changing society. This also has significant implications for the interpretation and constitution of a social history (see the discussion of historical location in Chapter 4).

Thirdly, like behavioural approaches, psychiatry is still largely based on a traditional scientific methodology which places the observer outside the theoretical framework. Most kinds of psychiatry, including the example discussed here, place special emphasis on the expert nature of the diagnoses offered on the basis of a scientific methodology, and also on the basis of clinical and medical expertise. In the case cited, Reder emphasises the expert contribution of the psychiatrist as an 'independent' observer of the various parties involved. This typical psychiatric stance is inconsistent with the concept of reflexivity in CA/B, and is in itself an illustration of the necessity of a methodology which can include the observer or assessor as participating in a specific set of structured social relationships. It is important to note that this is notwithstanding the reflexive concepts of transference and counter-transference which are deployed by psychiatrists and psychotherapists. These are also behaviours usually conceptualised as relating to intrapersonal and interpersonal dynamics, without *also* placing them within specific sociological and historical parameters. The psychotherapist remains the expert – even when (s)he recognises the possibility of 'learning from the patient' (Casement, 1990). However, the interactions between the values and perspectives of the assessor and of those being assessed and of others involved are central to the CA/B framework.

CA/B also highlights the issues of social difference and power, linking individual lives to social structures and examining the implications in assessment of cross-cutting uses and abuses of power. These issues are part of the 'cultural' background for the psychiatrist – the external stressors, which Reder includes as part of his theoretical framework. In fact, they are an *integral* part of the social situation in which the psychiatrist operates, and a social assessment is needed which can take full account of their complex influences. The realisation of this has led to many debates within psychology and psychiatry, and the following section indicates some aspects of theoretical development particularly relevant to social assessment and CA/B.

Lifespan developmental psychology

In the discussion of historical location and specificity in Part One, the use of lifespan developmental psychology was discussed as a contributing factor to CA/B method, especially when contextualised within critical, feminist and anti-oppressive social histories. It is therefore closer to the practice (as well as to the theory) of social assessment than the above examples of psychology and psychiatry. It is evident in the practice of workers in different professions that lifespan psychological theories which contribute to an understanding of the changes in people's lives and perceptions as they move through the life-course are often utilised, and are highly regarded (Gibson, 1991; Howe, 1995). There is thus inevitable overlap between workers who need to make use of psychological theories about personal change, and psychologists and psychiatrists who specialise in the study and practice of psychological change in people's lives (see the next section on issues of triangulation of approaches).

Some psychologists have made particular efforts to relate the psychological to the social and historical, especially Runyan, whose important study of idiographic methods makes connections between differing psychological methodologies and life histories (Runyan, 1982), and has been further developed since (Smith, Harre and Van Langenhove, 1995c). The development of connections between biographical approaches in psychology, sensitive to social history, will strongly facilitate a triangulation of social and psychological methodologies compatible with CA/B, and promises to be the most effective way forward in the holistic understanding and assessment of lives (cf. Josselson and Lieblich, 1993; Josselson, 1996).

An example of triangulation is given by Runyan in his explanation of Wachtel's early efforts to integrate behavioural and psycho-dynamic theory in the concept of 'interaction cycles', in which early psychological experiences affect later environments (Wachtel, 1977). He links this with the life-course sociology of Elder (Elder, 1974), and the changing person-in-situation interactions which Elder studies over the life-course of differing social groups – an appeal to precisely the kind of methodological resource utilised by CA/B, and carried forward recently in developmental and historical studies of children (Elder et al., 1995b). This complex approach to understanding lives is matched by the long tradition of social work theories also attempting to study the person-in-situation.

Probably the most significant factor in bringing psychological theory and practice closer to CA/B method is the contribution made in recent years by feminists within the disciplines of psychology and psychiatry. Some of the themes of feminist critiques of psychology connect directly with CA/B method. Primarily, there is the issue of social difference itself, upon which a feminist critique must be founded. Gilligan's work on moral development in girls (Gilligan, 1982) has subsequently been widely discussed and applied to other social divisions (Larrabee, 1993). The application of the concept of difference to other social divisions is also widely accepted in feminist psychotherapy, (e.g. Holland, 1990). Closely related is the emphasis on power, and both these themes can be found together in feminist psychologists (Burman, 1990a and 1990b; Burman et al., 1995) and psychiatrists (Benjamin, 1990). Feminists often highlight the importance of a concept of reflexivity that relates the psychologist to their own social experience, and advocate the importance of training which includes: 'encouraging trainees to examine the implications of their own gender role stereotypes for themselves and for their interaction with families' (Vetere, 1992, p.147). They have consistently argued for the importance of contextualising the psychological within wider disciplinary boundaries (Squire, 1989), and have also sought to explore the life-course aspects of psychology as part of that process (Gilligan, 1987).

As indicated at the beginning of this chapter (and Chapter 4), there is evidence of a general turn in psychology towards narrative and life histories. The lifespan approach to understanding lives from a social and historical as well as a psychological perspective, drawing on various theoretical resources, appears to be growing within psychology, thus facilitating integration with a social assessment methodology like CA/B. Unlike the more traditional forms of psychology and psychiatry discussed above, which still dominate the psychological discussion of assessment in health and social welfare, these more critical variants of lifespan developmental psychology overlap and integrate with CA/B, attempting to combine sociological and historical concepts with the psychology and psychiatry of individual development.

Triangulating/bridging practices in assessment: Multi-disciplinary issues

A common technique of social research practice is that of triangulation, in which the object of research is studied by using more than one research method. This is especially important in an age when research methods have proliferated, and is now an orthodoxy of social research (Denzin, 1978). It is also particularly germane to CA/B's conception of structured (and unstructured) differences in perspectives between groups and individuals. However, I have deliberately associated triangulation and bridging, following Miller's distinction between the two concepts (Miller, 1997a). She uses the term 'bridging' to refer to: 'using several methodological strategies to link aspects of different sociological perspectives, not to discover indisputable facts about a single social reality' (Miller, 1997a, p.25). By contrast, she takes 'triangulation' to be the endeavour to achieve an integration of different kinds of research evidence into a more comprehensive understanding of a common research object. Bridging is about reaching a dialogue between interpretative perspectives: 'to make different perspectives mutually informative, not to obscure or deny their distinctive features' (Miller, 1997a, p.41).

My contention is that in the relationship between differing professions and differing kinds of assessment, *both* triangulation and bridging are research concepts which are directly relevant. Unfortunately, it is often impossible in practice to be sure which is the most relevant, nor can the theoretical distinction be drawn too rigidly. I am also obviously using the concept to apply to interpretive practices that lie outside as well as inside sociology. Social assessment based on CA/B methodology is a social research perspective that offers a different understanding of human behaviour from psychology and psychiatry. The above discussion attempts to indicate some of the basic differences in theoretical perspectives, although this brief argument is obviously very limited in relation to the wide spectrum of debate in these subjects. However, my claim would be that *bridging* strategies are generally required for the kind of situation where professionals are using distinctive disciplinary perspectives (as in the above mainstream examples in psychology and psychiatry), which are not designed primarily with a social perspective in mind. Secondly, where there are shared perspectives which can be demonstrated by similarity of methods, concepts and values, then *triangulation* becomes a more promising possibility. In the real world of professional assessments of people and situations, it is often difficult to make such clear distinctions. For example, one cannot assume that differences between professions or organisations correlate with differences between basic methods. Multi-professional assessment does not necessarily equate with multi-disciplinary assessment. Nor does the use of different terminology necessarily preclude the possibility that similar methods are being used (Eisenberg, 1992).

A recent research analysis of multi-professional assessment and planning tends to support these claims, although from a more relativistic postmodernist position. Using narrative theory to analyse case discussions in 'multi-disciplinary' health teams, Opie concludes that: 'a significant aspect of team work is the recognition of interpretative differences', and thus 'the generation of different narratives moving ... to [the] possibility of their (temporary) meeting at nodal points, in a dynamic process which foregrounds the postmodern concepts of provisionality, incompleteness, and undecidability' (Opie, 1997, 3.38 and 3.42). She describes this as a 'rhizomic' model of teamwork, in which the different narratives interweave like spreading roots, and in which possibilities and constraints are 'made available to the team through its different constituent knowledge bases' (Opie, 1997, 4.4). However, she contends that the evidence suggests that in developing a team narrative, multi-disciplinary teams often failed to recognise the multiple interpretive possibilities that arose, and that an explicit organisational policy is needed to facilitate knowledge-creation. Using a study of knowledge-generation by teams in business companies (Nonaka and Takeuchi, 1995), she makes recommendations of wider relevance, based on the explicit recognition of interpretive differences in a team, which will be drawn upon below.

Unlike Miller's theoretical ideal of rational discussion between research methodologies, and unlike Opie's interpretive relativism, CA/B has built into it the view that to a significant degree, the methodologies themselves represent the values and interests of various dominant and oppressed groups. Therefore, there is a need for strategies that will support the perspectives of the most vulnerable to be a touchstone of the assessment process itself. This will not necessarily be easier when there *is* some agreement, since the status of professionals is involved, including the status of all workers in relation to service users. Opie asserts that the outcome of teamwork 'cannot therefore be a single authoritative narrative ... largely defined by knowledge deriving from one discipline' (Opie, 1997, 4.4). However, given the dominance of some social and professional groups over others, this may quite possibly be the case: her statement makes more sense as a recommendation or aim. However, Opie, Miller and CA/B theory broadly agree on the variability of interpretive perspectives within a dynamic process, and the importance of explicit organisational strategies to maximise the production of knowledge in multi-professional assessment.

It is not insignificant then that workers whose orientation has been towards the *social* aspects of assessment do in practice supply a different and critical perspective in those arenas where the management of risk and need are decided. Ann Davis refers to the recognition that recent Department of Health guidelines (DoH, 1994) have expressed – that social workers, along with probation officers, have particular expertise in the area of risk assessment and management on which other members of multi-disciplinary teams in the mental health field might usefully draw:

> This expertise reflects a perspective which strives to work with the complexity of risk ... It acknowledges and investigates the social, cultural and psychological factors which shape the experiences of people with mental health problems ... This *socially* informed, user-centred perspective can serve to extend and rebalance the diagnostically and behaviourally focused approaches to risk minimisation which [are] currently dominating this area. (Davis, 1996, pp.118–19; emphasis added)

The implication of this argument agrees closely with the perspective provided by CA/B methods. This means that the social assessment needs to be recognised as having its own methodology, and can therefore stand alone to a degree.

However, no form of assessment in the area of understanding lives can afford to stand entirely alone. Runyan makes this point strongly about theoretical orientations in psychology in relation to a life-course perspective: they each have something to contribute (Runyan, 1982, pp.97–9). This must be applied outside psychology as well as within it, but will depend on first evaluating the degree to which methods and values are in alignment, and the extent to which there is in fact a similar 'research object'. There are thus overlapping issues to be discussed both within and between professions and disciplines about the appropriateness of drawing on a given range of theoretical concepts in a particular case. This has always been an explicit issue within social work (Milner and O'Byrne, 1998). Awareness of issues of theory, methods and values should not be avoided, as one distinguished researcher into psychotherapy has found: 'If the biographical method is to be properly pursued by psychologists ... then *a priori* assumptions and value preferences will require examination and declaration' (Pilgrim, 1990, p.192). This will be a key factor in assessing whether qualitatively different research objects are being constructed, and different theoretical perspectives used both within and between various professions.

Implications for multi-professional teamwork

The practical circumstances of multi-professional teamwork can vary considerably, so the following are offered as principles which need to be translated into specific actions and policies feasible in those circumstances. The prerequisite for such an approach is the organisational intention to promote knowledge-creation by: 'problematizing the notion of team work ... and addressing team processes and organisational structures which could facilitate its development' (Opie, 1997, 4.3).

First, teams must regard *social* assessment as a specific theoretical perspective, and treat it as making a distinctive contribution equal in value to other disciplines. In Opie's terms, the team must sustain the 'presence of autonomy', for members who represent distinctive perspectives, in order to maximise their creativity and their understanding of their own and others' positions (Opie, 1997, 4.3). Thus each of the various professions represented has to be treated with respect – especially in relation to the specific academic disciplines and theoretical perspectives which they bring to bear in the analysis of a case. Social assessment has to be seen and treated as an autonomous theoretical perspective based on the social sciences, especially sociology, social policy, history and psychology. The social work assessment should be seen as the specialist 'social assessment', although other professions will unavoidably be using social concepts. The assessments made by other professions need to be contextualised by the social assessment, and in so far as they use social concepts, their evaluation of the case, especially in relation to any overall judgements, has to be critically assessed in the light of that context. In addition, it seems preferable to use 'social assessment' rather than 'psycho-social assessment', since this traditional phrase has historically connoted the dominance of the 'psycho' over the 'social', and has often had a specific psycho-dynamic gloss.

Second, there needs to be acknowledgement and consideration of the differences arising from the varied disciplinary perspectives (Opie, 1997, 4.3) and the values and life experiences of those involved in the assessment, including the users (Pilgrim, 1990). This ought to include acknowledgement of the social divisions that are relevant to those involved, and the differing perspectives that may ensue. In the legal context, social workers and others reporting to court are required to indicate the level and nature of their experience as well as their qualifications and level of contact with the assessed (Plotnikoff and Woolfson, 1996). A bridging strategy requires that professionals also indicate their *theoretical* orientation – their knowledge and value base – so that their assessment can be appreciated by others. An explanation of why people approach an assessment in a given way will illuminate differences in perspective, and thus the extent to which there is a shared research object. Further, the concept of *team reflexivity* needs to extend to the discussion of team values and assumptions, not only in relation to their interpretative methods, but also in the processual issues of team discussion. For example, there ought to be agreements about their own conduct, in order to avoid negative narratives about users, or unnecessary exposure of personal details (Opie, 1997, 3.11). There has to be at least a minimum appreciation of the values that are fundamental to a social assessment as set out here, together with their practice implications for the process and the outcome of multi-professional work.

Third, other bridging practices suggested by Miller in the research context are relevant to the multi-professional assessment context. For example, she points out that theoretical orientation and language may change over time within an agency, and cites the example of a family therapy centre which changed from ecosystemic language to a more user-centred problematising discourse (Miller, 1997b). It is also important to note that individuals within organisations may alter their theoretical stance between cases. Social workers, especially, are trained to be theoretically flexible (Milner and O'Byrne, 1998). The implication here is that there needs to be an organisational mechanism for monitoring changes in theoretical orientation over time, especially where personnel changes or external conditions affect organisational cultures, but also where the culture and discourse themselves undergoes endogenous development. Other professional assessors need to have some understanding of these changes, which are relevant to the relationships between local agencies. This is especially important when issues can be added to or removed from an agenda by a powerful agency without discussion.

Fourth, Miller also discusses the selection of minimally compatible perspectives, and the development of areas of compatibility (Miller, 1997a, p.41). However, it is very important to balance this *simultaneously* with the question of the representation of different perspectives. In Opie's terms, the issue is about 'the presence of requisite variety': the 'team's internal diversity must match the variety and complexity of the environment' (Opie, 1997, 4.3). In assessment practice, there needs to be space – particularly in the context of continuing relationships – to develop understandings of how differing perspectives may have some common ground, and where they differ, and to actively try to develop links between disciplines and professions and users, but this must include evaluation of the team's diversity, and the extent to which different perspectives are represented. This is therefore an important reason for developing dialogue with relevant user organisations – local children's, black, disabled, gay, lesbian and women's agencies, for example. However, there will always be practical and political problems about perspectives which are difficult or impossible to facilitate, or how well differing disciplines, users and professions are represented. The issues of power and representation of views need to be continually addressed, both in individual and organisational terms. Indeed, it has to be assiduously borne in mind that both failure to develop a minimal degree of consensus on values and methods and failure to take account of differing perspectives are risk factors, indicative of communication failures and inability of agencies and professions to co-operate.

Fifth, the optimum sharing of qualitative data is supported by both Miller and Opie, since this not only provides evidence for assessing validity, but can also be the occasion for discussing theoretical perspectives. Although differing disciplines are oriented to different sorts of data, there are always areas of overlap in assessing lives, and the presentation and theoretical interpretation of data should be used as an opportunity to compare interpretative methods. The sharing of information on life histories should therefore be used as fully as possible to facilitate both triangulation (providing cross-checks on validity, and information from different angles) and bridging (discussing differences of theoretical and interpretative approaches). Opie supports the 'utilisation of redundancy', (using information 'beyond immediate operational requirements'), because this enables individuals 'to sense what others are trying to articulate' (Opie, 1997, 4.3).

Sixth, a practical way forward is therefore to focus on the co-operative construction of *life histories*. The concept of the user's life history as shared data for multi-disciplinary and multi-professional work is not new, and has already been suggested by social workers and psychiatrists. For example, the use of life story work in childcare has been proposed as a vehicle to promote teamwork to support a multi-disciplinary approach and reinforce agency co-operation (Wolff, 1978; Lightbown, 1979; Beste and Richardson, 1981). Over half a century ago, a sociologist noted the commonalities involved in various disciplines and professions to understand life histories, but also commented on the variability of methods of analysis (Cavan, 1929). Little has changed in this respect, and given contemporary views about the plurality of different perspectives, it is unlikely to do so. However, this makes it all the more important to develop methods of 'working together' which not only respond to agency and government policies, but which are intellectually defensible, and clearly, the assumption of simple triangulation and consensus (or worse, the pre-eminence of one professional perspective) will not do.

The systematic collation of life history information, and especially the questioning of methods of collection, is crucial to an understanding of the *primary social construction* of the data. This means that there should be a systematic sharing of different types of evidence to create life histories: documentary evidence from various agencies and users; oral evidence from workers directly from their participation, or from colleagues' reports; third party evidence generally, and users' evidence. All of this needs to be rigorously assessed in terms of issues such as exactly *whose* evidence it is, and how reliable it is; when and where the evidence was obtained, and what that implies about the evidence; who actually obtained it, and why? Above all, the theoretical issue of the significance of selecting that type of data for collection in the first place, and how it is used and interpreted, should be explicitly discussed.

The life history format is relevant for a wide range of theoretical perspectives, even those like cognitive or behavioural theories, which focus more on current psychological circumstances. This is because any multi-professional assessment *must* deal with the whole person in their social situation in reaching a publicly accountable decision. If the life history is used as the basis for developing common data or sharing of information, then this may sometimes be more systematically organised if based on a life map, as illustrated in Chapter 1, so that key information inputs can be more accurately placed in time and space. (The author is currently engaged in developing a computerised version of the life map, to illustrate the complexities of multi-disciplinary and multi-professional CA/B assessment, and to facilitate the representation of lives at multiple levels. This may be developed for assessment as well as teaching purposes.)

Seventh, in considering the different perspectives, it is important to discuss whether bridging or triangulation is more relevant to understanding the differing inputs and interpretations being presented. Either way, there may be issues of disconfirmation which may be equally important if there *is* a degree of agreement about perspectives. It is important to search for disconfirming evidence, especially when there is a convergence of values and perspectives. It should already have been established whether there are significantly differing values and perspectives, and if so, then the presentation of differing kinds of evidence and differing interpretations of that evidence cannot necessarily be dealt with in terms of simple disconfirmation, since a different perspective will inevitably *reinterpret* the evidence, and/or use differing kinds of evidence to support those values.

A way forward would be firstly to build on the life history data to the extent that differing accounts of the 'facts' can be identified, and if possible clarified by means of confirming and disconfirming evidence. The second stage will be to identify the differing interpretations of the evidence, drawing on what should already be known about the different theoretical allegiances represented. Discussion of the extent of possible overlap, complementary interpretation, theoretical irrelevance or fundamental disagreement at the level of values should then help to determine what courses of action are likely to be justifiable in view of the current state of opinion. This may include the possibility of further evidence being acquired to help to resolve, or at least accommodate, differences of interpretation.

Eighth, the final stage must be the attempt to summarise the debate, and make recommendations. The ethics and politics of this decision-making stage are notoriously fraught with difficulties, and no assessment methodology can by itself resolve such practical issues. However, if the above principles have been realised in the practice of multi-professional assessment, then there is a much stronger basis for the conclusions reached if a *social* assessment based on CA/B methodology has helped to evaluate the reflexive social and political issues, including the power relationships present in and during the discussion.

The resulting decision should reflect the discussion, particularly in recording the existence of conflicting views, especially those views associated with the differing relevant perspectives that have been identified in the course of negotiation. Whether this actually happens obviously depends on who formally chairs the negotiations, who informally can wield influence, and who holds the purse strings. The absence of shared interpretive and value perspectives may need to be acknowledged and acted upon, either at organisational level (through a review of multi-disciplinary working, for example), especially when the conclusions are not agreed. Otherwise the existence of disagreement needs to be acknowledged, and steps taken for further information to be gained, or for alternative plans to be considered simultaneously. The potential for conflict is always present because of changing theoretical perspectives and values, and its presence *must* be acted upon at the planning stage, since the existence of conflicting interpretations and continued miscommunication is obviously a risk factor in itself.

It is in any case desirable to positively consider possible alternative futures to the life stories being assessed, particularly in relation to alternative perspectives. The carrying over of the past and present into the future cannot be a simple exercise in extrapolation, but neither can it be done without serious consideration of the historical evidence of trends and past influences, including risk factors and strengths. Given the crucial role of differing perspectives and interpretations of lives, one of the most recent developments in practice would appear to be very pertinent for a large range of multi-professional assessments.

Workers in fostering and adoption have begun to use the idea of *concurrent* planning, especially where users and workers may not share the same perspectives on what the best course of action should be (Katz, 1996). This seems a useful contribution to dealing with the problem of handling differing perspectives simultaneously, and interactive intervention over time in people's lives. Developing plans simultaneously with 'written agreements, clear alternatives, and time-focused reviews' (Byrne, 1997, p.54) should help to overcome some of the difficulties of sequential planning where one interpretation of the future is given predominance until it fails and another has to be considered. This technique recognises and allows for differences in perspective, interactive intervention through time, and plans for alternatives from the beginning. It could be more widely applied, including in circumstances where there are differing perspectives between professionals, as well as between professionals and users.

It is important to emphasise the point that the above discussion of implications for multi-professional and multi-disciplinary practice in assessment is intended as a set of suggestive guidelines. Translating it into practice requires a further effort of imagination and negotiation, but one that is much needed in view of the continual theme of public investigations into various scandals and tragedies: that professionals were unable to communicate, and that key social, historical and holistic aspects of case information had not been fully appreciated.

8 Assessing needs, risks and strengths

In this chapter, a general framework for practice in social assessment will be set out, based on CA/B principles, but elaborating them in relation to the practical concerns that generally need to be assessed in health and welfare – various kinds of needs and risks.

The significance of this argument is to demonstrate that the practical issues can best be managed if they are understood as consisting of interconnected concepts which relate to CA/B theory. It is becoming widely accepted that central concepts in assessing risk and need are socially constructed (Little, 1997, p.27), and thus a general framework for coping with the reflexive, sociological and historical nature of assessment is required. This framework will then be used in later chapters as a basis for discussion of specific issues of assessment practice in relation to differing user groups and settings.

The contention is that these issues are of *general* significance across different user groups and health and welfare boundaries. They therefore need to be dealt with at a general level, rather than repeated in each subsequent chapter.

CA/B methodology and concepts of risk and need

The definition of risk and need is always a social construction which expresses social values (Douglas, 1986 and 1992). Parton and colleagues have drawn attention to the ways in which risk has been increasingly used to allocate blame in an individualised way, thus meeting the requirements of an individualistic market economy (Parton, Thorpe and Wattam, 1997). Recent work in sociology (Beck, 1992; Giddens, 1991) has emphasised the way current social constructions of risk have become a prime focus of a 'risk society', where there is such a rapid pace of change and institutional instability that risk has become central to the way contemporary society functions.

A particularly significant aspect of their analysis is the way in which they emphasise the concept of *reflexivity* as a constitutive feature of the risk society (see Chapter 3). The modernist application of science to industry and social life has had unforeseeable consequences, and is no longer taken for granted – it is now subject to constant monitoring and feedback. The position of the 'scientists' as observers is no longer tolerated: they too are participants. There is no longer confidence that science can be relied on to provide satisfactory answers, and the logic of this drives people towards safety-first solutions where the avoidance of risk is the main aim, and those responsible for taking 'unnecessary' risk are held to account.

This is highly relevant to CA/B methodology, which accepts that the application of simplistic scientific concepts has never been appropriate, given the essentially value-laden nature of judgements about human circumstances. The emphasis here is on the way in which social divisions have always created rival knowledges and perspectives: the existence or otherwise of 'postmodern' or 'late modern' or 'risk' societies as such is *not* necessarily the main issue. However, the growth of the differing professions also leads to different perspectives and concepts of need and risk. The degree to which uncertainty may be part of contemporary society therefore does connect with CA/B, especially in respect of the undermining of empiricist or positivist assumptions about knowledge of the social world (cf. Parton, 1998). However, there are also other traditions in the social sciences (as well as postmodernism) which have questioned the possibility of certainty precisely because of the reflexive character of social theory.

The concept of reflexivity discussed in Chapter 3 includes the widely accepted idea that the social researcher/assessor is a participant whose ideas may be reacted to. There is therefore a close relationship between the concepts of power and reflexivity and the social assessment of need and risk. They are involved in both sides of the equation – in the definition of the concepts and values, and in generating the material dangers. Powerful groups are responsible for creating the structures of needs and risks in the first place by their control over the sources of wealth, income and status in socially disputed processes. Powerful individuals can alter the shape of particular needs and risks by their reflexive involvement and relative position in specific situations, using their powers abusively, collusively or supportively.

A specific implication of these considerations is that there can be no escape from the responsibility of making evaluative judgements in social assessments. 'Clinical' professional judgement used by itself has been rightly criticised as subjective and poorly predictive (Ryan, 1995, p.17; Milner and Campbell, 1995, p.21). However, statistically generated lists of risk factors also have their limitations in relation to predicting outcomes in specific cases: 'The value of any self-styled predictive checklist is negligible' (Dingwall, 1989, p.51). The most useful approach to assessing risks and needs will therefore need to combine the use of risk checklists with professional clinical judgement in negotiation with users, within the context of an explicit theoretical framework. There is considerable advantage in using checklists 'as an aid to, not a substitute for, clinical judgement' (Corby, 1995, p.22). There can be no automatic or mechanical adding of needs and risk factors to produce a predictive outcome. Furthermore, the use of 'explicit valuation systems' (Carson, 1996, p.10) is advocated to demonstrate the methodology that is being used in professional judgements about future directions.

The implications of CA/B theory include the importance of placing general predictive risk factors within a theoretical framework, and the necessity of making value-based 'clinical' judgements of specific cases. These two processes are firmly linked by the values and methodology of the theoretical framework. The existence of known risk factors in a particular field has to be applied in a particular case through the filter of the CA/B theoretical framework, an important part of which is the social and historical location of clinical judgements through the use of critical approaches to life history. This approach avoids the untenable and unhelpful 'theory-neutral stance' of checklists and DoH guidelines (Munro, 1998, p.101), providing guidelines for the collation and interpretation of evidence in relation to risk factors, needs and strengths. But it also ensures that the complexities of practice are indeed treated as central, and not marginal, to the process (Parton, 1998).

As well as being a premise of CA/B method, recent research into actual assessment practice bears out the beneficial effect of having a complex but consistent, multi-faceted theoretical framework for assessing risk and need (Farmer and Owen, 1995, Chapter 9). It is also a basic premise of psychological and psychiatric methods of assessment (e.g. McMurren and Hodge, 1994, p.2; Reder and Lucy, 1995, p.5). Thus all assessments should include elements of both risk and needs assessment within a comprehensive framework. This will enable the assessor to have some degree of assurance that the complex issues involved have been taken into account as consistently as possible. This applies in principle from the very start of any assessment process, and some of the practical aspects of ensuring this are indicated in Chapter 1 (see Figure 2). Continual review of pro formas, supervision of assessors, and reflective dialogical practice (involving assessors' active listening to the users and user groups at the same time as reflexive review of their own concepts) are all minimum requirements.

More lengthy assessments must include (CA/B-based) studies of personal and social histories, in which the assessment process is clearly viewed as itself providing a set of interacting (and possibly consciously interventive) variables. This implies taking account not only of the critical personal and social histories of those individual workers principally involved, but also assessment of the multi-professional personal and organisational factors which influence users, carers and assessors.

A comprehensive social assessment of risks and needs will need to consider how far it should be supplemented or complemented by specialist assessment or consultation from the perspective of another discipline, or from another profession (a decision complicated by the overlaps between academic disciplines and professions). Equally, when another discipline or profession is used to make an assessment, a *social* assessment should contextualise it, using the social assessment theoretical framework. Different kinds of assessments not only include aspects of the others, but also may originally be intended as one, but may end up as another. This needs to be as explicit as possible for service users as well as clear in the thinking of workers, and any significant change in this respect should be negotiated.

As far as any *social* assessment is concerned, whether carried out by social workers, health visitors, doctors or teachers, it needs to be related to an adequate theoretical framework. The degree to which assessors understand this, especially those making primarily medical or psychological assessments, will no doubt affect multi-professional teamwork and its local politics.

The interconnection of risk and need

Need is commonly conceptualised in terms of an uneven continuum, whereby some needs are not as important or as basic as others. The more important the need, the greater its objectivity and universality; the less important the need, the more it is regarded as related to subjective wants and wishes.

The concept of risk also has a continuum built into it. At the more positive end, the risk involved in certain actions may be regarded as worth taking if the potential for danger is relatively slight but the hope for gain is relatively great. On the other hand, a serious risk is thought of as universally compelling by definition: an indicator of the possibility of significant harm which demands avoiding action by whoever has responsibility. Risk is *now* usually associated with the more dangerous end of the needs continuum, and with negative rather than positive possibilities (Parton, Thorpe and Wattam, 1997, p.235). It concerns issues of basic need, such as physiological survival and safety, and whether a course of action is likely to meet those needs or not. The concept of need commonly remains a somewhat broader, less urgent concept, and more oriented to the present – though still with implications for the future and a tendency to be associated, like risk, with negative deficits. However, it is also linked to 'the accomplishment of a desired end-state' (Sanderson, 1996, p.23).

It is therefore important to recognise that both need and risk are part of a similar uneven continuum or range of human concerns which are based in common safety, physiological and psychological requirements, but exactly how and to what degree these are conceived depends on social constructions in particular times and places. It is important to recognise this continuity rather than infer that risk is just about serious harm and can escape the complications of social construction, as the contemporary overemphasis on risk and the individualistic allocation of blame tends to do (Parton, 1996b).

In both theory and practice, the two concepts of risk and need merge into one another in various ways. For example, the neglect and emotional abuse of children or adults is concerned with the failure to meet needs for emotional security and physical health. These needs may themselves constitute a dangerous circumstance because of the serious level of emotional or physical need, and therefore harm, that is involved. It is also the case that they are often linked to physical or sexual abuse. But it is clear that there is often no immediate, objective, precipitating event: the issue is often about the accretion of this type of need/risk as a result of numerous factors over a period of time. On the other hand, situations where there is a precipitating event, such as the use of violence or drugs, are usually designated as cases where serious 'risks' may arise in relation to either the person concerned or others. This use of risk does not disconnect it with need, but simply indicates differing *ranges* of needs and risks, often to do with physical safety. It may (if used without care) also distract attention both from other needs – including those which may grow incrementally – and from countervailing strengths.

Practitioners have sometimes not paid sufficient attention to the connections between risks and needs. Recent research has been critical of childcare workers for overemphasis on risk issues, at the expense of needs and family support (DoH, Dartington Social Research Unit, 1995). However, it seems common to emphasise one at the expense of another, depending partly on the social and political construction of the issues at specific points in time. Whilst childcare went through a phase of panic in the late 1980s about the varied risks of child abuse, workers with older people have focused on needs, only recently increasing attention to risks of abuse towards older people. On the other hand, in mental health, the risk of serious harm has been the predominant consideration, with the needs of mental health 'survivors' and the positive options for taking risks in the community sometimes taking second place.

Risk should therefore be understood in the broader context of need, and both risk and need require assessment of future potential – both positive and negative – and of past histories. Positive aspects of risk and need include the deliberate taking of risks where, on balance, the outcome is positively to be desired. Negative aspects include the minimisation of risks where the balance of outcomes is judged to be probably in the negative, or the danger is felt to be so serious as to require a very cautious approach to assessing its risk. In all cases, it is important in a particular case to *specify* exactly what are the range of needs and strengths, and *all* the risks arising from the whole range of needs, and their connection through time. Brearley's work (Brearley, 1982) is often used in risk assessment practice (Kelly, 1996; Kemshall, 1996; Pritchard, 1997) to distinguish between hazards (factors which are thought to cause or contribute to deplored outcomes) and dangers (the feared outcomes resulting from those hazards). It is certainly essential to be as specific as possible, not only about feared outcomes, but also the 'desired outcomes' (Sanderson, 1996, p.23) that correspond to the meeting of needs and the successful negotiation of positive risks. Both can usefully be distinguished from the factors contributing to the outcomes. A good current example of problems in this area is the evidence that child protection conferences often fail to specify the significant harms that are feared in a given case: 'It was the exception rather than the rule for the precise nature of the significant harm likely to occur to be clearly spelled out' (Thoburn, Brandon and Lewis, 1997, p.188).

Braye and Preston-Shoot (1992), again following Brearley (1979), distinguish between 'at-riskness' and 'risk-taking'. The former is essentially concerned with ascertaining the level of risk in a given situation – it corresponds to the assessment of need. 'Risk-taking' is future- and action-oriented – concerning the balance of risk between alternative courses of action, and between positive and negative outcomes that might both arise from a given course of action. As Braye and Preston-Shoot point out, this is rather a 'snapshot' approach, and assessments are in reality time-related and dynamic (Braye and Preston-Shoot, 1992, p.62). Further, the act of assessment is itself an intervention, and itself involves a risk, as also will the alternative of not assessing. The effect is a continuing 'balancing of likely benefits with likely risk' (Carson, 1996, p.9), taking account of past and current strengths and needs in relation to future potential dangers and goals.

The negotiation of the level and kind of assessment appropriate to a case (with the user, referrer and a supervisor) is thus a key element in assessment in which the assessment of needs, the riskiness of the situation and the risks of alternative courses of action (i.e. including levels and kinds of assessment) have to be tackled simultaneously. Given some assessment intervention over a discrete period of time, there will then be the need for further risk-taking assessment, taking account of the consequences and direction of the assessment process *itself* when balancing various alternative courses of action. This dilemma only reinforces the importance of seeing clearly the connections between the range of needs and strengths on the one hand, and the risks and opportunities on the other, in a dynamic, historical context, in which past, present and future are closely linked. In this sense, the predictive aspects of assessment of risk and need are bound into CA/B methodology, so that the information needed to make decisions about future events or trends is tied to a sociologically sophisticated framework able to reflexively account for the open texture of social possibilities.

Social difference and concepts of need and risk

Concepts of need and risk have sometimes been treated by health and welfare professionals as matters falling within their expertise in ways which leave them open to criticism from various sociological perspectives, including Foucauldian, critical and feminist theories. This is because of the tendency of some groups of professionals towards authoritative, 'scientific' approaches which take no account of either power or differences between ways of understanding social concepts. The medical and psychiatric approaches to need have dominated thinking in both health and welfare fields in this way. They have preserved the status of professional assessment by linking the implicit universalism in the concept of need to the universalism of biological functional imperatives, justifying a 'normative' concept of need – as defined by an expert. The dominant professions have tended to omit the element of social construction in concepts of need and risk, and thus have been able to sanction their own dominant values and implant them into the semi-professions. For example, in American social work, the 'diagnostic' school is associated with this approach, and its idea of need is exemplified in the title of one of its most famous books, *Common Human Needs* (Towle, 1965), a book and an approach which have been influential on both sides of the Atlantic.

Equally, in psychology, probably the most well-known concept of need is that of Maslow, who argued in favour of an objective and hierarchical concept of needs, from the most basic to less basic (Maslow, 1970). The most basic needs are said to have to be met first before the others can be dealt with, in his view. His well-known hierarchy of need begins with the physiological, and runs through safety, belongingness or love needs, with esteem, and self-actualisation at the higher end. His view of needs is psychologically and biologically oriented, based on the assumption that a need is a motivating drive getting its energy from within an organism. In other words, it is pre-eminently normative and individualised.

However, as Doyal and Gough have argued, this overly 'objective' concept of need is of limited value (Doyal and Gough, 1991, p.36). What we may have a psychological or physiological 'drive' for, may not be something we need (e.g. to drink alcohol), whilst something we need (like exercise) may be something we have no 'drive' for. The different 'levels' of need are often not in practice separable, and are influenced by social factors. By contrast, within conventional market economics, all needs are simply subjective preferences that happen to be shared by a large number of people who are expressing them by making a demand in some way or another. They are therefore both subjective, since their only justification is that they are the wants of individuals, and objective, since they can be measured in the same way that any consumer demand can be measured – through the mechanism of the market.

Some contemporary philosophers and sociologists take the view that needs are indeed socially defined, and that power issues help to determine that definition, but see these issues in highly pluralistic, interactive and relative terms. Individuals are constituted by their position in social interaction, and the language which they use to understand and define need relates to that 'discursive position'. This has the implication that traditional concepts of need are false, in that objective, measurable and static qualities are wrongly assumed. If there is no privileged knowledge, then traditional humanist social work is 'doubly damned', since it 'bases itself in a sphere of reality which does not exist, i.e. "common human needs"' (Rojek, Peacock and Collins, 1988, p.132). The danger with this approach is its openness to relativism and manipulation by the powerful (Doyal and Gough, 1991; Hewitt, 1993).

For example, the market economy assumes that individuals have equal access to information, and equal ability to make effective demands about their needs. But in reality, the awareness of individuals is limited by the particular historical period and geographical space that they happen to inhabit – and especially by which group(s) happen to be powerful at that time and place. So, for Marx, the market conception of need is a historical phenomenon which reflects the interests of the middle and capitalist classes (Lukes, 1985). For anti-racists, the definition of need in contemporary societies is based on white assumptions about the world, since white people control the institutions and media, and therefore the definition of need (Ahmad, 1990; Tao and Drover, 1997). Similarly, feminists say the same kind of thing about needs in a male-dominated world (Croft, 1986; Fraser, 1989), whilst Oliver contends that in a disablist society, 'providing welfare services on the basis of individual need has failed disabled people' (Oliver, 1996, p.76). Older people's views of their own needs are often depressed, and the idea of negotiation of need solely depending on their individual views is therefore also questionable (Key, 1989). Professional groups whose concepts of need can predominate through their expertise also help to (over)determine in various negotiations what needs are officially recognised, and may reinforce dominant concepts.

Given the CA/B construction of understanding changing human situations in terms of interconnected social divisions and power relationships, it is clear that a compatible concept of needs should take account of the social, historical and discursive aspects of need, and elements of commonality in relation to physical survival, human development and the experience of oppression. As I have argued elsewhere (Clifford, 1984), it is the ability of dominated groups to use their experience of deprivation and oppression – their relatively privileged knowledge – to provide a critique of the currently dominating definitions of need, and reach towards commonalities of need which can also recognise and accept difference. It is therefore imperative that an adequate and anti-oppressive concept of need grasps both parts of this dilemma: to be aware on the one hand of the relative nature of any definition of need, especially towards dominant social discourses at particular times and places, and on the other hand, to be equally aware that this must and can be limited by reference to the physiological, economic and psychological realities of need (Doyal and Gough, 1991), and by dialogue between individuals and groups to help to establish what those commonalities and differences are.

Needs and risks are thus essentially a matter for political and ethical debate: a 'struggle over needs' (Fraser, 1989, p.161) in which values and power collide in a material world. This is consistent with the CA/B premise of critical commitment to values which attempt to prioritise the perspectives of (needy) dominated groups. It is therefore not surprising that recent major research efforts in childcare have identified issues related to the social divisions as matters which are problematic in current assessments – for example, the over-representation of black children as being at risk of abuse (Thoburn, Brandon and Lewis, 1997, p.171; Thorpe, 1997, p.75); the underestimation of the risks resulting from male violence (Farmer, 1997, p.151); the over-representation of risk of abuse arising from poverty and social class (Thorpe, 1997, p.76) and under-recognition of the role of poverty and the social divisions in creating need and risk (Parton, 1997b, p.11). Most difficult of all are the issues which arise when the needs arising from differing social divisions pull in different directions. This is commonly the case when adult needs and children's needs come into conflict. In most children and family cases, the needs of the adult woman are often seen only through the lens of appropriate motherhood (Urwin, 1985, p.196; Tunstill, 1997, p.43). This tension may be exacerbated by the woman (and/or child) having other specific needs relating to social divisions such as disability or 'race'. The complexity of relating needs and risks to social difference thus requires considerable understanding and subtle analysis in social assessment.

Risks, needs and interacting social systems

The practical issues of assessment by professionals are primarily about how to assess individual human circumstances in order to make a decision about the identification and nature of strengths and weaknesses that can be as acceptable as possible to users, carers and assessors, but above all, be supported by the agency for which the assessor works. The reality of the assessor's own circumstances is that their employment is based on a contract in which their duty is to make proper assessments (amongst other things). What constitutes a proper assessment is therefore significantly related to what that particular agency is prepared to accept, and that in turn is bounded by the law and central government. In the fields of law, health and welfare, there are numerous agencies with varying responsibilities, all using concepts of human needs and risks. That definition of need and risk is partly made by central government, which indicates in broad terms in the legislation on health or childcare or community care what ranges of need and risk should be given attention.

However, broad guidelines concerning assessment such as exist in various official documents always have to be interpreted by local agencies, and by individual professions and professionals. The current advice in community care makes clear the link between agency interpretation and concepts of needs, which are defined as: 'The requirements of individuals to achieve, maintain or restore an acceptable level of social independence or quality of life, *as defined by the particular care agency or authority*' (DoH, 1991, p.12; emphasis added). Legal concepts such as 'significant harm' and the welfare checklist in the Children Act also provide a framework set by central government when assessing needs and risks. However, the inter-relationship between different levels of organisations and social systems is very apparent in the claims that have been made about the role of needs assessment, both in community care and in childcare.

It has been argued strongly that the function of needs assessment is so defined and controlled by the agencies involved that although it is represented as a humane relationship between the individual and the assessor, in fact it is a way of rationing resources, by local agencies and by government (Browne, 1996, p.60; Parton, 1997b, p.10). The word 'need' itself 'has become a smokescreen to ... camouflage policies which in their intention and effect have the purpose of increasing inequalities' (Bradshaw,

1994, p.49; quoted in Percy-Smith, 1996, p.8). Ignoring the impact of different agencies at different levels of the social system on the process of assessment itself is thus inadequate and unrealistic, either from the perspective of explicit law and policy or in the light of their more 'latent functions'.

As well as making sense to themselves as employees of an agency which may itself be responsible to local and/or central government, and as members of a profession, the assessment of need and risk has to make sense to professionals as individuals, and also to the users with whom they have to negotiate. There is therefore some interpretative space within which differing kinds of power and knowledge can operate, influencing and constituting the nature of assessment: what is to be assessed, why and how. It is also important to remember that there is a continuum of professional status and expertise in relation to assessment issues, ranging from the socially accepted professional status of the medical consultant to the semi-professional and voluntary work of various care agencies, whose assessment work may or may not receive wider recognition – especially in the courts of law, where assessments may be tested. The ability of professionals to get their interpretations accepted will thus vary in time and place, depending significantly on the organisational and social systems within which they operate.

In addition to the interacting systems and organisations of the world of the professional, there are numerous other layers of interacting systems which interlock and/or conflict with them, and affect both the reality of risk and need, and the concepts involved. The overlapping worlds of service users – their families, friends, relatives peers and communities – involve, to varying fractured degrees, systemic elements which support or undermine users' abilities to cope, as well as their perception of what it is to 'cope'. In addition, the broader social structures and divisions in which users and workers participate can also be partly taken as systemic factors imposing constraints and possibilities. No one system, such as the family, should be analysed in isolation from other systems, as though the latter are external and environmental. Social systems interpenetrate even when they are functioning 'successfully', as well as when they fracture and conflict. Systemic rather than linear causation can never be assumed, but is a possibility to be considered in assessing risk and need, and it is potentially dangerous to do otherwise, since significant sources of risk (or strength) may thus be ignored.

A significant aspect of the broader systems are the varied organisations and movements which purport to represent dominated social groups, such as children's organisations, black organisations, women's groups and societies, working-class political parties and clubs, disability organisations, and gay and lesbian groups. In all cases, there are complex issues about the representative nature of the organisations in relation to the dominated groups for which they sometimes claim to speak. Nevertheless, the existence of social divisions and their varying degrees of self-awareness and organisational cohesion are significant aspects of the interaction of social systems, and may contribute to, or problematise, issues at the local level in relation to perspectives on risk, strengths and need.

In various ways, therefore, the numerous social systems in which assessors and users are enmeshed will affect how needs and risks are conceived and constructed, and how their negotiations are conducted. There thus needs to be a theoretical framework which can integrate evidence from the social sciences and from user groups, to work towards commonalities of need, whilst recognising significant differences, the vested interests of powerful organisations and social systems, and the shaping of needs and risks by small and large groups and systems at different social levels.

Power, needs and risks

The creation of risks/needs by powerful groups and individuals has to be systematically analysed in both negative and positive ways. Negatively, the relationships of power which emanate from social differences create needs/risks because of the vulnerability of members of dominated social divisions, and the potential threat that is posed by those more powerful, and the circumstances they help to create. These interconnecting and overlapping differences of power therefore have to be studied carefully to establish the potential needs/risks inherent in specific situations. This includes not only the generation of needs/risks as a direct (and indirect) result of vulnerability, but also the definition of concepts of risks/needs which will express dominant rather than oppressed concepts of need relevant to specific circumstances. For example, any adult is a potential personal risk to a physically vulnerable young child to whom they have access, by virtue of their superior physical strength. However, male-oriented images of vulnerable young women in cultural products and the media help to create concepts of gender relationships which are particularly risk-producing for female children and young people. Concepts of risk which are focused on individual responsibility may also produce risky situations by ignoring the range of wider social contexts.

Conversely, the positive aspects of power include the abilities and powers which individuals and groups develop in their everyday resistance to domination, and in their development of co-operative working towards shared goals. This will include oppositional values and perspectives, as well as personal and group strengths which have been built up over time. These strengths will also relate to complex interconnections of social divisions in specific circumstances, and need to be just as carefully studied, rather than read off from a set of labels. The judgement of *which* needs and risks are pertinent to a particular instance will thus need to balance the way power creates both vulnerabilities and strengths if any assessment intervention is intended to remedy dangers arising from power differentials. Balancing positive powers and strengths against negative powers which create risks and needs does not imply naively summing risk/need factors, but assessing their different weights in context.

An important aspect of power in assessment concerns acknowledgement of the power relationships which the involvement of the user in the assessment process implies. In the introductory negotiations, and periodically at subsequent stages, especially if there are significant changes which affect the user's position, an understanding of the politics and ethics of the situation needs to be shared as far as possible with the user. This includes an appreciation of the powers of the assessor and of the agency and the law in respect of the proposed assessment, and the degree and kind of participation that can be negotiated. Although community care guidance stresses the importance of needs-led assessment, it is important to include an understanding of the power conferred on the assessor and the agency by virtue of their control over a range of resources which can be used negatively or positively in relation to needs, risks and strengths.

It is clearly important to make a conceptual distinction between needs and service availability, and this is an official requirement (DoH, 1991). Indeed, a commitment to a comprehensive concept of human need sensitive to social difference remains a buttress against oppressive bureaucratic management of needs (Morris, 1997). Logically, in any needs-led approach there is the 'requirement ... to begin by building systematically a comprehensive picture of need before tackling priorities' (Lightfoot, 1995, p.112). However, pretending that there are no powerful vested interests in controlling the definition and satisfaction of needs is also unrealistic and unhelpful: 'it is nonsense to undertake assessment as an activity divorced from seeking a reasonable response to meeting the individual's requirements. It is arguably unethical to do so' (Middleton, 1997, p.9). It is also nonsense to pretend that ordinary user-defined 'needs' are the only consideration, when plainly the social assessment is also concerned about *risks*, either to the users themselves or to others. The power structures underlying social assessments by professionals will not be fully acknowledged unless these cross-cutting power issues are taken into account and negotiated with the user – as far as they can be. It is an implication of the CA/B concept of power that assessment should neither be 'resource-led' nor conducted without awareness of the realities of resource availability, of control over resources, and of statutory obligations and powers.

The ethical judgement and skill required of the assessor to be able to negotiate these issues, gauging the feasibility, appropriateness and manner of discussing the difficult implications of power, is of a very high order in complex cases, especially those involving any kind of abuse. The relative power and position of the worker necessitates an unavoidable, existential responsibility for using that power as ethically as possible.

Risks, needs and reflexivity

The concept of reflexivity has to be examined as thoroughly as possible to identify significant problems about assessing risks and needs. In particular, the power of the professional as an individual personality, as a member of various social divisions, as a trained professional and as a representative of an organisation has to be reflectively considered in the way needs/risks are being construed, and especially the way they are being presented to the user and/or carer.

Assessment *itself* constitutes an intervention which may or may not increase the needs/risks, depending on the circumstances. In most statutory investigations or assessments of alleged abuse, it raises anxiety, intensifying the dangers, and all the issues of power just listed will have a bearing on the way needs/risks are inflated simply by the involvement of the assessor. In voluntary psychotherapeutic assessments, it may be that intervention has some immediate positive impact on needs/risks, simply because of the intervention of an assessor who is willing to listen, thus meeting a need. However, the essential point here is that whatever the circumstances of the assessment, there are likely to be both positive and negative effects on risks/needs from the reflexive involvement of the professional making the assessment. The point is that the assessor must be as aware of that as possible, and must monitor those effects in dialogue with the user/carer and supervisor, as appropriate.

The impact of the assessor's own membership of various social divisions not only affects their ability to conceptualise needs and risks of people who have very different lives, but may also add to the degree of risk by virtue of their involvement. They may make users feel threatened, misunderstood or alienated through their inability to understand or empathise with experiences they themselves could not possibly have had. They also have to recognise that the particular circumstances of their own lives may contribute to these effects. For instance, if an assessor is recently qualified and inexperienced at making assessments, or is under a heavy workload or personal pressures, then these are personal reflexive factors which alter the nature of current risks and needs. Conversely, there may be positive features in a particular assessor's relation to a given user: this also needs to be recognised as a valuable reflexive element in assessment. For example, the ability of people in dominated groups to empathise with users in similar positions has long been recognised, but even here there may be attendant dangers.

In addition to the individual assessor's recognition and accounting for self in the assessment process, there is also the wider aspect of representations of need and risk as they affect this process. On the one hand, the various sources of social and political power are able to write concepts of need into legislative frameworks and government advice, as well as relying on cultural and media dominance of discussion. This translates into clear expectations for practitioners, users and carers that the assessment of needs/risks should be understood within the dominant perspectives. At a local level, it means that the agency has the power to define needs and risks, and to make those definitions stick. Thus the reflexive aspects of assessment must include the dangers arising from the involvement of agencies themselves. Recent childcare research confirms that the involvement of agencies in the assessment process is itself a needs/risk factor: 'the process of investigation further damages children when it is experienced as abusive in its own right' (Hearn, 1997, p.226). Occasionally, some agencies may be seen in a more positive light by users, and may have a beneficial effect. Either way, the impact of the involvement of agencies in the assessment must itself be taken into account.

On the other hand, there are oppositional perspectives on needs/risks that have no such legitimising authority, and may not even be communicated to the user and/or carer. This is well exemplified in the views of anti-disablists about the assessment of disabled people. Oliver's dismissal of current individualised assessment as having failed the disabled (Oliver, 1992b, p.204) is echoed fully in another paper on disability: 'The individual model of voice in decision-making has been easily incorporated into, and reinforced by, the individual models of disability which are readily apparent in the terminology of "assessing needs" and "individual programmes"' (French and Swain, 1997, p.202). In contrast to this dominant perspective, oppositional values would involve different considerations: 'A say for the *collective* voice of disabled people however, would involve the recognition of disability culture, the inclusion of the representative voice of disabled people in formal decision-making, and the promotion of a social model of disability as integral to the processes, relationships and content' (French and Swain, 1997, p.203).

The assessor should therefore consider how far the collective voice(s) of the disabled can be brought to bear in a particular situation in the light of his or her own experience, understanding of and relationship with disability. The individual consciousness of a disabled person has to be understood in the context of the contemporary disability movement (Campbell and Oliver,

1996, Chapter 6), and ethical and political choices have to be made. Clearly, this kind of logic applies, with adaptions and variations, to all the social divisions, requiring openness on the part of the assessor to the contrary views of users, carers, and other professionals and voluntary organisations, especially those representing dominated social groups. This implies the importance of reflexive ethical and political choice by assessors in the context of listening to the voices of users, not only as individuals, but also in relation to wider social groups to which they belong.

History, time and needs/risks assessment

The importance of the historical dimension of needs/risks assessment is not only that it begins at a specific point in time – when the referral is first made – but also that it takes place over a particular period of time, and draws upon an array of information about the past in order to inform the present and influence the future. It is crucial for the assessor to try to compare present and past specific contexts of events, and to understand the historical directions of development both before and during the assessment: needs/risks are dynamic, and may change quickly or slowly over time. It is also crucial for assessment of future options to take into account the element of time, and the period over which risks and needs may be increasing or decreasing before another assessment will be made. The assessment of the riskiness of a specific situation can both be distinguished from and connected to the assessment and balancing of risk options for the future (Braye and Preston-Shoot, 1992, pp.60–3): how are current needs to be met, and when? What are the risks and benefits compared to non-intervention over a period of time, in consideration of the timing of the assessment in the lives of the user(s)? The time dimension is an essential part of the process of assessing both needs and risks. But the specific nature of the needs or risks has to be explicit, as must the time periods.

The assessment must of necessity start as an initial investigation, and gradually it may become more comprehensive in scope and quality as it proceeds. It is unavoidable that all initial assessments will be *constrained* by time, and will only be able to consider some issues very superficially. The use of the CA/B framework ensures that the main dimensions are being considered, that major information shortfalls are identified, and that there will be continuity with any later assessment. Within the theoretical framework proposed, the assessor is required to monitor these questions simultaneously: how much assessment needs to be done (if any), and how deeply, how quickly? In addition, the processual aspects require assessing interactions over time between all personnel involved, including the assessor, possibly including intentionally interventive interactions where assessment and 'treatment' or 'training' occur simultaneously. Given the theoretical framework, there seems no automatic distinction that can be made between 'initial' versus 'comprehensive' assessments, except that these issues have to be the subjects of continual ethical and political review, in discussion with the parties involved, with an awareness of changing circumstances, directions and power balances.

Within the CA/B framework, the potential for comprehensive assessment is present at the beginning of any assessment, and the endpoint is not theoretically given. In a specific context, it has to be agreed what is comprehensive enough in the light of government and agency requirements – and in the view of the service users and carers. The process of any assessment must also lead to clarification of what *focus* is appropriate for any particular assessment, and the assessor must negotiate with those involved what that is likely to mean in terms of time constraints, intrusiveness and the range of needs/risks. This is also an ethical and political process that often involves difficult and complex issues in relation to conflicting needs and risks. Part of an 'empowering' approach to assessment must include: 'a rigorous approach to reflecting on practice and reformulating goals and methods of working as the action proceeds' (Adams, 1996, p.38). However, there is no way of avoiding the possibility that conflicts of power and interactions over time may empower some but not others. The historical dimensions help to provide a wider context within which to evaluate the overall costs and benefits to those involved, and take the least damaging course. However, the variability of risks and needs over time is an important concept for understanding the complexity of professional judgement that is necessary (and thus the advantage of a theoretical framework). Both the categories themselves and the situations to which they refer are changing entities which are not easily assessed (Hearn, 1997, p.229).

It is essential to understand the relevance of history for the assessment of risks and needs. Both in childcare and community care, the importance of risk indicators has been widely recognised, but what is not so often recognised is that these risk indicators depend on the gathering of oral and life history information, and the interpretation of historical events. For example, the standard psychiatric assessment criteria for identifying the risk of harm to other people constituted by mental health patients is almost exclusively about historical factors in their lives (Lipscombe, 1997, p.153). Equally, reviews of research in childcare (e.g. Hallett and Birchall, 1992) tend to support critically aware use of risk indicators in assessment *within* a detailed social history, but the inadequacy of history taking in child abuse cases has also been criticised (Hill, 1990).

The fundamental historical issues of assessment methodology raised by the CA/B framework indicate the importance of a theoretically informed socio-historical interpretation of historical evidence, through life history and oral history methods, and integrating a critical lifespan psychological understanding, reaching up to the present, and anticipating the future. This negotiated construction of social histories will be realised at the level of practice in various ways, depending on time constraints, settings and circumstances. The use of particular methods such as geneograms, time lines and other social history formats has to be considered within this theoretical context.

Implications for assessing risk, needs and strengths

Methodology

Methods for assessment have to be consistent with a methodology that is sensitive to the range of various kinds of needs strengths and risks, and their interconnection, and encompasses their reflexive, evaluative dimensions. This means that historical risk factors will be used within a theoretical framework that demands ethical and social judgement.

The statistical evidence of risk and need has to be weighed in context, taking account of interactive systems and differing perspectives, especially those of user and oppressed groups. All assessments have to focus on key issues which are dictated by the circumstances and by professional judgement, and the legal and policy framework.

Social difference

Assessment requires the systematic consideration of all the social divisions in relation to the development and definition of needs, risks and strengths. This must include the differing perspectives of users, carers and workers in differing agencies, but also the views of user and oppressed groups and organisations relevant to the needs of a specific situation. The major social divisions need to be considered, both separately and together in their interconnections in individual and group lives.

Reflexivity

Assessment of risks, strengths and needs has to take into account the values and social location of the assessor and the agencies involved. The assessor needs to recognise, in discussion with the user, the ethical and political issues involved in identifying and assessing needs, strengths and risks, in attempting to agree kinds and levels of participation.

The assessor should be conscious of the way dominated groups define need and risk in different ways (especially those groups to which s/he does not belong), negotiating this both with users and carers. The assessment should take into account the risks (and/or support) constituted by the agency and the workers themselves.

Historical location

Needs, risks and strengths should be understood within a historical context, since assessment of them all involves reference to past, present and future potential. Social histories are essential to assessing the directions and trends of development and contextualising differing historical risk factors. In addition, the assessment takes place at a particular point in time, and the assessment is an interactive, and often interventive, process which lasts for a period of time.

The historical context should link all these aspects together, providing a framework for interpreting psychological, psychiatric and medical histories. The changing nature of need in relation to serious harm requires monitoring over time, prior to and during the process of assessment, assessing the direction of developments over time, and the *likelihood* of differing outcomes occurring. There should be some indication of what period of time assessment will take, and over what future time periods need and risk is being considered.

Interacting social systems

The assessor needs to be aware of how both the generation and definition of needs, risks and strengths are shaped by the influence of the range of social systems at different levels. The assessor has to take account of positive and negative implications of the agency system's policy and functions, including its broad range of resources and responsibilities.

The family and related social networks have to be placed within other contexts of neighbourhood and wider organisations, and the agency itself, in order to understand the complex interaction of localised and wider social systems and networks, including links with other agencies and with organisations of user and oppressed social groups.

Power

The analysis of power differentials needs to be rigorous and systematic to encompass the positive potential of individuals and families (strengths and opportunities), as well as the negative aspects (hazards and dangers). The vulnerabilities and powers of differing individuals and agencies have to be considered across different system levels and social divisions within their changing historical context.

The aim is to assess as clearly as possible the historical evidence of use and abuse of power as it affects the present, and the changing *balance* of outcomes for alternative interventions which might have various consequences in terms of needs, strengths and risks. The assessor also has to acknowledge and judge the impact of his/her own power, (and their agencies), as well as the reciprocal powers of users and carers on themselves.

The following diagrams (Figures 4A and 4B) attempt to summarise the relationship of CA/B principles to the assessment of risks, needs and strengths. Figure 4A emphasises the details of the CA/B framework within which the assessment takes place. Figure 4B gives more detail of the process of assessment against the background of the CA/B framework.

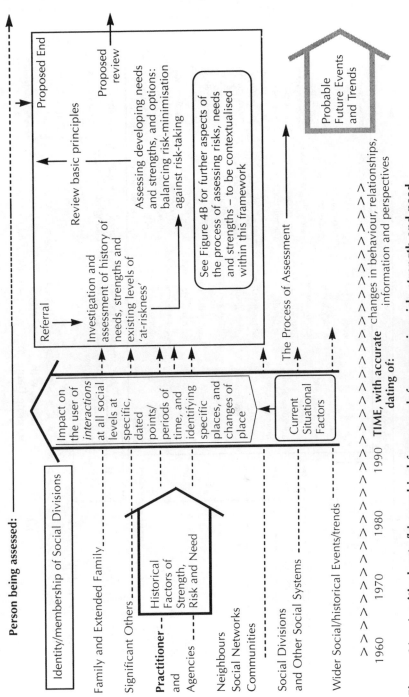

Figure 4A   A critical auto/biographical framework for assessing risk, strength and need

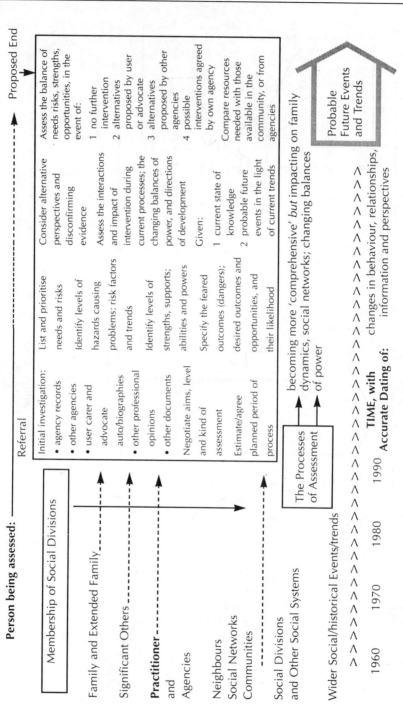

Figure 4B   A critical auto/biographical framework for assessing risk, strength and need

9 Children and families

Introduction

The importance of assessment in childcare as an issue has grown dramatically with the increasing publicity over childcare tragedies. It has been argued that social work assessment is now central to the processes of for caring for and controlling children and families (Parton, 1991 and 1996b). The government issued guidelines for comprehensive social work assessment which have been heavily relied upon by social services and the courts (DoH, 1988), and the development of better methods of assessment has been widely studied (Corby, 1995). However, despite assessment in childcare being 'multi-disciplinary', and the government strongly encouraging the idea of 'working together' (DHSS, 1988), problems of assessment and working together remain.

This area of work has been the subject of damning criticisms of the assessments made, and the decisions and planning based on them: there is no need to detail the various scandals – they are public knowledge. There has also been criticism of the way government has directed resources first towards 'comprehensive' assessment, then towards 'risk assessment', and lately towards 'needs assessment', with little effort to work out the relationship between differing types and purposes of assessment, or to test their theoretical or practical adequacy, at the level where it actually matters – where the assessments are applied by professionals in complex human situations (Parton, 1996c). The impression given is one of government departments responding to changing political pressures and values to ensure the identification of 'dangerous' cases, to safeguard the care and planning of care for children for whom the state has responsibility, and to secure the maximum involvement of the community, and cost-effective methods.

Above all, the state has sought to protect its own interests in appearing to promote the right mix of values in the light of media coverage at any one point in time, balancing the rights of parent voters against the wrongs done to children, and using the professionals as ready scapegoats for various systemic inadequacies whenever possible. In this context, the issue of social assessment is crucial – particularly for social services, whose role is now centre-stage (Parton, 1985 and 1991).

Developing practice in childcare assessment

Early Social Assessment

Traditionally, assessment methods drew their inspiration from psycho-social theories, with the emphasis on the psychological factors. However, the influence was not unidirectional: Bowlby's theories of attachment were first suggested to him by two women social workers, who were colleagues at a child guidance clinic before the war (Bretherton, 1991). However, the predominance of the psychiatric and psychological professions over predominantly nursing and social work carers meant that the post-war years were guided by attachment and psychoanalytic theory and by child psychiatric specialists such as Winnicott (Winnicott, 1971a; 1971b; 1980), but their concept and use of the *social* was rarely explicitly studied, except through the lens of psychiatric theory. Indeed, it appears that one of the strengths of the psychiatric or medical history that the nurse or social worker constructed was that it helped to incorporate the social into the psychiatric assessment – but usually in a theoretically unexamined way, from the perspective of sociological theory or social research methodology. This is not surprising in view of the predominance of psychoanalytic concepts as the 'groundwork' of assessment in social work (Payne, 1991, p.38). Nor is it any more surprising that a more practical culture has in fact been dominant when it is acknowledged that the diffusion of trained psychiatric social workers has been very limited in Britain, and the 'pragmatic and common sense provision of service' has been even more significant in practice (Payne, 1991, p.83).

The tradition of assessment in childcare has thus been an amalgam of psycho-dynamic theory and pragmatic common sense in the study of cases, with an infusion of social systems theory. This was principally the case in the influential psycho-social theories of Florence Hollis (Hollis, 1964). The diagnostic approach to the assessment of the person-in-situation drew principally from medical and psychiatric models, laying particular emphasis upon assessment. It has been pointed out that: 'the second and third editions of the book use systems theory to analyse action in the "situation", and psychoanalytic theory for "stress", which is given more attention' (Payne, 1991, p.83). This combination of factors, using psycho-dynamic ideas concerning child development (and sometimes later also behavioural and cognitive psychologies), social systems concepts and pragmatic common sense has been characteristic of the social assessment of children and families. It has had both strengths and weaknesses, promoting great variability in assessment practice, but at its best, in the hands of experienced women social workers, capable of producing sensitive assessments of complex situations. Nevertheless, what has sometimes been achieved has had a precarious theoretical basis, and has often lacked sufficient grounding in sociological and historical analysis.

Psychiatry and life history assessment

An early paper by the psychiatrist Sula Wolff expresses her belief in the importance of the life history that social workers construct in the process of 'multi-disciplinary' assessment of children: 'In eliciting and interpreting the case history to their colleagues, whether as long-term members of a clinical team or in relation to a single shared case, social workers fulfil a major educational role' (Wolff, 1978).

The traditional psycho-dynamic and/or medical orientation of psychiatry placed emphasis on the importance of knowledge about the early childhood experiences of parents and children, sometimes assuming a naive concept of retrieving social and historical information – the lower-status worker merely recording the facts for the psychiatrist to consider. However, in making her observation, Wolff had taken the trouble to draw on neo-Wittgensteinian philosophy of the social sciences (Toulmin, 1970) and a phenomenological account of the life history (Watson, 1976). She argues that there should be a 'common clinical and social history' for social work, child psychiatry and paediatrics (Wolff, 1978, p.106), and that this will facilitate inter-professional work, providing a shared framework, and allowing workers to: 'predict the effect of interventions' (Wolff, 1978, p.102). She cites evidence that narrative accounts by parents provide a more reliable guide for work with children than other methods, such as questionnaires. She contends that these methods can take into account the cultural issues of interpretation, and stresses the importance of a systematic approach to coverage of the life history. She is still using a limited, medical, diagnostic framework, however, as becomes evident in her assertion that the life history 'should not be read by children and their relatives, nor by adoptive and foster parents, nor indeed by anyone without professional knowledge and skills' (Wolff, 1978, p.105).

The recommendations made by this psychiatrist may have had some effect, but they did not become central to childcare assessment, partly for reasons she anticipates. Both the support for genericism in reorganised social services departments and rapid promotion to management undermined the development of social workers as specialists in childcare, leaving basic-grade workers vulnerable to the childcare tragedies of the late 1970s and 1980s.

An official report on social work assessment and decision-making in the mid-1980s concluded that: 'Social workers quite often misinterpret natural parents' behaviour at the time of admission because the psycho-social study of the family is not sufficiently thorough' (DHSS, 1985, p.8). Part of the problem was that not only were new social workers unable to develop expertise and unsupported in doing thorough life histories of children and families, they often had little time in which to write up a 'comprehensive' family study, and no adequate guidance on how to select the most significant aspects to study, and on which to base intervention.

Psychodynamics and assessment

However, in contrast with the psychiatrist's advocacy of life history studies as the basis of social work assessment, a psychotherapist's more programmatic approach with its simplified examples met the current need for a brief guide to assessment in childcare, and fitted well with the social work tradition of drawing on psycho-dynamic theory. Vera Fahlberg's publications under the British Association for Adoption and Fostering imprint had a considerable impact on social work, and continue to do so (Fahlberg, 1981; 1982a; 1982b; 1988; 1994).

Work that was originally developed in the late 1970s for use in Michigan became the basis for childcare social work practice across Britain, and was officially cited in the government's advice on comprehensive assessment (DoH, 1988). However, in Fahlberg the social and historical aspects of life histories were made secondary to a distinctive interpretation of psycho-dynamic theory and its application to child development. This meant that one could read off what the psycho-social stage *should* be from the child's chronological age, and then compare it with evidence of the actual psycho-social development according to this scale. Any failure to exhibit the appropriate signs could then be attributed to traumas evident in the family history, and/or discoverable through direct work with the child.

The scale used to measure child development was very old (Gesell et al., 1940; Gesell and Ilg, 1946), and based on a small sample of above-average white New England children (Thomas, 1979, Chapter 6). Wisely, the 1988 government advice on assessment used a more up-to-date scale, but Thomas's comment remains valid: 'Group averages are of limited use in explaining a child's past, predicting his future stages, and suggesting what should be done to guide his development' (Thomas, 1979, p.124).

In addition, the use of a particular child development scale was subjected to the application of Fahlberg's psycho-dynamic interpretation. For example, she describes the case of Rhonda, a sexually abused 7-year-old whose mother had died two years earlier. The father was found to have sexually abused her before and after the death of her mother. Fahlberg's suggested analysis refers explicitly to a psychoanalytic stage of development: 'Rhonda lost her mother during the "Oedipal" stage', when she needed to feel that her mother was not upset by her feelings for her father', and she concludes that Rhonda needs to 'identify with a woman and accept her femininity' (Fahlberg, 1988, pp.145–6).

Fahlberg's assessment appears to ignore social issues of power between genders, and between age groups. There can be no *a priori* assumption that the abuse was specially linked to an Oedipal stage: it might well have been going on earlier. Indeed, it could reasonably be argued that Fahlberg's explanation – the daughter's infantile fixation on her father – comes very close to blaming the victim, as she is seen as inviting a sexual response from her father because of her stage of development.

The advantage of her method, however, was (and still is) that the guidelines offered have some kind of theoretical basis, even though disputable, and they are capable of relatively easy application, helping workers to understand the processes of child and family development as they relate to care systems.

Attachment theory and assessment

The pattern of using psychological developmental assessment methods in work with children has relied heavily on the use of attachment theory combined with developmental scales. An example of an assessment done along these lines was published in the same year as the government's 1988 guidelines, and demonstrates the sociological and historical inadequacy of this particular way of combining psychology and sociology (Clifford, 1992/3). In this assessment (Adcock with Lake and Small, 1988), the social worker, Roger Lake, used well-established techniques developed by the British Association for Adoption and Fostering. Within the Aldgate and Simmonds collection in which this assessment was published, there was also a useful paper on the assessment of black children (Brummer, 1988). However, it is precisely because the BAAF guidelines for assessment do not attempt to seriously consider the sociological and historical issues central to CA/B methodology that in practice, Lake et al.'s assessment inevitably concentrates on the social psychology of individual children and their families – in isolation from the social factors, and ignoring some of the advice suggested by Brummer.

There are many sorts of questions that need to be answered from a CA/B perspective. After initially describing the child concerned in this example as of Black Afro-Caribbean origin, they totally failed to refer to it again, except where the 'cultural and racial experiences' (Adcock with Lake and Small, 1988, p.25) of children are paid due lip service without any attempt to consider how this applies. For example, there was no mention of whether both parents had the same ethnic origin, nor whether a sibling (by a different father), mother's boyfriends, fosterparents, teachers or schoolfriends had similar ethnic origins, so the question of whether some of the behaviour might be related to racism does not arise. The authors did not discuss whether the mother or father were born in Britain, or whether they had suffered traumas of settlement and separation: the role of the extended family and friends in the community was therefore ignored. There was no awareness of the impact on communication between social worker and client that arises from the ethnicity and age of the worker: issues of reflexivity and social division were ignored. The various events in the mother's life, as far as we are told, make it clear that much of her behaviour could be attributed to sexist behaviour by her partner, and by the sexist and racist social structures within which she had to survive. The whole assessment was geared to the evaluation of attachment between mother and child, regardless of 'race', gender or other social divisions, or histories or reflexivity.

Recent work on attachment theory in a social context (Howe, 1995) emphasises the importance of a thorough understanding of the history of relationships between children and their parents or carers: feminist critiques of attachment and development theories (discussed in Chapter 4) are relevant at this point. The point here is that in a social assessment such a history must be based on CA/B principles if it is to be an adequate social history, rather than a limited psychological account of interpersonal attachments.

The Orange Book: Official guidance for assessment

The psychiatrist Peter Reder has made significant contributions to the area of child protection assessment in recent years (Reder, Duncan and Gray, 1993a and 1993b; Reder and Lucey, 1991 and 1995). In the introductory chapter to Reder and Lucey's 1995 edited work on the assessment of parenting, it is stressed that a theoretical framework is essential to all assessment, but the authors comment bluntly that in contrast with their own clear theoretical framework, the problem with social work assessment based on the Orange Book (DoH, 1988) is that the latter 'provides no theoretical framework' (Reder and Lucey, 1995, p.5). They make no attempt to say what a social assessment theory should be, but focus on attachment theory and intra-family interaction as *their* theoretical framework.

Ironically, these are the two main theoretical perspectives that did in fact underpin the Orange Book. Although they are not explicitly and systematically set out and discussed as theories, relevant literature is cited both in the body of the text and in the bibliography. For example, Fahlberg is used and cited in the context of assessing emotional development and attachment (DoH, 1988, pp.38, 39 and 43), whilst the systemic approach to family interactions of Dale and colleagues (Dale et al., 1986) is used in relation to assessing family interactions, (DoH, 1988, p.55).

However, the absence of explicit discussion of a theoretical framework is clear, and its impact on practice is evident. A recent paper on social work assessment argues that the problem is that: 'there is no conceptual framework which adequately embraces the range of assessment tasks' (Lloyd and Taylor, 1995). Recent DoH research confirms the unacceptable deficiency of theory in assessments and case conferences (Farmer and Owen, 1995, Chapter 9), and another recent study criticises both the inadequacy of social workers' grasp of theory and the unacceptable 'atheoretical stance' of DoH guidelines and other checklists (Munro, 1998). However, as cognitive-behavioural psychologists are quick to observe, it has been found in several meta-analyses that assessment programmes 'are more likely to be effective if they are *explicitly* based on a theoretical principle, (McMurren and Hodge, 1994, p.2; emphasis added). Explicit awareness (and preferably working towards integration) of *alternative* theoretical bases for assessment in health and welfare is also very much to be desired (Corby, 1989).

Criticism of the limitations of theoretical guidance in the Orange Book is compounded by other criticisms. Some of these obviously arise from its origins in the pre-1989 Child Care Act period: for example, a lack of focus on children, and very few questions being actually directed towards them. Children's rights in the legal process were increased in the 1989 Children Act, and children's rights issues have been given greater prominence in recent years. The question-and-answer format is not always appropriate, suggesting to parents what the 'right' answer should be, but at least it implies some form of partnership with parents – an issue of increasing official importance – and also a relationship which is highlighted and problematised within the CA/B framework. However, it does not help to clarify difficult issues of power and responsibility if the whole assessment is based on this format alone.

There need to be alternative perspectives and sources of evidence for an assessment of continuing needs and risks, in addition to answers to the set questions. CA/B methods include the relevance of documentary and third-party evidence, which may or may not be confidential. Such evidence may be crucial in forming judgements about the life histories which are involved in studying family situations. There is also a general weakness on sociological issues involving social division, including how childhood itself is oppressively socially structured. The importance of 'cultural sensitivity' is noted (DoH, 1988, p.13), but in a subsidiary way that leaves assessment open to the kind of psycho-social treatment given in examples already discussed above. The assessment has a relatively static format (not conducive to encompassing changes during the intervention process, and unhelpful for considering interventive assessments), and fails to consider adequately the reflexive issues of worker–user dynamics.

Above all, it is a long, time-consuming document, containing 167 questions, which has been difficult for social workers to follow in any consistent way, resulting in great variations in actual practice. Yet magistrates and solicitors have expected social workers to have substantially reproduced its patterns and prescriptions. Corby remarks that: 'it is hard to see how the current document could be usefully applied in most practice contexts' (Corby, 1995, p.25), yet this has had to be done. In addition, there has been confusion arising from the title of the Orange Book, which refers to comprehensive assessment and child protection, yet clearly states inside that: '*the purpose of the assessment is not to determine whether a child has been abused or there is other serious cause for concern* as that will already have been established during the initial investigation' (DoH, 1988, p.21). The contradictory messages that on the one hand this is a comprehensive model of assessment, but on the other it does not include initial assessment of abuse or the risk of further abuse, has led to the Orange Book being used for child protection assessments at various stages, increasing the inconsistency and variability of childcare assessments. Although it is explicitly about child protection, it does not include reference to the most well-known presentation of risk factors in child abuse, which was published the year before (Greenland, 1987), and only refers to a variety of indicators in relation to the parental history, and none in relation to the child (DoH, 1988, pp.49–50).

At the time of writing, there are plans for the Orange Book to be revised, and brought up to date with the legislation. However, this will not be sufficient if there is again no attempt to discuss what is most evidently needed – a theoretical basis for comprehensive social assessment. There is no simple stage at which an assessment becomes 'comprehensive' – the very idea suggests a static concept of assessment. The constraints of time mean that the idea of 'comprehensive assessment' is also very ambitious (Platt and Edwards, 1997), and the values and reflexivity involved mean that it is always open to further comment and debate, especially in the light of the differing assessments of other professions, and the perspectives of users and carers.

It will normally be essential to have a *focus* on particular aspects of child and family circumstances that should have been identified (e.g. in supervision, or at a case conference). It is evident that any initial assessment should focus on understanding the urgent needs of a referred child, including its need for protection. The CA/B framework helps to question and check the kinds of assumptions being made, and provides support for the idea that the social assessment is comprehensive in principle, and consistent with a rigorous social research methodology, even though all the information is not yet available.

A 'comprehensive' social assessment, if it is to mean anything, must be one in which a substantial amount of detailed information has been assembled, and a thorough examination made of a child and family's circumstances, in the light of known risk factors and children's developmental needs, contextualised by a full social history, and assessment of the current interactions and interventions between family and workers – all based on CA/B principles.

Looking after children

Until research in the early 1990s highlighted the point (DoH, Dartington Social Research Unit, 1995), needs had been relatively overshadowed by assessing serious risks in initial assessments, and 'comprehensive' planning assessments had focused on family relationships and psycho-social development. Another twist is for assessment of needs to be centred on an even later stage, when a child is being 'looked after'. Beginning from this perspective, the research described by Parker and colleagues (Parker, et al., 1992) concentrated on assessing the outcomes of intervention over time, and has strengths in its structured involvement of parents and professionals, as well as its age-related and multi-dimensional guidance on children's needs. However, there is still an absence of a theoretical framework to help interpret and evaluate the multitude of issues that arise in complex situations. There is an attempt to address theoretical issues, but it is limited in scope and usefulness. There is an awareness of the legislative framework: reference is made to the concept of a 'reasonable parent' and the duty to promote children's welfare under Section 17 of the Children Act.

The theories used to support the assessment of needs in this context are of limited use, however. They rely on interactionist psychological 'theories of competence', which stress the 'interplay between a person's abilities ... motivation, and certain qualities in the impinging environment' (Parker et al., 1991, p.59), focusing on how compensation can be made for past deficits. This is combined with a 'production of welfare' approach to evaluating final outcomes in relation to intermediate outcomes and resource inputs, enabling some concrete measurement of success. Little attention is paid to the complexity of social situations and the value-laden decisions which are involved in understanding and assessing disputed concepts of need. It is thus not surprising to see, on the one hand, the 'Looking After Children' material being attacked for its potential insensitivity across a wide range of social divisions issues (Knight and Caveney, 1998), nor to see it defended on the grounds that it provides a basis for the defence and improvement of living standards amongst the very same social groups (Jackson, 1998). The CA/B theoretical framework provides a way of being aware of the complex issues of interpretation which should be used to critically underpin instruments like the 'Looking After Children' documents which, being relatively atheoretical, are open to questionable use.

There is little guidance on how this assessment relates to the assessment of risk in child protection, possibly because its original focus is upon children already being 'looked after', rather than in the initial stages of assessment. However, the protection issues do not go away: there should be an integration of assessment of needs and risks, and *continuity* between them, as explicit in the CA/B framework. Conversely, the strengths of this focus on needs and outcomes should be utilised throughout the assessment process, not only when children are 'looked after'. However, the lengthy pro formas that are provided, whilst suitable at a later stage, may well lead to the kind of variability of application associated with the lengthy questionnaire in the Orange Book in situations where organisational, legal and time pressures do not permit the space for the procedures envisaged.

Practice research is required to establish how the various elements of assessment can be properly integrated in the difficult situations which are common in childcare practice. Whilst CA/B provides a theoretical framework, it requires practitioners to develop techniques for specific situations, and ways of integrating theory consistently in practice, throughout the 'care career' of a child, from initial assessment to assessments at later stages.

Assessing parenting

Recent work by psychologists and psychiatrists on the assessment of parenting can also be used to illustrate how CA/B methodology helps to make assessments of people currently caring for children, building on good practices that have been developed by childcare workers in this field, and supplying a theoretical basis for *social* assessment. Chapter 7 has already referred to the work of Reder and associates in developing psychological and psychiatric methods of assessing children and families, and their criticism of the Orange Book's lack of a theoretical framework has been noted. One of the works cited (Reder and Lucey, 1995) focuses especially on the assessment of parenting, and provides an influential guide in this area – not least because of the social status of the authors. The discussion in Chapter 7 drew attention to both distinctions and connections between their approach and *social* assessment: this can be seen also in relation to the assessment of parenting.

On the key issue of how to predict the future prospects for good parenting, one of the authors agrees with the view that research evidence based on socio-demographic risk factors has to be taken further by clinical forms of assessment (Browne, 1995, p.123). He lists five aspects of parental evaluation, all of which can be viewed through the lens of a psychological or a psychiatric but also a *social* perspective, and all involve social components. For example, understanding the 'caretakers' knowledge and attitudes to parent–child relations' (Browne, 1995, p.123) can be constructed through the telling of life stories by the parent/carers themselves, by third parties, and from documentary evidence. All these need to be socially and historically located within CA/B principles, as well as linked to a psychological theory.

The 'observation of parent–child interaction' (Browne, 1995, p.123) is another key aspect of evaluation, but within the CA/B framework, the reflexive social locating of the participants in this social interaction is equally as important as the psychological interpretation of inter-personal relationships. Similarly, the other components of Browne's list of aspects of parental evaluation all inevitably involve considerations of the fundamental principles of CA/B method, since what is being described is not just a psychological but also a social interaction.

It is thus not surprising that Lucey and Reder, in their attempt to summarise a 'balanced' view of assessing parents/carers, conclude that: 'the *histories* of their relationships in general, and of child care in particular, are reasonable predictors of future behaviour' (Lucey and Reder, 1995, p.271; emphasis added). Furthermore, in order to construct such histories, they reiterate 'the value of meeting the social worker … in order to draw up a genogram of the family, and a chronology of relevant events' (Lucey and Reder, 1995, p.273).

One of the key psychological components of Reder's assessment of parenting is the meaning of the child for the parent/carer. This also makes it 'necessary to collate information already known … and the nature of their problem over the years', in order that 'patterns may then become apparent' (Reder and Duncan, 1995, p.50). This is all reminiscent of Sula Wolff's valuing of the social work construction of social histories discussed earlier in this chapter, but without her awareness of the different theoretical perspectives necessitated by social and historical interpretation. It is also of critical importance in relation to recent evidence of social workers' failure to make use of past history (Munro, 1998, p.92).

Other important factors identified which resonate with the CA/B framework are the nature of interventive assessments in which parenting strengths and needs are seen in a process of both treatment, training and assessment (Lucey and Reder, 1995, p.268). Here, the changing social context and socio-historical aspects of the interaction also need to be interpreted in terms of CA/B theory as well as psychology. They refer to the importance of avoiding 'prejudice' in assessing parents with certain characteristics such as learning disabilities, psychological disorders, being gay or lesbian, single-parent families, or teenagers (Lucey and Reder, 1995, pp.268–9). Such matters are clearly of considerable social importance, and need to take into account CA/B principles concerning the interpretation and understanding of social difference. Avoiding prejudice is an admirable but limited approach to the social issues involved.

In sum, the way parenting is assessed by contemporary psychiatrists and psychologists is in fact surrounded by assumptions about and investigations into social and historical factors. Such inquiries must of necessity therefore be closely related to social assessment of parenting, drawing on CA/B principles. In using the products of social assessment, psychologists need to remember that they are not simply incorporating 'factual' information about the past or present social events, trends or structures. The social assessment is itself already a construction of reality based upon theoretical principles. If it is not, then it will be drawing on relatively unexamined social assumptions.

Conversely, although social assessors will doubtless learn from their colleagues, the worker making a social assessment of parenting must beware of simply taking over psychological concepts without critically examining the theory that lies behind them, or the social concepts that should be informing their own assessment. They should, of course, be working together to understand and develop their differing values and perspectives, working out ways of bridging or triangulating their analyses (see Chapter 7).

Assessing potential carers

There are obvious links between long-term childcare planning, in which there is 'comprehensive assessment' of needs and risks; rehabilitation, where assessments of parenting and family functioning need to be made, and fostering and adoption assessments. Similar kinds of judgements must be made about the potential of the adult carers involved, and about the needs of the child to be looked after. However, there has sometimes been a compartmentalising of assessments in this area, without the benefit of an over-arching framework within which to judge their differing contributions.

As elsewhere in social work, earlier concerns with psychodynamic and developmental assessment of potential carers gave way to ecological systems theory (Hartmann, 1979). Recent discussion of the assessment of potential carers in fostering and adoption has been partly about the advantages or otherwise of traditional individual investigative assessment compared to groupwork (Howell and Ryman, 1987; Lee and Holland, 1991; Rhodes, 1991; Stevenson, 1991; Selwyn, 1991). There was a swing away from regarding social workers as experts, and more emphasis on working in partnership with applicants, partly as a result of the 1989 Children Act and its stress on partnership with parents and carers. There are certainly strong arguments for guarding against insensitive 'expert' individual investigation, and welcoming the positive contributions that potential carers can make to their own assessment process. There are also good reasons for using groupwork, both as a method of assessment and as a means both of providing information and creating a self-supporting group.

However, the (then) government's assumption that 'common sense human judgements' should guide assessment (DoH, 1993) and some writers' support for methods of self-selection (Ryburn, 1991) ignore a whole range of difficult issues about assessment of needs and risks in individual and family life for which professional workers have to take responsibility to ensure as best they can the meeting of children's needs, including safety, as in other areas of social work (Cain, 1992; Boushel, 1995). Whatever methods are used, there needs to be a consistent theoretical framework which can provide a basis for assessing issues of risk and need, as well as strengths, in which partnership with actual or potential parents/carers is tempered by a thorough analysis of the power relationships and social differences which may support or neglect the role they have (or may have) in relation to vulnerable children.

Research into assessment of potential parenting by the author (Clifford and Cropper, 1994; 1997a; 1997b) has explored ways in which good practice can be both understood and strengthened by consistent use of CA/B principles. For example, issues of power cannot and should not be avoided (Selwyn, 1994). The CA/B framework provides a systematic focus on power, to fully assess its place in the lives of potential carers, providing a check on potential child abuse in relation to historical risk factors, as well as other important issues about the differential impact on, and use of power by all the parties involved.

People's lives may also be explored for strengths as well as problem areas (sometimes two sides of the same coin). Their experiences in specific social contexts may have prepared them for caring for children in particular valuable ways. For example, the experience of disability may be an area of continuing problems for a disabled person in a disabling society. However, the strengths gained from having survived these experiences, and the personal knowledge involved, may be an invaluable asset to the potential fosterer or adopter of a child – including (but not only) a disabled child.

Another issue which has caused concern is the problem of how to assess the social values of prospective carers. It is integral to the CA/B framework that anti-oppressive values encompassing both respect for persons and understanding of oppression in different social groups, and especially attitudes towards children, have to be assessed by drawing on personal and family histories, also taking into account the values and personal history of the worker. There can be no guaranteed outcome, but there needs to be some evidence from individual histories that applicants have a *minimum* understanding of the personal and structural nature of oppression (especially of children), and a 'willingness to examine their own values and behaviour' (Clifford and Cropper, 1997a). These issues can be best assessed in terms of a CA/B methodology which sets values in real historical and social contexts, as well as in the reflexive context of worker(s) and user(s). What are really of interest are actual personal and family experiences, and how they have processed and reacted to social trends and historical events: for example, reactions to events involving gays and lesbians (Brown, 1992).

Effective functioning in family and personal relationships has always been regarded as a key set of criteria, and these are indicated by the CA/B framework in the personal and political links between informal and formal social systems, in the present and the past. Neither negatives such as aggression or social isolation, nor positives such as the ability to communicate and negotiate can be assessed exclusively by psycho-dynamic histories of childhood, by systemic assessments of current functioning, or by observation of communication skills in group sessions. Sufficient assessment requires the systemic, developmental and current factors to be socially located within detailed and continuous life histories: the CA/B framework, within which differing psychological factors can be located in a social context.

Assessment of risks and needs in childcare: The CA/B framework and contemporary issues

Methodology

The previous sections in this chapter have shown how disjointed and haphazard the practice of social assessment has been in childcare, varying over time and in different settings, and even in similar settings where differing purposes have been in mind. There has been little in the way of an overall theoretical framework to hold the whole range of issues together or to help integrate alternative perspectives. As a result, various items tend to get lost. Sometimes the needs of various participants have been overlooked, sometimes risks have not been properly dealt with, sometimes key variables such as changes through time or the reflexive impact of the assessment have not been properly considered. The practice of assessment has thus been very variable, and in need of a comprehensive theoretical framework. Recent research confirms this view: there has been an absence of theory in assessments and case conferences, and the research suggests strongly that there would be a very beneficial effect on assessment of having a complex but consistent, multi-faceted theoretical framework which can cope with interaction over time (Farmer and Owen, 1995, Chapter 9).

At its best, social assessment has been full of insight and awareness of a variety of factors, and practice theory has developed from what practitioners do in the course of assessment, assisted by some of the theories discussed above, especially systems and psycho-dynamic theories (Curnock and Hardiker, 1979). The intention of practitioners was to understand the person in a dynamic social situation in which they were themselves involved, and the development of practical methods of working produced good assessments with theoretical implications that began to be drawn out and combined with social science theory (Curnock and Hardiker, 1979, pp.163ff). However, rapid developments in social theory, in social research methodology and in the various practices of social assessment during a turbulent period of change have meant that the development of a methodological framework at a theoretical level, combining contemporary social theory and research methodology with the experience of practitioners and the perspectives of users and oppressed groups, is now long overdue.

It is important to understand that CA/B theory applies to initial assessment as a guiding framework to assist professional judgement, not as a rigid, detailed blueprint. The actual constituents of procedures are bound to vary greatly with the circumstances and time available, and many detailed pro formas, checklists and risk factors are available for assisting workers in initial assessment (Taylor and Devine, 1993; Corby, 1995). However, the framework affects not only the way initial assessment is carried out, but also its content and development into later stages of assessment and review (see Chapter 1). It provides a justification for taking user and carer perspectives seriously, not only on the basis of individual rights, knowledge and respect, but also because of the integral concern of CA/B theory for understanding socially structured differences in perspectives. This is a matter of considerable concern in view of current research evidence on the importance of full understanding and clear presentation of carer/parental views, and on the importance of allowing contrary views to be expressed, both by parents and by differing professionals (Farmer and Owen, 1995, p.101).

'Childhood' and social difference

General issues concerning the assessment of risk and need have already been discussed in Chapter 8. The dynamic and socially constructed nature of risks and needs and their close interconnection requires considerable thought and skill in assessing children. The reflexive nature of sociological theory noted by Giddens (see Chapter 3) has already affected views of child abuse (Little, 1997), and practitioners are often aware to some degree of the negotiated and constructed nature of the 'realities' involved.

The central concept of 'childhood' itself has become a current subject for discussion amongst sociologists, with an emphasis upon its socially constructed nature, and a 'theoretical focus upon the plurality of childhoods' (Jenks, 1996, p.121). This has been accompanied by increased concerns about the rights and welfare of children, not only as individuals, but as a social group (Franklin, 1986; Archard, 1993; Scraton, 1997).

The orientation of the CA/B framework is towards a concept of childhood that is sensitive to these issues in a particular way. It inevitably accepts the (much discussed) historical evidence of changing concepts of childhood, as exemplified in celebrated studies of past childhoods (Aries, 1962), and emphasises the elements of difference between childhood and other social divisions, and within childhood itself, between gender, race, class and all the other fragmented identities which impinge on specific groups and individuals. This will include the important consideration that children themselves have powers which may be used positively, but they may also be abusers of other children, especially those younger than themselves, or belonging to different social divisions, vulnerable in other ways. Childhood itself is socially divided between age groups, with distinctions often made corresponding to different stages of schooling, with the approximate fracturing line of adolescence marked by adopting the term 'young people'.

However, CA/B method will also place these differences within historically specific commonalities of experiences that children have as a result of the social structures of power and discourse that influence their lives. These commonalities can extend globally (Jenks, 1996, p.122), partly as a result of the economic power of Western commercial, political and voluntary agencies to impose expectations and demands which can simultaneously exploit child labour (including sexual services) and impose standards of parenting and child welfare on indigenous cultures. As in the example of the black child given earlier in this chapter, the importance of systematically taking account of social difference in relation to childhood as a social division and in relation to the other social divisions relevant to this specific child and his relationships can only be ignored at the cost of an effective assessment.

The social construction of risks and needs in the assessment process must therefore proceed in the uncomfortable knowledge that 'realities' are partly being constituted by adults within the situated process itself. This is not only in the sense that the adults are responsible for defining the terms of the relationship, and constructing the concepts involved. Even more troubling is the reflection that the adults concerned, both personally and as members of the group, have continuing power over the children concerned. They both are and will be perceived as authority figures with power to do harm as well as good, and it is well known that much harm is actually done by professionals entrusted with the care of children (e.g., Staffordshire County Council, 1991).

A reflexive awareness of the issues concerning the methods and values involved therefore necessitates a level of theoretical and ethico-political engagement with social difference: assessments need to be understood as taking place within such a framework. CA/B method is explicitly oriented towards this consideration, attempting to draw deliberately on the perspectives of oppressed social groups, including those of children themselves, even though this aim is fraught with difficulty.

Historical location

In Chapter 8, the importance of contextualising indicators of risk, need and strength within a detailed social history has already been emphasised. Researchers have been critical of the inadequacy of history-taking in child abuse cases (Hill, 1990; Munro, 1998). Thus a social research methodology tailored to studying the histories of microsocial situations in health and social welfare is clearly required as a framework within which risk factors and related developmental evidence can be understood and weighed.

Corby summarises recent evidence, pointing out the importance of understanding the interaction between individual risk factors, many of them having historical dimensions in individual and family lives (Corby, 1995). The historical dimension of CA/B method directs attention to this aspect of understanding the relationship between risk factors, and between risks, needs and strengths. A rounded view of service users' lives will attempt to situate their life stories within wider family, peer and community histories, making use of documentary evidence, third-party evidence as well as oral history, addressing strengths in addition to risks and needs, and taking account of differing perspectives. This justifies much good practice as it already exists, whilst encouraging further reflection and effort towards a more sophisticated social and historical awareness.

For example, oral historians have given credit to social and health workers for their good practice in developing life story work with children (Thompson, 1984, p.161). It has been used as a means of therapy and of assessment (Ryan and Walker, 1985), and the basic principle of eliciting a life story from a service user has to be one of the essential criteria of CA/B method, even though imperfectly realised in difficult situations. It is a crucial way of understanding the perspectives of children themselves. However, the aim of constructing a life story for the purposes of assessment involves a complex balancing of the life stories of parents and children, and an understanding of relevant documentary and social history.

Many of the risk factors pertaining to a child's needs will have arisen as a result of parenting patterns which will involve the gathering of adult life stories and other perspectives and values. These histories have to be interpreted by the worker within the CA/B theoretical framework, drawing upon an understanding of difference, power relationships and interacting social systems which influence the perceptions of both service users and workers. The therapeutic use of a life story with a child thus needs to be carefully distinguished from the construction of critical social histories by the worker, even though they will inevitably overlap in significant ways, depending on the particular context.

Factors which accrue over a period of time are specially significant in relation to the development of a sensitive historical account of people's lives. The element of *neglect*, common in many child abuse situations, requires an awareness of historical developmental change, which workers have been able to tackle in terms of chronologies of individual lives, documenting how physical and emotional neglect accumulates over a period of time. Recent childcare research stresses the importance of comparing present and past contexts of events and directions of development, and assessing interactions over time (Farmer and Owen, 1995, p.148). This requires CA/B histories of interacting social systems and power relationships in which patterns of neglect relate to varying combinations of social and personal circumstances. This social account of the life history provides a context for both the psychological and developmental information, attachment, other psychological theories and any relevant medical history.

Reflexivity

Good practice in social assessment has frequently emphasised the importance of social workers taking account of themselves, and including this within the assessment. This issue has traditionally been seen in social work and in other related professions in terms of a psycho-dynamic understanding of the self (Ferard and Hunnybun, 1962). Using the Freudian concept of 'counter-transference', the worker transfers their repressed emotions about mothers and fathers onto the client – depending on the gender and age of both parties. This necessitates the worker's self-examination (and, originally, the requirement to be psychoanalysed oneself before doing it to others). The CA/B framework includes consideration of the intra-psychic and inter-personal psychological issues in assessment. However, the framework emphasises the social aspects of reflexivity. The fact that the worker belongs to a specific combination of social divisions and occupies a specific location in socio-historical space has particular social as well as psychological implications.

The basic issue about reflexivity in childcare has to be the workers' recognition of their own adult status and the particular kind of power and authority this give them, for good or ill, over a child's life. Recent guides to good practice in assessing black families or anti-sexist working with women have laid considerable emphasis on the importance of the social assessor taking account of their own membership of particular social divisions, and thoroughly analysing the implications. The advice tends to focus on one or two of the social divisions, for example when challenging white assessors to consider 'what steps have you taken to critically examine your values and perceptions of black families?' (Ahmad, 1990, p.27), or in furthering anti-sexist assessment, requiring students to demonstrate 'how your gender affects who and how you are and how that affects your practice' (Phillipson, 1992, p.49). The insistence on addressing issues of value reflects CA/B's acceptance of the values of workers, users, and the concepts and methods used as central and unavoidable, requiring self-aware positioning. In this case, the recognition of the worker's own adult status and the barriers that creates for a particular child is obviously a central issue, but has to be placed in the context of all the social divisions to which the worker belongs.

Within the CA/B framework in relation to childcare assessment, the whole range of social divisions needs to be considered, and the overall social and historical location of the worker needs to be analysed. In particular, the worker's earlier biography and experience of childhood is specially relevant – not (just) for psycho-dynamic reasons, but because the worker's experience of a specific socio-historic childhood is a significant parameter in the assessment process, and the more clearly that is identified in its particularity, the better. More recent periods of the worker's biography are also important, since the formation of their present changing identity, and how that will be viewed by a particular child, has to be grasped as well as possible in order to anticipate children's reactions, and make oneself as accessible as possible across the social divide of age. Supervision and discussion with third parties is obviously pertinent to this objective.

The reflexive principle focuses attention upon the intervention itself as a risk factor, including the person of the assessor, as well as the involvement of the agency and what it represents to the users. CA/B method requires such an understanding of the interaction between social systems and individuals over periods of time. Recent research confirms the importance of assessing interactions between the family members and the social worker over time, and for the worker to be discussing this and receiving support in supervision (Farmer and Owen, 1995, p.65). The principle applies to all workers involved, and has been at the root of failures in childcare where the issues of reflexivity have not been seriously addressed by the group of adult professionals and users supposedly working together for the benefit of the child.

The principle of reflexivity does not only apply to the intervention of the worker as an individual and the impact their particular identity has in a specific situation, but it also applies to the 'team' that is working on the case. There needs to be a self-awareness at an organisational level that has been described in recent research as 'team reflexivity' (Opie, 1997), and is extremely relevant to both intra- and inter-agency team meetings. Issues such as how teams are socially constituted, where the power lies, how different perspectives are represented (and may be changing – see Chapter 7), what values are being supported, and how the team impacts on the child concerned, on carers and on families are not matters which should be brushed under the carpet, but need to be explicitly monitored and reviewed.

Power

Risks, needs and strengths are about power – the ability and potential to arrive at desired or feared outcomes in changing circumstances. The current childcare legislation separates out risk and need in Sections 17 and 47 of the 1989 Children Act, and this corresponds to ordinary language usage, in that (negative) risk is usually thought of as the possibility of something seriously undesirable happening unless there is an intervention which prevents it. But there are close links between need and risk, as discussed in Chapter 8: they are better considered together, with every need having a corresponding risk of a consequent danger if that need remains unmet.

Thus, all the different kinds and levels of power discussed in Chapter 6 need to be considered in assessing complex childcare situations, and continually reviewed throughout the process of assessment as fluid power relationships change over time. Who has the power to meet needs, and to protect or to abuse? How can the powers of different individuals and groups (including professionals) have positive or negative affects? Who can control the situation? How have balances of power been changing, and how will they change?

However, in childcare there seems to be a tendency to see risk as something often considered at the initial stages of assessment, whereas need is sometimes looked at more closely at a later stage, when a more comprehensive planning assessment is required. However, the best assessments seen by recent researchers were those that were able to indicate a firm basis for a proper plan to meet the needs (and therefore reduce various risks) at the outset – including the needs of the carer/parent, as well as those of the child. Farmer and Owen contend that: 'It is a major disadvantage of the present system that the assessment of risk to the child is not necessarily an assessment of need' (Farmer and Owen, 1995, p.159).

It is well known that *Messages from Research* (DoH, Dartington Social Research Unit, 1995) indicates that many children are being investigated for child abuse risk but receive no services, staying at home with the powerful impact of a child abuse investigation alienating parents, disrupting families and contributing little to meeting their needs. This research suggests that there should be a better balance between looking at childcare needs and protecting the child – and thus the need for an overall theoretical framework for assessment. The research also shows the importance of assessing the needs of carers/parents as well as children, and offering support to mothers, especially in the early stages of any assessment; of balancing strengths against needs, and of not naively summing risk/need factors, but assessing their different weights in context (Farmer and Owen, 1995, Chapter 9).

The CA/B framework stresses the interconnection of ethical and political issues, providing a framework for examining the risks, needs and strengths affecting the whole situation consistently, from the beginning and throughout. A rigorous examination of changing relationships of power is therefore essential to this kind of assessment. A typical example of its crucial practical relevance is in the way recent research highlights the importance of changing pre- and post-conference power balances (Farmer and Owen, 1995, p.260). The power of professionals varies in the light of the legal context and the stages of assessment. Carers and parents may at one point be anxious about the outcome of an investigation, but having seen the result of a child protection conference, may feel confident to reassert their control. Such changing balances of power have to be assessed and anticipated. The CA/B framework alerts workers to the range of both needs and risks – including risks posed by workers, both as individuals and as members of agency or inter-agency groups: for instance, the possibility of various kinds and levels of abuse of power by professionals, as well as carers and users. It also includes the positive aspects of power and the support and strengths that may be offered by users, carers and/or workers. Only a systematic conceptual grasp of the multiple dimensions of power (see Chapter 5) will enable workers to adequately assess the social context of children's needs risks and strengths.

Interacting social systems

Social assessment in childcare has drawn on various kinds of systems theory for a long time, especially in analysing family systems, and to a lesser extent the systemic relationships in which professionals are engaged within and between their agencies and with service users and carers. From a CA/B perspective, the interacting systems are viewed as interpenetrating and systemic only to an uncertain and partial degree: they are socially constructed and changing phenomena. The other social concepts drawn together in CA/B theory mean that interacting social systems are problematised, exposing conflicts of power and reflexive understandings. This uncovers differences between the phenomena that are given the label of 'system'.

The nature of differing family systems will itself vary enormously depending on the degree of closure within a family, but the relationship between the worker and the users is also called a 'system' (Siporin, 1975). In the latter case, it is obvious that how far the behaviour of actors within the 'system' can be explained in systemic, circular terms by other features of that system is open to question, and cannot be assumed simply by identifying the possible existence of a system. This is by no means to deny the importance of the concept, but to question its over-facile application.

On the contrary, CA/B method requires a more scrupulous attention to the whole range of systems, their change and interaction. This appears to be supported by recent research into childcare practice which underscores the significance of putting the family situation in a broader context of changing social systems, as well as the importance of assessing the interaction between the family members and the social worker over time (Farmer and Owen, 1995). The 'social systems' involved in these interactions are not only the immediate ones, but include the range of networks, organisations and social structures which impinge directly and indirectly on everyday social life. Such an approach is a seriously social rather than (just) a psychological analysis, and thus requires a developed social research methodology.

The family as a social system is a field of psychological, psychiatric and sociological study in itself, which is often undergoing periods of transition in order to take account of the difficulties of relating these differing perspectives (Goldner, 1991). Part of that difficulty is precisely the ways in which the family and its individual members variably interact with other social systems. The impact of social networks 'outside' the family includes the extended family, various peer groups, neighbourhood and community networks, and specific agencies and the individuals who represent them.

The organisations within the multi-agency network itself either have or can develop systemic relationships with them and with each other. It is important to note that many social systems are both 'inside' and 'outside' the family system and its members, especially where they may be regarded as participants in wider groupings. This spatial metaphor does not seem adequate to characterise the nature of communities, social classes and other social divisions, nor the national and international organisations and systems in which individuals and families are caught up.

CA/B method encompasses the (sometimes) 'systemic' social relationships involved, with a particular emphasis on the structuring of lives by the wider contexts of the social divisions, including the lives of the professionals and their interaction with users and carers. In fact, this approach draws attention to the membership that individuals and groups have of wider 'social systems' and social divisions, making workers and users more aware of actual and potential memberships. This will include not only the more diffuse but highly significant membership people have of broad social groups, including oppressed groups, but also their actual or potential membership of local groups and organisations that are particularly relevant to them. For example, the existence of children's and parents' rights organisations is of both national and *local* importance for childcare cases, as well as women's groups, gay and lesbian organisations, disability groups, black and ethnic organisations, and so on.

The task of working together actively encourages the setting up of local social networks, yet there is often inadequate assessment of the impact of these systems on the child's networks. A central feature of recent research has been the enormous negative impact of child protection systems on families (DoH, Dartington Social Research Unit, 1995). CA/B method strengthens the analysis of interactions between the systems, and promotes both individual and team reflexivity as part of that analysis (see above). For example, the legal system has to be included in the assessment not only as a set of rules and procedures to be followed, but must also be analysed sociologically as a local and national organisation which has specific social systemic characteristics, and representatives whose particular identity and social status carry varying degrees of weight.

Summary

Social assessments may vary enormously in length and detail, but the following elements should have been considered in all.

A checklist of CA/B principles

Have the basic theoretical principles of social assessment method been systematically incorporated in professional methods and judgements? They should be used on every social assessment, however brief or however comprehensive, and all pro formas, methods or checklists need to be examined for consistency with these principles. All assessments require an explicit negotiated focus that meets the needs and interests of the users as far as possible within the legal framework of responsibilities of the agency, and identification of areas where more work/analysis or information is needed.

Social difference

There must be an analysis of the range of social divisions represented across the whole situation, including the workers, and assessment of the implications of that for needs and risks to the children and carers, and for the understanding and possible action of the worker. Tentative assigning of identities from information immediately available must be made, then further study of the identities of the key individuals in the light of their own life stories (as far as possible and appropriate), with a focus on the changing identities of children. There should be consideration of alternative perspectives available from community organisations or independent advocates.

Reflexive assessment of interaction

This must include service users and other agencies, and consist of personal and professional self-evaluation, as discussed with the supervisor, and perspectives and attitudes of, and relationships with:

1   parents/carers
2   child(ren)
3   other professionals.

It must emphasise identification of changing differences over facts and opinions, taking account of other professionals' expertise, and carers'/parents' values, knowledge of their children and themselves, and children's own perspectives as conveyed in direct work with the assessing professional.

Social histories

These must be taken for the child(ren) and carer(s), or anyone with access or responsibility, especially information regarding risk/need factors – including strengths – up to and including recent past and present situations, attempting to distinguish between facts, hearsay and opinion as far as possible. Medical and psychological histories, including attachment histories, need to be integrated into these accounts as far as they are known. The perspectives of users, carers and others with information about the past need to be taken into account, together with any evidence from agency records. Assessment of the trajectory of individual and family life-courses, and changing family interactions should be attempted, with anticipation of continuities and discontinuities over time, including during the course of the assessment.

Interacting systems

There should be consideration of interacting risk areas associated with the differing social systems involved within the family itself, the sub-systems of the child and the parents/carers, other children in the household, other people outside the family as appropriate, the professional worker, and inter-agency relationships. Assessment should identify levels of risk and need created by these systems, and the strengths and supports offered by them. The assessment must consider the impact of continuing interaction between different systems, and the appropriateness of further interventive assessment, compared to not taking further action, or alternative interventions, including action concerning immediate risk (if any), childcare welfare/protection plans to meet needs, and the implications of recommendations, time-scales and responsibilities for different system members.

Power

A rigorous analysis of the complex power factors should begin with a consideration of the range of strengths and vulnerabilities involving:

1 a checklist of children's needs – for example, using the *Looking After Children* criteria (Parker et al., 1992).
2 a checklist of serious risk factors (Greenland, 1987), or some other risk checklist (see lists in Corby, 1995; Taylor and Devine, 1993).

There should be assessment of parents'/carer's needs, as well as the child's, and identification of strengths as well as problem areas. The *interaction* of risk factors is a serious issue which needs to be evaluated in terms of any possible multiplying effect. But it needs to be placed within the context of social histories of the individuals and groups involved, and examining the positive and negative aspects of their changing powers through time.

Assessments which contain all these elements can claim to be comprehensive in principle, in that all the relevant methodological principles have been covered, and all the relevant substantive areas have been considered. In the event that there is insufficient time to gather information to reach agreed conclusions, or if there are other problems about its availability, then the assessment will identify its own shortcomings, and the reasons for them. A 'comprehensive' professional social assessment might reasonably be regarded as comprising a thorough study of all the issues identified by the CA/B principles, with special reference to the professional's responsibilities under the law for assessing the full range of risks, strengths and needs, including a full CA/B social history, and preferably a negotiated and planned 'interventive assessment' of parent/carer ability to change.

Case study discussion

Note: See Figure 3, and compare with the practice questions at the ends of the chapters in Part One. The following is only intended to be indicative of issues that could be considered. The comments are fragmentary and incomplete.

Social difference

The social difference that is obviously relevant to working with children is that of age, and in this case the needs and risks of Debbie, the youngest child, are clearly of paramount importance. CA/B is in this way consistent with the 1989 Children Act and its concern for meeting children's needs as well as their protection. Debbie's stepbrother is also a young person with specific needs arising from his status both in the family and in society.

However, this basic social difference is intersected by others of equal importance which need to be considered both separately and together. Debbie's black father and her white mother, and their particular ethnic origins, mean that Debbie is a child of mixed parentage (or 'dual heritage'), and what that means for Debbie, her identity, and the reactions of others to her is of fundamental importance (e.g. how is it seen by her white stepbrother?).

The childcare social worker is also black, and that has different implications for different members of the family – and also for others involved in the case.

Debbie is female and speech-impaired – both issues relating to major social divisions which both connect and separate her from others in the family and outside it. For example, given the apparent history of domestic violence, important gender, disability and age social differences exist between Debbie and her father which would have made her very vulnerable. Both language delay and domestic violence are risk indicators for child abuse.

Historical location

It has been a standard part of assessment practice in this area of work to take social histories. Direct work with Debbie and her brother to understand their life stories, and social histories of other family members are clearly essential, in conjunction with medical and other histories.

Many of the classic risk indicators for child abuse are to be found in accounts of the past (leading up to and including the present) – the history of the parents' relationship, their own experience of parenting, the history of incidents and events relating to the child, the medical and developmental histories, and so on. All these need to be seen together and in the context of wider social histories of relevant social networks, including the history of neighbourhood changes, agency involvement and agency changes, in addition to legal and social changes that have affected this particular family.

Interacting social systems

This has also traditionally been part of assessing children and families. CA/B method builds on it by placing the question of thoroughly examining interacting systems in the context of the other related principles. The family is not seen as a unitary system to be scrutinised by 'outside' observers, but both internally intersected by other social systems, and in interaction with them, including the agencies and their representatives. The impact on the family of various social systems – the family itself as a system, the local neighbourhood, agencies which have been involved, and the wider systems – has to be examined to assess their contribution to the possible construction of the needs and risks in relation to these children.

This family is a recently reconstituted family with all that means in terms of coping with past losses and current adjustments. It is also a three-generation family with widely differing membership of age categories with very different needs. Most of the family has also recently relocated itself, leaving behind not only individuals but also social networks and communities, and having to deal with new social systems. The losses and gains made by differing members of the family need to be considered separately as well as jointly taking into account the changing nature of the surrounding social networks.

In this case study, even international systems may be directly relevant – for instance, if Debbie's father is a refugee or immigrant. If Debbie's father was born in the UK, she may still have significant paternal relations living abroad. In addition, other organisations representing the interests of oppressed groups are also significant social systems. For example, in this case children's rights groups, black people's organisations, family rights groups and disability organisations are all relevant.

Reflexivity

The different social and health workers will need to assess their own personal membership of social divisions in relation to the different members of the family, and the organisations have to be aware of the reflexive effect of their involvement. In this case, the childcare social worker is black, and will need to take account of his own social location and what it will mean to the white female mother, grandmother and stepbrother, as well as to Debbie and her father. In addition, his middle-class, educated, employed status as a representative of a powerful bureaucracy has to be acknowledged as having both negative (frequently) and positive (sometimes) implications for different members of the family. For instance, how well will he be able to work with a white female carer, and will she be accepting of him, given her recent experiences?

This aspect of CA/B assessment is sometimes taken into account in practice, but with difficulty, since individuals often find it hard to assess themselves and their impact on situations, and it is also hard to develop team reflexivity where other professionals have some awareness of their individual and joint social location and its impact on the service users. The use of professional reflective analysis in supervision, contact with organisations representing different oppressed social groups and pro-active team procedures can assist.

Power

The adults and older children all have greater power over Debbie, but the social group of children and young people are discriminated against and oppressed at structural as well as personal levels. Children's rights and child poverty groups draw attention to some of the ways that society and the law can oppress children. In this case, Debbie's needs are multiple, and in danger of not being met because of her relatively powerless position, both within the family and in society. A working-class black father would not be in a strong position in relation to welfare organisations or the law, but within the family he would have been a relatively powerful figure, and might remain so if he tries to maintain links with the family.

The occurrence of domestic violence is a risk indicator which reflects on Debbie's vulnerability and her father's physical and social power. The reasons for her hospitalisation need to be investigated. Debbie's white stepbrother will have personal and socially resourced power over her as a potential sexual, physical and cultural threat to her identity and welfare. Joan may be a powerful source of support for Debbie, but that power may also be abused.

The agencies and the workers clearly have varying degrees of power in this situation, and this has to be taken into account when assessing both the support available and the increased stress, compared to control that is possible as a result of assessment and intervention. There are numerous other considerations here which could be discussed further.

Methodology

In child and family work, the social services department has responsibilities for protecting children and attempting to ensure that their needs are met. The methods used have often drawn on attachment and other psychological and psychiatric theories, with some social systems theory and 'social work values' welded to them. The CA/B framework offers a consistent concept of social assessment, drawing together the major theoretical principles of a social research model relevant to micro-social situations, and containing an explicit value-slope compatible with both the social science and the ethical parameters of working with and respecting users including children. It supports workers creating critical narratives of life histories in partnership with service users and co-professionals, cognizant of the different interpretative lenses being used, and the perspectives of those oppressed groups whose social problems are encountered.

In Debbie's case, the child's perspective has to be accessed through sensitive and specialised skills of direct work with the individual child (including life history work), but also by studying the views of others, and liaising with them, including organisations representing children's interests.

The CA/B principles thus provide a comprehensive theoretical framework suitable as a basis for a social assessment of the needs and risks of a childcare case, and gives the practitioner an intellectual base to work from in multi-professional settings. The following diagram (Figure 5) attempts to summarise the relationship of CA/B principles to the case study, with particular attention to the implications for children and young people.

Interconnected assessment principles in Figure 5

1 Identify the membership of all major *social divisions*, as far as possible, of all relevant individuals. Consider the possibility of non-visible social divisions. Take account of specific social differences within and across major social divisions, and their interconnection in this particular child's or young person's life, and for other 'family' members.

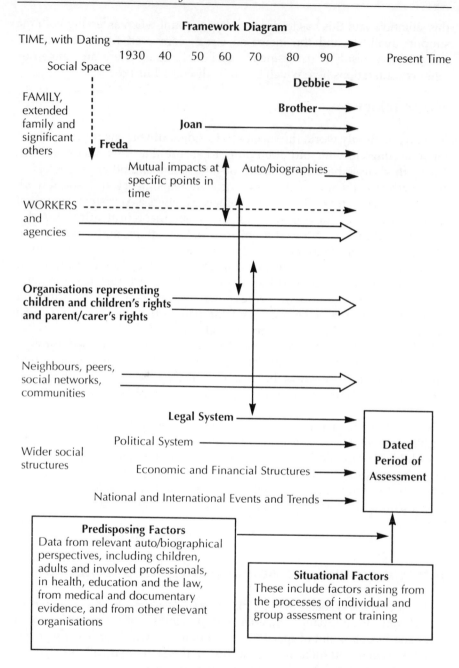

Figure 5   Critical auto/biographical assessment in work with children, young people and families

2 Examine your own membership of social divisions in relation to this child or young person and their family. Consider impact of *yourself* on the user's situation. Where possible, share perspectives, including views on the purpose, content and procedure of assessment. Acknowledge the agency's function in relation to yourself, and assess implications with service users.

3 Note the timing and place of significant events and processes, social and developmental factors in personal and family *histories*. Review life stories within concrete historical contexts, including changing legislation, and historical indicators of risks, needs and strengths.

4 Connect personal lives to various levels of *social systems*, and assess the degree of positive and negative interaction in the 'family' and social environment – continuing support, or danger of increasing stress, including in the processes of interaction with agencies and workers, and in changing family and other social networks.

5 Looking both vertically and horizontally at the framework, assess the changing differentials of structural, organisational and personal *power*. Identify, as far as possible, the shifting vulnerabilities and strengths of the person concerned, and those near to them. Note different agency legal and informal powers in relation to children, young people and families, and consider the outcome and impact with the users as far as appropriate and possible.

10 Mental health and distress

Introduction

The discussion of social assessment in relation to psychology and psychiatry in Chapter 7 is particularly relevant to this chapter, as is the discussion of a critical approach to lifespan psychology in Chapter 4. The aim here is to examine practical issues about assessment in mental health, building on the theoretical discussion, and learning from the practitioners who make assessments.

Clearly, the whole issue of the status of mental health as a socially constructed practice in which assessments and diagnoses are key instruments of labelling and social control has been discussed for a long time, and the values and ethics of it also continue to be discussed (e.g. Hopton, 1997). There has already been a reference to Foucault's concept of power in relation to disciplinary practices, and the social construction and control of 'madness', and particularly the use of biographical methods, has been a central part of the debate (see Chapter 4).

However, in addition to considering theoretical issues, the concern here is how social assessment should be put into practice within the context of psychiatric and psychological services, given that these systems exist, and that social assessments are variously used within them. It is not being suggested that the wider critique can be ignored: on the contrary, it is assumed that the continuing quandary of professional social assessment is that it is inherently implicated in the social construction of reality, and in issues of discipline and control. This is basic to CA/B's methodological concern with a reflexive, value-based orientation to social assessment.

However, the orientation of CA/B methodology towards sociological and historical perspectives, rather than the medical and individual, means that the key issues concern the ways in which social assessment offers a radically distinctive perspective which does not triangulate easily with the domain assumptions of clinical psychology or psychiatry.

The first point must be that any social assessment needs to be self-aware of its different status and orientation. CA/B methodology necessarily entails a critical perspective on mental health assessment processes, and the ways in which they may stigmatise, label, construct and control, as well as their limited potential for positive change and personal growth. It is often mistakenly assumed by workers of all professions that the contribution of a social assessment can be directly assimilated into a medical or psychological assessment. This is not the case, for reasons discussed in Chapter 7. The 'research object' of a social assessment is often qualitatively different from that studied by means of research methods drawn from other disciplines (although different *professions* may sometimes use similar disciplinary research methods). The object of CA/B research specifically and reflexively includes the social process of assessment in mental health itself, together with the wider social environment within which it is set. This means that the presentation of a social assessment needs to be organised as strategically as possible to demonstrate its relative autonomy as an intellectual product, both in the way it is textually produced, and in how it is juxtaposed to other assessments.

In practice, this means claiming as much space and time as possible for consideration of social assessment (within the limits set by the ethics and politics of intervention in users and carers' lives), and also delineating its territory and claims as explicitly as possible. This will obviously depend on the organisation and politics of different settings where social assessments are offered. The example given in the previous chapter about reporting the social assessment to a court is relevant here, as social assessments in mental health may well take the form of a report to court. Clearly, the relative but specific 'expertise' of the social assessor needs to be evidenced in terms of explicit qualifications, level of experience and levels of contact with service users, carers and other professionals. In other words, the basis for this particular piece of social research needs to be set out clearly.

The details about the author's biography are particularly important in view of CA/B principles – in relation to being able to understand the social world of the service user and conveying a sense of the levels of quality of experience and competence of the assessor to the report reader. Clearly, exactly how this is done will be dependent on the sociology and politics of the relationship between the writer and the audience(s). Other ways of marking out specifically social assessments will be discussed further in the course of examining practical aspects of social assessment in the field of mental health.

Assessing needs and risks in mental health

The distinction that Ann Davis makes between risk-minimisation and risk-taking approaches in assessment relating to mental health and mental distress in the community (Davis, 1996) is a useful starting point, because it helps to make connections between issues of practical assessment with this service user group and the framework developed here. In terms of the discussion in Chapter 8, what she is talking about are the negative and positive aspects of need/risk.

Risk-minimisation is about the negative possibilities of dangers arising from the situation in which a person exists, both to themselves and to others. It concerns the needs of individuals and those around them for physical safety and protection from violence or harm, including self-harm, and it may also include a whole range of other significant needs where there is a risk that they may not be met. *Risk-taking* is about meeting the needs that people have to develop autonomy, to learn from experiences, and to be free to make choices in their social lives, but also to live safely, without harming themselves or others.

These two aspects of assessment are found in official guidance to mental health workers, following the community care legislation. The Care Programme Approach was intended to provide a basic model for all workers, and begins with the essential element of 'systematic assessment of the health and social care needs of the individual' (DoH, 1990). In addition, the political agenda formed by media attention to fatal assaults by those being cared for in the community led inevitably to additional advice on identifying risk (DoH 1994), and to further measures such as registers to assist in their supervision. It therefore follows that mental health workers should be simultaneously oriented towards the whole range of needs/risks, with the attendant ethical and political evaluations and dilemmas that this orientation entails, in line with the discussion of needs/risks in Chapter 8. The distinction represented by Davis may reflect differing professional discourses, as she claims. Conceptually, however, the two apparently different orientations are closely linked, even though politically they may be used by differing groups with different interests and purposes.

Davis's discussion associates the policy of risk-minimisation with official policy guidance discourse – especially that emanating from the investigation of public scandals when mental health care appears to have gone disastrously wrong. In particular, she cites the five components of effective risk assessment and management advocated by the Blom-Cooper Report:

- 'an assessment of mental state ... designed to identify potentially dangerous thoughts or actions';

- a decision made as a result of the assessment about 'who might be harmed and how';
- an evaluation of 'whether current arrangements adequately address the risk';
- 'to record ... what risks are thought to be present, what action has been taken, and what level of risk is being accepted';
- 'a regular review system' (Blom-Cooper, Hally and Murphy, 1995, pp.175–6).

This risk assessment includes the risk of self-harm, and through the use of supervisory registers and prioritisation of people in specific legal and institutional circumstances (such as being on the point of discharge), enables mental health workers to identify and minimise risk for this organisationally identified group. However, as in childcare, the focus is on narrowly defined 'high-risk' cases. There is some inconsistency between this narrow definition of implicitly potentially dangerous people and the advice against using a static concept of dangerousness, together with the admission that risk changes over time (Blom-Cooper, Hally and Murphy, p.176). The narrow focus in effect identifies a small group of dangerous people – often men – whilst downgrading the significance of the needs of the large majority of mental health service users – often women (Buck, 1997).

Equally important is the assumption of the separability of high risks from other risks, and the failure to recognise the close relationship between the whole range of needs, and how they interact and change over time in complex ways, influencing all potential behaviours. This connects with Davis's second category of 'risk-taking', which is concerned with meeting the needs of people suffering various forms of mental distress, by delivering 'normalizing experiences' of autonomy and social participation. She characterises it primarily in terms of the values which seek to challenge institutional stigmatising and dependency. It is thus associated with 'user literature and campaigns for service and/or social change' (Davis, 1996, p.115). The concept of interconnected needs/risks, as discussed in Chapter 8, is consistent with the more 'socially informed and user-centred perspective' on the 'complexity of risk and risk-taking' that Davis advocates in her conclusion (Davis, 1996, pp.118–19). It is certainly the case that there are issues of value here, but the binary opposition between official risk-minimisation policy on the one hand and popular risk-taking policy on the other does not best serve the need to understand the complex relationship between differing kinds of risk/need.

'Official' and 'popular' policies have interests in *both* risk-minimisation and risk-taking. The official policy of the mental health system is just as interested in taking risks as it is in risk-minimisation. The whole community care programme could fairly be described as an exercise in risk-taking, and its rationalisation in terms of normalisation, integration and 'social role valorisation' has been well documented and discussed (Ramon, 1991). One problem with it lies in the absence of an adequate theoretical base for social assessment.

It has been remarked that although social role valorisation owes a lot to symbolic interactionism, it tends to ignore social control and social division issues, assuming that labels can be reversed, and that users *can* integrate. However, it is very clear that 'sociological knowledge is indispensable ... because social role valorisation is aimed at introducing change at the individual and at the social levels' (Ramon, 1991, p.20). In addition, 'personal change has a temporal dimension', with transitional crises (Ramon, 1991, p.22), so the whole process obviously stands in need of a social research methodology of needs/risk assessment such as CA/B which can deal with these dimensions. These considerations also clarify that risk is of concern to users who are being encouraged to live amongst a potentially hostile 'community' environment where powerful forces will impinge on their attempts to 'integrate'. The risk to their own safety and well-being is considerable.

The point is that professional assessment in this area, as elsewhere, should be taking account of needs/risks within multi-disciplinary and multi-professional perspectives, fully informed by a social as well as a psychological and psychiatric assessment. The function of CA/B method is to supply a theoretical framework that is complementary, not supplementary or subordinate to the psychological, and offers an integrated social assessment in which the whole range of risks/needs of service users and their perspectives are included. A 'multi-method' approach to assessing the family context is strongly indicated in the literature (Wilkinson, 1987, p.375). It is also particularly important that social divisions which condition broad vulnerabilities and strengths are taken into account, and this essentially requires going beyond the medical definition of needs towards a 'multi-systemic' approach to assessment (Fernando, 1995, pp.209–10), sensitive to interconnecting social oppressions of the kind that CA/B provides.

Davis rightly refers to recent DoH guidelines which note the expertise that social workers and probation officers have developed in risk management (DoH, 1994). She also notes the focus of this expertise in the area of developing service and practice principles by experienced workers in conjunction with service users, and how this helps to rebalance the 'diagnostically and behaviourally focused approaches to risk minimisation which is currently dominating this area' (Davis, 1996, p.119). The proposed CA/B framework helps to clarify and justify the kind of approach experienced workers use in a way which takes account of both risk-minimising and risk-taking approaches, putting both risk and need firmly within historical and social time frames. However, it goes beyond 'service and practice principles' to a theory of social assessment which *can* 'accommodate the complex social and interpersonal factors which are relevant to understanding risk in the context of an individual's life' (Davis, 1996, p.113).

The latter requirement is exactly what is lacking in the Blom-Cooper guidelines, which depend heavily on a psychiatric or psychological clinical interview, combined with risk factors. Given the narrow clinical orientation, over-determined by a legal perspective, it is hardly surprising that the recommended approach to assessing risk defines it narrowly in relation to individual mental states of institutionally defined 'dangerous' people. In terms of methodology, there are obvious objections to any assessment of human situations which fails to use qualitative social research methods to support a social (as well as psychological) evaluation. To ignore social and historical factors or assume that they can be encapsulated within a psychiatric account is to repeat mistakes that have been made in the past by psychiatry and psychology. The diverse disciplines have different perspectives, and constitute distinctive research objects, which make it highly questionable to assume the possibility of simple correlation or even triangulation of research evidence (see Chapter 7).

The Blom-Cooper Report stresses the importance of understanding complex histories for all high-risk patients. It further recommends that inquiry teams should construct: 'an extended psychiatric and psycho-social summary, or chronology of the case, listing all significant events and all contacts between the patient and professionals and with independent sector services and organisations' (Blom-Cooper, Hally and Murphy, 1995, p.181). However, the example given in this case is from the perspective of a psychiatrist writing *after* the event, with little evidence of awareness of other perspectives, or of social research criteria. In fact, what is necessary is for CA/B methodological principles for complex social histories to be considered (at least in principle) in relation to *all* assessments, thus requiring inter-disciplinary and inter-professional parity in constructing assessments.

This theoretical framework potentially applies to any mental health setting, whatever the nature of the needs/risks, since the circumstances always consist of a person in specific socio-historical settings which require social analysis, whatever other clinical assessment may be appropriate. The Blom-Cooper admission of the importance of a chronology, and the reference to a 'psycho-social' contribution (see above), insufficiently recognises the pertinence of a suitable social research methodology as a framework for all assessments, and not only for special inquiry teams to consider when things have gone wrong. Exactly how the CA/B framework would be positioned in practice would depend on particular settings, and would be subject to organisational and political pressures, as in other health and welfare fields.

However, this contention itself should serve to strengthen the hand of those whose task is to provide a specifically social assessment, such as social workers. It also supports those psychologists and psychiatrists who do attempt to integrate their assessments with the social.

The more clearly a social assessment identifies its distinctive methodology, with its characteristic interpretations of socio-historical evidence, the more impact such a methodology will have. Accordingly, the CA/B principles will need to be employed consistently in providing reflexive social histories – or partial narratives from social histories – which do not construct the individual primarily in intra-psychic or even inter-psychic terms. They will necessarily need to consider closely the CA/B principles in relation to the accounts of people's lives that are offered for consideration at all stages during the course of any assessment, monitoring the range and levels of needs, risks and strengths, and evaluating appropriate courses of action for assessment and/or intervention. In addition, they will need to use those methodological principles to question the status of explanations of behaviour by other professionals that impinge on the social where a social methodology is not being deployed, and where CA/B principles are being ignored. In these circumstances, bridging strategies (see Chapter 7) as well as practical and organisational strategies designed to raise the profile of social assessment will be necessary, with monitoring of the depth of social analysis needed in any particular case.

The example of compulsory admissions assessment

The importance of a social perspective on the assessment of risk in mental health, and the relative autonomy of this perspective, is recognised by Sheppard, and is an integral part of his CASH system of assessment (Sheppard, 1993). It is a good example of a social approach to assessment in mental health, and I use it as a means of demonstrating the relevance of CA/B methodology. The additional value of having a broader-based theory is that it can be applied outside the particular range of applications that Sheppard is concerned about, and thus can provide consistency of approach in different settings, as well as critically underpinning his approach. His insistence on the relevance of social research in mental health assessment and his support for social research methodology as a basis for assessment (Sheppard, 1995) agrees with CA/B theory. However, as indicated in Chapter 1, the argument needs to be developed further, and the more distinctive social research methodology of CA/B theory needs to be used for social assessment.

In developing this particular method of assessment, Sheppard was concerned on the one hand with the importance of social factors in making mental health assessments where there is compulsory sectioning of patients. He was equally concerned with the lack of a knowledge base to balance the formidable knowledge base of medicine (Sheppard, 1993, p.232). His method is described as a 'social risk' orientation, giving the assessment of the health and safety of the patient and the protection of others equal status to mental disorder criteria, examining dangers, hazards and risks as precisely as possible in their social context (Sheppard, 1990).

The value of his approach also lies in the validating role his research gives to practitioners, whose practice wisdom he draws on in action research (Sheppard, 1993, p.233) as well as in terms of research methodology (Sheppard, 1995). Also consistent with CA/B is the way dangers, hazards and risks are placed within a broad framework that links risks to needs, and both are placed in a social context. The importance of gaining information from all relevant individuals is emphasised, thus gaining from the availability of differing perspectives, and increasing understanding of the social interactions between individuals and various social systems.

The development of this assessment theory on the back of both practice wisdom and social theory is a major step forward, but can be usefully situated within the wider CA/B framework. The CASH system rightly gives attention to developing consistency of ratings between approved social workers – particularly in the context of making a compulsory order, where someone's liberty is at stake. However, it also needs to attend to interpretative issues, and their integration within the judgements being made. The CASH framework positively addresses the social factors, avoiding the vacuity of excessive constructionism, and its results appear to justify this approach. Experienced workers are reported to have found that the schedule usefully confirmed and aided their assessments (Sheppard, 1993, p.250). However, the issues of interpretation and evaluation in making social judgements do not disappear, and the CA/B framework would critically support CASH assessment by giving it further social research methodological principles to deploy in the process of making the evaluative judgements which are still central to the assessment.

Many of the judgements that approved social workers have to make are inherently value-based. Within the CASH framework, assessors have to judge the relevance of individuals within the social network of the case, and the potential contribution their information could make. They have to assess the seriousness of a range of needs in particular contexts, and interpret the meaning of statements. For example, Sheppard notes that in two cases, an approved social worker rated the threat of death as 'quite' rather than 'very serious' (Sheppard, 1993, p.248). It is perfectly possible that in the context this was a reasonable interpretation, given the common use of exaggerated threats, but clearly it requires careful evaluation of the person and situation: a matter upon which there could presumably be disagreement. Conversely, the approved social workers who interpreted such threats as very serious needed to have made the judgement that the context and behaviour of the person involved justified that level of categorisation: that the meaning and intention was sufficiently clear. Either way, disputable judgements are being made which require reflection and some theoretical basis.

Similarly, another judgement by an approved social worker involved the view that a person was exhibiting 'extreme religiosity' (Sheppard, 1993, p.246). This not only plainly raises the issue of judgement, but also the matter of reflexivity. It will certainly make a difference to whether an approved social worker comes to this conclusion if the worker is religious or not, and if so, from what kind of religious tradition s/he comes. The differences within and between black and white ethnic groups in their approach to religious issues also warns of possible racist, religious or other discriminatory evaluations being made in this area.

In order to make judgements like these, the assessor needs a socially based theoretical framework which will draw attention to the parameters involved. CA/B does not solve these problems in the sense of providing 'objective' criteria which avoid value issues, but it does support social assessment by providing a methodology which combines a critical awareness of, and means of coping with interpretive issues. In this way, the CASH basis for assessment in mental health would be strengthened in exactly the area where it lays claim to having relative autonomy: as an assessment of social as distinct from medical or psychiatric factors.

Psychotherapeutic and social assessment

The focus of this chapter so far has been in the area of making assessments particularly influenced by issues concerning serious risks – whether to people themselves or to others. The remainder of this chapter will examine the issues surrounding assessments which are less constrained by media attention, but are nevertheless important: the social assessment of people in mental distress who do not need compulsory treatment, but who may voluntarily agree that they need help. They may or may not also require medical or specialist psychological or psychiatric treatment, but they receive interventions which may be described broadly as psychotherapeutic. This will involve two kinds of assessment: firstly, to establish the suitability of the user for psychotherapy in general, and for a specific type of psychotherapy in particular; secondly, there needs to be assessment of the user's presenting problems, and some initial exploration and evaluation of underlying issues, sometimes including 'trial interpretations' of the user's predicament (Holmes, 1995). These assessments are commonly undertaken by a range of professionals, including counsellors, nurses, social workers and psychotherapists, as well as psychologists and psychiatrists.

The distinction between assessment and therapy, however, is not clear-cut. It is especially difficult to disentangle in practice because much psychotherapy is concerned with helping the user to explore their relationships, their past, their feelings and behaviour (though clearly, the balance of elements varies in nature and emphasis with the type of psychotherapy). Conversely, social assessment, and especially that based on CA/B methods, will certainly be covering some apparently similar areas.

In practice, assessment is always an intervention which has either beneficial and/or harmful potential, and therapy always contains an element of social assessment, and is itself a social practice. This is a well-known parallel, and it has been suggested that assessment itself may be an adequate therapy for some people (Barkham, 1989). Tantam has observed that people coming to psychotherapists often want to make sense of their lives, and the effort made in the assessing interview to create a comprehensive narrative of their life story is itself 'profoundly reassuring', bringing order and coherence to the meaning of their life (Tantam, 1995, p.17), and there is research evidence within psychotherapy that this is the case (Tibbles, 1992).

It therefore follows that CA/B assessment is likely to produce 'an immediate improvement' (Tantam, 1995), simply because it may involve a process of life history-taking and the production of an organised narrative. However, there are some serious qualifications to be made which help to distinguish CA/B assessment from psychotherapy, which limit potential therapeutic effects, and which illustrate important issues concerning the practical implications of CA/B-based social assessment. Firstly, CA/B assessment does not necessarily involve the production of any life history, since it is a methodological theory, the *principles* of which should underlie social assessment, but whether they are fully and overtly expressed in any particular assessment depends on various factors and evaluations concerning those specific circumstances. It may be either practically impossible or inappropriate to spend time developing a narrative of someone's life story. This is obviously true in emergency situations, but may also apply where assessment is only required for fairly definite purposes which may not require extended discussion or detailed social study, or where the service user does not agree to it.

Secondly, there is no assumption that the social assessment will be necessarily therapeutic, because the theoretical model is not medical or psychological, and the purpose of the interaction presupposes an analysis of power relationships where the needs and vulnerabilities of other than the interviewee may well be prioritised by the assessor. This may lead to difficulties in the process of negotiating the assessment, possibly leading to conflict and breakdown, and even the use of formal and informal pressure, including compulsory assessment. CA/B social assessment does *not* only involve an interview with the client (which is often the case in psychotherapy); it explicitly raises the issue of interviews with others who may have a relevant perspective, including relations, friends and other professionals. It also includes within its scope the various kinds of documentary evidence which could be brought to bear from various sources. Whether and how *any* of these other sources of information are brought to bear is, of course, itself part of the social assessment and evaluation process, but they are in principle ruled in. The focus is on the sociality of multiple perspectives, rather than on the sole individual, and on the complexity of needs/risks, of which the individual user's are of central importance, but only a part.

Thirdly, even where the interviewee's needs and feelings are prioritised, it does not follow that the construction of a life story will have the beneficial effect that has been presented as typical in psychotherapy. The existence of past traumas, and the differing evaluations that people have of their recent or distant past mean that sometimes it will be painful or simply distasteful for some to have to consider things they would prefer to forget. This will include not only predictable circumstances where interviewees may not be ready to recall past abuse, but also where the interviewee is the abuser, and may not be willing to acknowledge responsibility. Given the overlapping interconnections of social divisions in people's lives, it is likely that both circumstances will pertain at various times in any individual's life-course.

Coleman's research (Coleman, 1986; 1991; 1994) suggests a variety of responses to life review are possible, and social assessment which involves people in reflecting on their own life may well be of little interest or benefit, or may be damaging or painful. This applies less to psychotherapy, in that the decision as to whether treatment is 'indicated' should help to exclude inappropriate referrals, whilst the process of treatment should be able to deal constructively with painful issues, thus helping to ensure a beneficial outcome in the majority of cases, at least in theory, and at least for the interviewee directly concerned. However, it is impossible to separate out the social from the psychological so conveniently in practice.

A psychotherapeutic assessment certainly needs to establish as carefully as possible whether psychotherapy is likely to have a positive outcome for the 'patient'. However, a social assessment should also contribute to a psychological assessment in this regard. There is always a social context within which intervention occurs, and which conditions it: 'psychotherapy is a form of practice which is shaped in form and content by its social context' (Pilgrim, 1990, p.183). The very question of whether the outcome of psychotherapy will be beneficial therefore depends not only on a psychological assessment of the intra-psychological state of the user, nor even on the inter-psychological factors, but on a series of social issues and judgements which can be understood in CA/B terms. It raises issues such as:

beneficial for whom; who else might benefit, and who else might be harmed, or whose need might be greater? What sources of information are available, and how are they constructing the social interaction in this case? Is the individual being seen in isolation from peers and family, and what reactive impact will psychotherapy have? Who is making these judgements, and how far is the individual in an informed position to agree or disagree with the psychotherapist? What role and function does the therapist and the agency have, and how far is this understood and shared by the 'patient'?

The practical implication of CA/B method in mental health is therefore that there should be a much more carefully considered and wider role for social assessment. This should be undertaken by a specialist in social assessment such as a psychiatric or a hospital social worker, especially for complex or potentially dangerous cases. It could be done by other workers satisfactorily if they have had appropriate training in social assessment.

Psychotherapy and critical auto/biography

A further practical implication is that social assessment understood in CA/B terms has much to offer people in the area of socio-psychological understanding of self and others as a form of supportive social practice (I deliberately reverse the usual term 'psycho-social', indicating the connection between the parts, but the priority of the social in this configuration of the concept). In this case, the use of CA/B principles mainly for assessment purposes, with the supportive(?) relationship process as a major sub-theme, is reversed, so that the supportive review of someone's life history is the main objective, with continuing assessment of the situation as a necessary accompaniment. This is not just a theoretical possibility, but has been a growing reality of practice in various fields where workers without psychological or psychiatric qualifications have been able to create effective 'therapeutic' practices, based primarily on ideas that are similar in orientation to CA/B social assessment.

For example, the principles of method in social work assessment and those in oral history, particularly where the practice of *reminiscence* is concerned, are closely related (Clifford, 1995). Although reminiscence work with older people owes much to the interest and support of psychologists, and Butler's paper (Butler, 1963) is often quoted as one of the sources of the method, it has developed outside the confines of psychology and psychiatry, as a social movement amongst service users themselves, social workers, oral historians and others (Bornat, 1989). As a positive method of intervention, it is user-friendly, and relies on the recall and review of life experiences. It owes much to the influence of oral history, but also needs to be critically used in the light of CA/B principles. It is itself profoundly reflexive and social, emphasising the right of older people to have a voice.

It has been argued by supporters of a discourse analytic perspective that: 'Research approaches which reduce reminiscence to an individual psychological process ... marginalise the sociality of the reminiscence enterprise' (Buchanan and Middleton, 1994, p.73). The interconnection between principles of oral history, reminiscence and CA/B method show that the social activity of negotiating an understanding of a person's life history is inevitably more than either a research project or an assessment. It is itself a form of intervention or 'therapy' which draws on the socially constructed situation in which people interact to understand the meaning of their mutual circumstances and lives.

This would be better understood and more effectively practised if it were more consistent with CA/B principles. In particular, CA/B methods would need to be engaged first to decide whether this type of intervention was appropriately supporting the person being interviewed, or whether the ethics and politics of the circumstances were such that this would not be desirable.

One of the dilemmas of the assessment situation is precisely the tension between the supportive relationship-building aspect of the process of understanding a life and the distancing professional responsibility for assessment of various social needs and risks. This issue might have to override the potential gains of a CA/B intervention which was the social counterpart of a psychotherapeutic intervention. However, there may well be circumstances where the use of a CA/B methodology for understanding lives might properly focus on the value of a socially 'therapeutic' intervention, although, even within a therapeutic rather than an assessment framework, there would still have to be continuing assessment. Not only should the review of people's lives include assessment of the social, political and ethical issues that arise in social situations, but also the possibility that specialised psychotherapeutic support might still be needed. This should clearly be an area of useful multi-professional and multi-disciplinary discussion where triangulation and bridging strategies are both needed (see Chapter 7).

The activity of life review is neither solely psychological nor should it be exclusively concerned with older people. It has been pointed out that in the course of assessment, the process of support and insight can be equally beneficial for people of any age (Clifford, 1995). As a constructive social intervention, oral history has a number of uses, especially with people whose voice has often not been heard, such as ethnic minority groups (Martin, 1995). It has been used in practice for a long time by social workers and others in adult care and childcare, and for once they received some recognition of this in one of the foundational books on oral history. Thompson asserts that: 'the practical breakthrough ... has come from social workers and hospital staff who have provided the frontline in caring'

(Thompson, 1984, p.161). The use of life story books with children (Ryan and Walker, 1985) and reminiscence and life review with older people (Fielden, 1990) has been widespread in the caring services. This observation is consistent with the discussion of CA/B principles in Chapter 1, where it was suggested that the social experiences of women in caring services are an important source for developing adequate methods and theoretical concepts for understanding people's lives. It is also possible for psychologists to utilise the perspectives of social carers in life story techniques, as in the example of clinical psychologists who have reported their successful use of life story book methods with people labelled 'criminally insane' (Hossack and Jackson, 1991).

The conclusion, therefore, is that critical auto/biography can be used as a basis for various forms of life history work and counselling that can be done on a social or socio-psychological basis, rather than with narrower psychotherapeutic or 'biopsychosocial' approaches (Ruddell, 1997, p.13). Pilgrim's verdict on psychotherapists (as a psychologist with a sociological training) is that: 'The centring of attention on individual psycho-pathology and the more general reification of the individual ... produces practitioners that are psychologically sophisticated and sociologically weak or incompetent' (Pilgrim, 1990, p.191). Given the divisions which often characterise academic disciplines, this verdict, though strong, is not surprising, and no doubt the reverse is also true – that many social workers and others whose grasp of the sociology is very strong may not be so well-informed in other areas. However, the situation in the health and welfare services is such that it is medical and psychological expertise which predominates.

A more productive and equal partnership between disciplines and professions is thus seriously needed, in which there can be space for autonomous methods of intervention and assessment, but also co-operative discussion in bridging and triangulating the differences between the professions. This obviously takes no account of the politics and sociology of the organisations or professions concerned: this can only be a matter for debate and struggle in practice, but at least there is a clear intellectual basis for social life history-based assessment and intervention.

Case study discussion

Note: See Figure 3, and compare with the practice questions at the ends of the chapters in Part One. The following is only intended to be indicative of issues that should be considered. The comments are fragmentary and incomplete.

The most obvious target in this case study for psychiatric intervention is Freda, the grandmother, who is alleged to be acting 'strangely'. Using the CA/B framework, there needs to be an examination of the following factors.

Social difference

This should be carried out not only in relation to her but also the others involved. Freda is a white, working-class woman, who may or may not have a 'mental health problem'. The CA/B framework can encompass various possibilities from a medical/psychiatric condition involving brain degeneration to social circumstances such as poor neighbour relationships (in which case it may be more appropriate to find ways of relieving stresses within the household, and/or with neighbours). In *either* case, her specific membership of social divisions is significant, and this particular combination reveals her as apparently a very vulnerable person, easily capable of being misunderstood.

She has mobility and hearing problems, and being categorised as having a mental health problem also places her in a stigmatised and oppressed social group. The importance of this CA/B principle is to be as systematically aware as possible of the structural social differences that may be contributing to her behaviour, which may in themselves explain much or part of it, especially when compared to the social-division membership of the other people in the family and neighbourhood.

There are a range of needs and risks relevant to Freda, as well as risks and needs that she might impose on her daughter and granddaughter. The history of her relationship with her daughter will be especially significant, and there are many possible social division issues which could have a bearing on their relationship.

Historical location

An important point to be made is that even if the health workers diagnose a case of senile dementia or some other disorder affecting the brain, the relevance of an autonomous CA/B construction of the life histories involved is in no way diminished. The pre-morbid personality of Freda, and her previous life experiences, will be relevant to understanding the form any illness would take. Eliciting and evaluating such information independently of the health workers on the basis of a social analysis of the narratives collected and the documentation available would be of major importance not only in assisting diagnosis and treatment, but also in planning for future care, and helping to make decisions which protected the interests of the various vulnerable people in this family.

CA/B histories of other people in the family would help to understand the pattern and direction of their relationships and provide a basis for multi-professional discussion for development of a 'team narrative' drawing on past and present life stories, and indicating the likely future course of events. The timing of the assessment in their lives, and its process over time would also constitute 'historical' factors, and become part of the story.

Interacting social systems

The impact on her of the various social systems of family, local neighbourhood, agencies which have been involved with her, and wider systems have to be examined to assess their contribution to the possible construction of her as having a 'mental health problem' – *including* this assessment itself. Her own social and psychological state has to be analysed within this wider context, and the different professional perspectives have to be integrated, (see the case study discussion concerning multi-professional working at the end of Chapter 7).

The changing neighbourhood over time and the arrival of Debbie's family within it will be significant in relation to understanding the way local social networks function – for example, in local attitudes to 'race' and class, and the allegations that neighbours have made. Freda's needs in the community as an older, working-class woman, apparently in some mental distress, would have to take account of both the supports and the strains in all the social networks involved. Her own role in the family system might itself be endangered if her strange behaviour extends to her grandchild, or puts too much strain on her daughter.

The CA/B principle thus supports a thorough examination of the interacting social systems and their implications for specific individuals.

Reflexivity

The social and health workers will need to assess their own personal membership of social divisions in relation to the grandmother and the carer, her daughter, and the impact of the involvement of their own agency.

In relation to the grandmother, they will both be younger and lack the experience of impoverished, disabled, confused and distressed old age. They will benefit from the support of informed agencies outside their own familiar networks that will support the users and carers, such as mental health service users' organisations. They will certainly have to examine and monitor closely the effect of their own involvement in creating and maintaining a mental health problem, and the multi-professional team will need to be aware of and discuss their own cultural values in attempting to evaluate what is 'strange' and what is not.

Power

The power issues in this case involve consideration of cross-cutting power structures at various personal and social levels.

This is Freda's house, so she will have had some initial authority over what happens within it. How long this will last will depend on what kind of relationship she has developed with her daughter and grandchildren, her level of mental functioning, and any supportive network systems she has in the neighbourhood. It would be a crucial issue if she were found to have a mental disorder which meant that Freda was no longer financially responsible for herself. The power issues in the relationship would only be adequately understood by paying attention to the history of it, and the accounts of events and trends given by those involved, and by people who had known them.

Her status as an older, disabled woman would itself be a significant disempowering factor to take account of in addition to the control issues stemming from her mental health. However, her possible inability to control her own actions and moods might also produce other kinds of power and control issues in relation to her vulnerable grandchild. The various risks of abuse, and of significant needs not being met would also be more adequately understood within the context of a systematic review of the politics of the family and its social networks and history, as supported by CA/B method.

Methodology

The tradition of some psychiatric social work has been for the 'patient' to be seen exclusively by the medical staff, and the carer to be seen by the social workers (Oliver, Huxley and Butler, 1989, p.77). However, there should be no pre-determined assumptions about this method of collaboration.

If the social assessment is to be constructed adequately, it will be essential to have Freda's perspectives on her own history and knowledge of the history of others – as much as she is able to offer. Some of this could be collected by health staff, but they are likely to focus on aspects of her medical and psychological history, and a full social assessment may be particularly important in some cases. In addition, it might be also appropriate for a therapeutically oriented social history to be taken as suggested above, by a specialist in reminiscence or life history work. Exactly how this might be progressed would depend on whether the multi-disciplinary team practised according to the principles laid down in Chapter 8, sharing their theoretical perspectives on a basis of equality.

In general, the social assessment needs to have equal access to the service users and their carers – unless there is an overriding objection concerning the effect on the user's health, or unless there is an agreement about sharing work in the light of an understanding of theoretical perspectives.

In respect of the community care package which might need to be put together, the CA/B method offers a framework for connecting the past to the present and the future, using a methodology which provides a specifically social aspect to assessment but is able to incorporate and engage with alternative professional and disciplinary interpretations.

The following diagram (Figure 6) attempts to summarise the relationship of CA/B principles to the case study, with particular attention to the general implications for people such as Freda who may be referred to mental health professionals. The CA/B framework also directs attention to her status as an older woman (see Chapter 11).

Interconnected assessment principles in Figure 6

1   Identify the membership of all major *social divisions*, as far as possible, of all relevant individuals. Consider the possibility of non-visible social divisions. Take account of specific social differences within and across major social divisions, and their interconnection with mental health as a social location in this particular person's life.

2   Examine your own own membership of social divisions in relation to this person. Consider the impact of *yourself* on the user's situation. Where possible, share perspectives, including views on the purpose, content and procedure of assessment. Acknowledge the agency's function in relation to yourself, and assess the implications with the service user and/or carers as appropriate.

3   Note the timing and place of significant events and processes, social and developmental factors in personal and family *histories*. Review life stories of the person within concrete historical contexts, including their history of treatment within the changing mental health system.

4   Connect personal lives to various levels of *social systems*, and assess the degree of positive and negative interaction in the social environment, and the likelihood of continuing support, or danger of increasing stress, including in the processes of interaction with organisations and workers, in changing family and social networks.

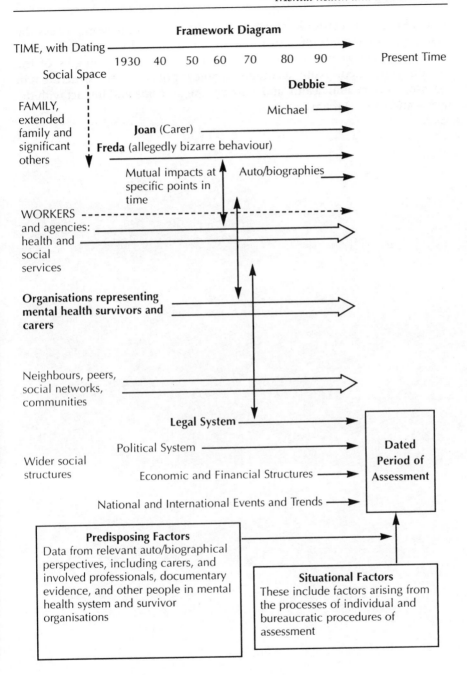

Figure 6 **Critical auto/biographical assessment in mental health**

5   Looking both vertically and horizontally at the framework, assess the changing differentials of structural, organisational and personal *power*. Identify, as far as possible, shifting vulnerabilities and strengths of the person concerned. Note changing agency policies and structures in assessment of mental health, and consider the outcome and impact with the user – and carer(s) if any.

11 Older people

This chapter will concentrate on a critical evaluation of existing theories and practices in the light of the framework produced in Part One, especially issues relating to life-course concepts, and the social construction of age and ageism.

There are many examples of research and practice involving the use of biography and life history in understanding and assessing older people, (Birren et al., 1995; Bytheway, 1989; Bury and Holme, 1991; Coleman, 1991; Cornwell and Gearing, 1989; Gearing and Coleman, 1995), and the chapter will include particular reference to the use of biographical methods of assessment in the Open University's Gloucester project (Johnson et al., 1989), and the use of simple and complex methods of assessment in community care.

The development of recent critical approaches to assessment in this area, against the background of changing theories of ageing (Hughes, 1993 and 1995; Thompson, 1996), and growing awareness of the abuse of older people (Biggs et al., 1995; Whittaker, 1996; Baumhover and Beal, 1996) have also contributed to the developing importance of the process of assessment. Positive implications for assessment practice in relation to the CA/B framework, together with an awareness of the consequences for professional intervention, will be discussed.

It is sometimes suggested that social and health workers have often been unable or unwilling to give sufficient time and expertise to the assessment of older people, especially in comparison to that given to younger people. Hughes makes the point that: 'There has been no impetus at the local, regional or national levels to develop the kinds of model of multi-disciplinary comprehensive assessment which have characterised developments in working with children and families' (Hughes, 1995, p.67).

It is true that the health and welfare of older people has often been entrusted to nurses and assistant social workers, and that working in this area has not had the same status as other areas in either health or social services. However, official support given to comprehensive assessment in childcare is in fact limited.

As already shown above, the government's guidelines for childcare workers are conspicuously free from theoretical guidance or, until very recently, relevant research into practice. In addition, the judgements of social work assistants and other health care professionals dealing with older people prior to the community care legislation may well have been variable in quality, but like childcare workers, they have also demonstrated some strengths. The structural factors which segregate women's work from higher-paid male roles, and which also help to ensure the survival of older women, meant (and still mean) that in practice much assessment of older women is done by 'middle-aged' women.

As in childcare assessment, therefore, part of the aim of the CA/B framework is to support and build on the best practice of experienced women workers who have used their judgement and experience of life to make sensible assessments with their users and carers in difficult circumstances.

Community care and assessment

In Britain, the 1990 National Health Service and Community Care Act ushered in a period of administrative and cultural change for health and social service workers, but increased rather than diminished the focus on the importance of assessment. The professed aims of the legislation were to centre on the assessment of need, taking account of: 'the wishes of the individual and his or her carer ... and where possible should include their active participation' (DoH, 1989b, p.19). This was regarded as being in opposition to previous practice, where the availability of resources was taken into account rather than people's needs. There is also a connection with the responsibility of the local authority to assess the macro level of needs – which should be informed by the assessment of need at the micro level. Assessment thus remains a central issue in the care of older people as well as in other areas of social and health care, informing the planning of individual care packages as well as the commissioning of services by the authorities.

In addition, the recent legislation has made a point of the 'multidisciplinary' nature of complex assessments in working with older people. The guidance to practitioners refers to six types of assessment, often collapsed into three: simple, complex and 'multi-disciplinary' (DoH, 1991), with the assumption that, as in childcare, different professions should be working together to produce a holistic representation of need. However, early attempts by 'multi-disciplinary' panels established to undertake development work experienced great difficulties in producing satisfactory assessment schedules (Hughes, 1995, p.68). As in childcare, there remains a theoretical gap where social assessment is concerned, which a multi-professional meeting cannot easily resolve.

The power differentials between and within multi-professional work groups make the concept of working together just as difficult here as in other areas of health and welfare. The medical perspective is as dominant as anywhere else, and the social status and administrative authority of senior health officials and consultants is very influential. However, these power differences between professions are complicated by the truly multi-*disciplinary* differences arising both within and between the professions. Chapter 7 discusses the difficulties which arise from the normal use of different discourses based on medicine, psychology, psychiatry, sociology and politics. It stresses the importance of recognising the need for triangulatory and/or bridging practices between interpretive perspectives, and the use of shared life history narratives. However, assessment in community care also involves problems of resources for workers, including lack of time and heavy caseloads.

The difficulty of making good assessments in the time available, and with the inevitable bureaucratic constraints of strict eligibility criteria, followed by lengthy pro formas and assessment schedules which must be completed are major practical issues which will be addressed in this chapter.

Theories of ageing and assessment

Key theoretical developments have concerned changes in emphasis away from medical and biological concepts of ageing to psychological, and then historical and social concepts which have permitted the encouragement of a more inclusive biographical understanding. More extended discussions of social gerontology can be found elsewhere (Peace, 1990; Hughes, 1995; Payne, 1995), but recently, significant themes relevant to CA/B method have included the use of life-course and cohort or social generational theories. Pilcher's summary refers to five main sociological theories of ageing, with particular emphasis on the socio-historical context of both ageing and theories of ageing (Pilcher, 1995, pp.29–30). There have clearly been moves away from concepts of ageing which assumed stereotypical and ageist ideas about inevitable decline and withdrawal applied to a whole range of age groups over 60 years. Recent theory has become much more sensitive to social divisions within age groups, as well as variations in the nature of age as a social construct itself (Bytheway, 1990).

Phillipson has discussed a symbolic interactionist concept of the life-course, and indicated the contributions as well as the limitations of this approach (Phillipson, 1982). It is important to note here that CA/B methodology does *not* rely solely on subjective interactive concepts of biography, but does include this dimension. It also specifically requires attention to be paid to the structuring of life stories and subjectivities by economic and political systems, at the same time as taking into account the multiple subjectivities involved in making an assessment. It emphasises the kinds of issues raised by life-course and cohort theory concerning the importance of relating lives to historically changing social structures, and takes account of the power differentials at the various levels, from the personal and beyond to widening, interacting social systems.

There are thus connections between some of the recent developments of social theory about age and the idea of CA/B method as a basis for assessment of older people. These connections will be further illustrated below.

Auto/biography and older people

The fact that older people have a long history behind them has lent itself to the possibility of exploring individual's life histories for a variety of purposes, including qualitative research (Bury and Holme, 1991; Wallace, 1994). Especially important has been the use of reminiscence for its psychological and social benefits to older people, from the psychiatric perspective of Butler (Butler, 1963) to a multiplicity of contemporary approaches with differing groups of older people (Bornat, 1994).

From the perspective of the CA/B theoretical framework presented here, these developments have sometimes been fragmentary, and have clearly focused on therapy rather than assessment. They have also been associated with changing theoretical approaches to older-age issues, including biographical and critical theories relevant to CA/B method.

The importance of the life-course to understanding ageing has been well documented (Arber and Evandrou, 1992), and the development of oral history has made major contributions in both theory and practice (Bornat, 1989; Martin, 1995). The contribution of Erikson has been widely acknowledged (Hughes, 1995), including his later work on older age (Erikson, 1986; Erikson et al., 1986). He also had a keen awareness of the place of a life-course within the wider framework of history (Erikson, 1975). This inter-relationship of history and psychology has been taken up by

Runyan, and provides an interdisciplinary resource for understanding the lives of older people (Runyan, 1982). One of the limitations of psychology has been its lack of appreciation for social structural factors, but that has been put into perspective by further developments of recent social gerontology (Arber and Ginn, 1995; Blakemore and Boneham, 1995). These more recent developments have added to the critical edge of social gerontology by studying the interconnection between different social divisions and their impact on ageing.

The Gloucester project (Boulton et al., 1989) is the major example of the explicit use of biographical method in the assessment of older people, and this succeeded in getting quality information. The project involved the taking of detailed biographies as part of the assessment of people living at home when referred for social and health services. Although it has been suggested above that good practice in social assessment has always included a strong component of life history-taking, this project was based on the explicit recognition and valuing of oral history as a basic part of assessment. The aim was to understand current needs in the light of past experiences, hoping for an improvement in the appropriateness and acceptability of services offered, as well as enhancing the self-esteem of the users by their active participation in the assessment. Care co-ordinators were given a biographical interview schedule, with prompts to enable users to explore aspects of their experience. They were also offered lifetime charts and biographical summary sheets to help record the information (Johnson et al., 1989).

It was found that the quality of information was much improved, especially in the area of understanding family relationships, older people's attitudes, and a range of issues relating the past to the present in ways which helped the professional worker assess the current need for services. The main problem was the amount of time taken over the work, valuable though it was. Under the current circumstances of service delivery, the common complaint is that there is never enough time to listen to people, and the organisations concerned place a great priority on the completion of standard checklists necessary for monitoring the overall provision of services as well as checking and recording the services offered to an individual.

However, the problems of time allocation are avoided to a degree, in that CA/B method is presented as a set of principles which applies regardless of the length of duration of an assessment. The question of the extent to which it is possible, appropriate and desirable to develop extended oral history interviews with users or carers is not clear-cut: it requires additional judgements about the ethics and politics of the situation. The service user or carer might have good reasons to object to detailed biographies, considering them inappropriate to the task. However, if organisational time constraints make the appropriate sharing of biographical information impossible, then that issue might itself become one of the unmet needs of the user which should be recorded. It is certainly not assumed that extended social life history-taking is necessarily appropriate (see Chapters 1 and 12). Issues of intrusion, confidentiality, possible trauma and relevance must all be considered and negotiated (Smale et al., 1993, p.54).

The Gloucester project clearly showed the value of an assessment based on social biographical methods. It would have been more compatible with CA/B methods had it included other of the basic principles. It failed to deal with issues of reflexivity, and did not lay much emphasis upon issues of social division or power in understanding oral history or the process of taking it. Possibly, this was partly because the planning for the project began in the early 1980s, and it was itself bounded by time. However, it laid some useful foundations for appreciating the importance of a more critical auto/biographical theory of social assessment for older people.

Critical auto/biography and assessing older people

The previous paragraphs show how various developments in the area of professional work with older people can be seen in relation to a CA/B theoretical model, but these various threads need to be drawn together, and their implications for practice made clear.

Note that the purpose is to guide and support professional judgement, not replace it. It is also intended that CA/B principles should operate in combination with more narrowly defined pro formas and risk factors, which help workers to assess specific situations. These may be more or less detailed, depending on the needs and requirements involved, but they need to be consistent with CA/B methodology. It is essential that the principles and their practical implications be taken together. The reader may thus need to refer back to the general issues for practice that have been discussed in the first part of this book, especially the chapter summaries, as well as Chapters 7 and 8.

Methods and methodology

One issue that arises in practice is the continuity between simple and more complex assessments, and between initial and more comprehensive assessments. The CA/B framework has continuity built into it, and foregrounds the issues of time and inter-related social systems and organisations. It therefore requires the use of a theoretical framework as a template against which to check all assessments, *however limited* their scope in temporal, 'disciplinary' or organisational terms (see the case study discussion below). Thus the method of assessment may be a simple checklist, pro forma, interview or rating schedule, but the methodological framework remains as an interpretative guide for all assessment, however brief. This can be made effective in various ways, through training and supervision especially, but firstly through the personal responsibility and professionalism of the worker in self-review of their own work. More complex forms of assessment will need to draw more directly from the CA/B framework. However, a biographical interview or a multi-professional meeting should also be subject to methodological review using the CA/B framework. In other words, the actual methods used to assess may vary enormously, depending on circumstance and appropriateness, but the CA/B methodology underpins and critiques whatever methods are used, since it is the basis for any *social* assessment.

It is implicit in this methodology that different views should be taken into account – especially those of users, carers and representatives of user and carer groups. This also requires different tactics and strategies, depending on specific circumstances. Multi-professional views are sometimes accessed in meetings where team narratives of the user's history and circumstances are constructed to help determine future care plans (Opie, 1997). However, it is important that:

1 a social assessment is given equal weight to other kinds of assessment, and that the 'team' narrative is not dominated by medical or psychiatric criteria;
2 there is an effective way of including the users' views and perspectives, and also a way of accessing the views of users' organisations, especially those expressly positioned as on the side of the user, such as 'grey power' organisations (Ginn, 1993).

Unless *different* views are explicitly sought from colleagues, users and dominated groups, then the value of any consensus achieved is minimised: the views offered by alternative positions are invaluable in gaining a perspective on one's own assumptions, especially when professional networks sometimes develop their own culture and immunity to dissent (see Chapter 7).

Social difference

The nature of age as a social division has been discussed in the literature as an important issue in the process of assessment (Bytheway, 1990; Pilcher, 1995). Ageism has been of growing concern to practitioners and theorists, and the evidence for treating older people as an oppressed group is well known, as well as the way old age is a changing, fractured concept, differently constructed in different times and places (Bytheway, 1995; Thompson, 1996). It needs to be seen as a specific but dynamically changing category of analysis, which constantly needs to be reinterpreted in the context of social and historical developments.

The status of older age groups as being oppressed in 'objective' terms in relation to income, wealth, welfare, stereotyping and other factors also needs to take into account the subjective experience of old age and oppression, which will vary between different older age groups and between different individuals. Workers need to be aware of specific circumstances of oppression, and the user's perspective. The subjective meaning of being an older person will clearly depend on qualitatively different specific experiences. These will undoubtedly be significantly influenced by the interconnection and overlap of old age with other social divisions, as well as the differences within and between different cohorts of older age groups. For example, many older people also come within the category of 'disabled', though they might not define themselves thus (Morris, 1997, p.6). It is essential that *all* the social divisions should be considered systematically, even if the information is not available, especially differences that may be hidden or not obvious. For example, it should not be assumed that an individual is heterosexual or able-bodied.

Recent postmodernist interpretations of social difference in relation to age have the merit of raising awareness of the complexities of difference, the positive and negative facets of individual membership of multiple social differences, and the heterogeneity of age (Featherstone and Hepworth, 1990; Phillips, 1996). However, other recent sociologists and theorists about age are also concerned to maintain the importance of the commonalities as well as the differences which affect older people, and a balance between unity and diversity is more compatible with the CA/B framework.

Bury's discussion of the relationship between age and gender acknowledges the relevance of other social divisions, and the complexity of social relationships over the life-course, but views the postmodern emphasis on plurality as of limited validity. The crises in public expenditure on old age 'may exacerbate inequalities in old age, rather than ushering in a more pluralistic and non-hierarchical, let alone "playful" scene' (Bury, 1995, p.28), thus providing a common experience of poverty for many older people.

Similarly, Bradley's review of social inequalities notes the postmodern contribution to the discussion of ageing, but concludes that its stress on identities as 'fluid, multiple and chosen appears less revealing when we are confronted with the stigmatised and non-negotiable social identities of the poor and frail elderly' (Bradley, 1996, p.161).

A recent proposal for a comprehensive framework for assessment of older people therefore appropriately recognises the importance of holding on to the commonalities as well as the differences in the varied experiences of older people (Hughes, 1993).

There is thus no alternative in principle but to systematically consider all the major social divisions, and assess their detailed complexities and interconnections in the context of concrete life histories. This interpretation of social difference thus needs to underpin the practice of assessment throughout the process.

Reflexivity

In relation to older people, one specific issue stands out in distinction to other social divisions – it is simply that the worker is usually in a different age group from the person being interviewed. Age is unlike other social divisions in this respect, where the assessor may share most or all major social divisions with the user. The same applies to childhood and youth: however, all assessing workers have had the experience of being young, but none have had the experience of being old.

This consideration certainly raises an issue of reflexivity for the employing agencies concerning their recruitment policy in relation to age: how far is age seen as a positive advantage, and how much positive action is put into the recruitment of older people? However, professional workers are quite often in the same age group as the carer involved. The implications are important: the worker must be aware of the gap in experience, not only of lived time but also of the oppression associated with older age, and must also be aware of possible bias in understanding in favour of the carer, with whom the worker may have a more similar range of experiences.

The kinds of issues raised by reflexivity for workers involve recognising differences in values and experience, and endeavouring to listen to the perspectives and values of the older person. This necessarily includes actively taking up value positions, without which the whole enterprise of understanding is impossible. The values specific to this social division are clearly about anti-ageism, but the values of a specific older person may or may not be consistent with an anti-ageist perspective. Even if they are, their own conception of what actually is anti-ageist in a specific context needs to be considered carefully, as it may well reflect different priorities and perspectives from an assessing worker who has never experienced old age. It may well be that a specific older person may not be able to articulate their needs positively enough, for either physical or psychological reasons. Equally important is the likelihood that they will not be able to do so for reasons to do with ageism itself.

As workers in this area have recently been making clear, not only do older people have 'the right ... to have their unique identities and histories properly acknowledged in any assessment process' (Key, 1989, p.70), but the worker also needs to overcome communication blocks and value assumptions which ignore the internalised depression of need. Ageism suggests to older people themselves that they do not or should not have many needs, and many have learnt to expect or defer to this. Unless careful attention is paid to this, 'practitioners will be unwittingly reinforcing the widespread depressed level of desire found in elderly clients' (Key, 1989, p.75).

This pattern of issues in assessment is common across differing social divisions, and connects with the CA/B concepts of reflexivity and power, especially in relation to the importance of oral history-taking. This involves actively listening to the stories of the other, and especially being alert to the clash of perspectives within a life story account between concepts and values that reflect dominant positions in the culture, and ideas informed by the more immediate realities of personal experience (see Chapter 6). Hughes and Mtezuka make a related point, referring to the age *and* gender of older women: 'assessment must ... incorporate her views of her situation and her needs and yet not be limited by her low expectations and internalised acceptance of the consequences of ageism and sexism' (Hughes and Mtezuka, 1992, p.236).

The need to value differing perspectives yet at the same time attempt to discriminate between them illustrates the unavoidable necessity of the assessing worker themselves having considered their own values, their own membership of differing social division, and having to make difficult value judgements and decisions. This applies in relation to older people as with other social divisions. The pre-eminent value here must be one concerned with overcoming ageism, and affirming the value of the lives of specific older people. Part of this reflexive aspect of assessment needs to be understanding the impact of the worker on the user and their situation in the process of assessment.

The dilemma of making judgements in which the worker assesses the ethics and politics of social situations is not something which analysis of risk factors can resolve. The personal values and position of the worker in relation to the users, and their skill in making judgements and in handling conflicts in these relationships remain decisive (Hughes, 1993, pp.362–3).

Historical location

The importance of biographies within historical contexts affecting lives differentially is central to social assessment, and should be a fundamental principle regardless of how much time is available. The point has been made above that the group of older people should not be stereotyped as one monolithic mass, and that the concept of age is best understood as part of a life-course theoretical framework which places a cohort of people born at a specific time within their historical period.

The views and behaviour of particular older persons therefore have to combine an understanding of their individual biography (and biographies of kin and peers), placed in the context of the cohort or social generation effects, and in turn placed within the specific historical period (Pilcher, 1995, p.143). This theoretical guidance has to be translated into practical situations where the project of biographical understanding, and especially of seeking *further* historical information, may or may not be appropriate and/or feasible.

In the context of assessment, it is also essential that the user's and carer's relationships with particular agencies should also be seen in terms of a history of contact between them, and that the history of changing agency policies and personnel be taken into account. The perception of the agency by an older person may have significant historical roots in personal, family or community life. The relationship with biography of individual workers is also a key factor (Bradley and Manthorpe, 1997, pp.23–5). Their life experiences will not only differ from their users', but may change and be influenced in the course of doing assessments, and the impact of their changing relationship on the assessment itself is particularly important in more complex assessments. The process of time – and ageing – has an impact on both workers and users during the period of the assessment. The CA/B framework provides an articulate foundation for understanding these complexities of time and timing.

The importance of a historical approach to assessment of older people has already been discussed earlier in this chapter in connection with the Gloucester project. There is no need to discuss at length the advantages of understanding older people's lives in the context of their personal and social histories: this has been established clearly through that programme. The combination of oral history with other kinds of historical information needs to be considered, and the therapeutic implications of using oral history interviewing also need to be assessed and monitored.

The use of reminiscence therapy in work with older people has already been noted in this chapter, and the relationship between the therapeutic aspect of an interview and its assessment function needs to be carefully examined in practical situations, and clearly understood from a theoretical perspective. The tangled relationship between CA/B methodology and reminiscence as a psychological or social therapy has been discussed in Chapter 10.

The use of other kinds of historical information over and above oral history interviews is clearly essential to social assessment. The use of documentary material, and especially the involvement of other professionals and carers in the construction of social histories, means that there needs to be a development of a 'team narrative' about a person's history that the workers (and carers) involved must negotiate between them in the light of the ethical and political considerations of partnership with the service user as much as is feasible. The multi-professional issues relating to this have been discussed in Chapter 7, and the historical principles in Chapter 4.

Interacting social systems

A training manual discussion of the needs of older people in the assessment process stresses the importance of 'the views of the family (immediate and extended), the neighbourhood and community networks' (Ahmad-Aziz et al., 1992). The position of an older person within the context of interacting social systems is certainly an important aspect of social assessment, and has been a feature of good practice in this area for a long time (Smale et al., 1993, pp.25–6). The obvious micro-systems of carer(s) and immediate family (if any) also need to be placed in their various systemic contexts, including local social networks (Sharkey, 1989), the organisations with which they are, or have been, in contact, and the legal, economic and political systems which contextualise them.

The CA/B framework supports and extends this aspect of assessment with its focus on the complex, partial and historically situated nature of systems at all these levels. Understanding and assessing the nature and appropriateness of social ties in which dependency and abuse are so closely connected requires a sophisticated theoretical framework to underpin professional judgements about actors and social systems. It has been argued that in assessing the dependency of older people: 'The fundamental failing of most existing instruments is their treatment of dependency as an individual attribute, rather than as a social relationship in which the behaviour and perception of all the actors contributes to the construction of the situation' (Wilkin, 1990, p.30). The actors concerned will include professionals making the assessment, as well as the users and others.

CA/B theory supports a sociological approach to both theory and assessment of old age which can 'address the relationship between micro and macro levels of analysis, the nature of the links between agency and structure, and especially focus on the notion of social hierarchies' (Bury, 1995, p.16). This requires the identification of the social systems relevant to a particular situation being assessed. This perspective also requires an evaluation of how relevant actors relate to those systems and to each other. What micro-systems appear to exist in a particular older person's life, and how do they function within them? What mezzo- and macro-systems impinge on their situation, and how do they perceive themselves in relation to them? This needs to include systems at differing social levels, and to take into account their changing historical nature, including possible malfunctioning and breakdown. Is the family and/or caring system continuing to operate in a stable way, or are there problems which impact upon various actors? How do actors help to maintain or to undermine stability in various systems? All social systems are in a state of flux, therefore good assessment will be wary of facile assumptions about them. The 1995 Carers' (Recognition and Services) Act gives carers (who are often themselves disabled) an entitlement to separate assessment (Morris, 1997, p.9). The CA/B principle indicates the importance of an inclusive approach to critical assessment of all relevant micro-social systems, and their varying interwoven interests and conflicts, thus theoretically taking into account the crucial and often complex relationship between users and carers.

Broader social systems are not to be regarded as distanced, and therefore irrelevant: they impinge upon, and are partly constituted by the concepts and behaviour of actors in micro situations. The values and concepts of relevant community networks and wider social movements need to be understood in relation to particular locales. Does this specific older person have any membership of differing community networks, such as ethnic groups, women's or disabled organisations? What are the views of these groups about assessment in general, and is there any possibility of their contributing to this assessment, with the consent of the user?

It is often impossible to fully research the range of relevant views, but strategies need to be devised to take the principle into account in the procedures and policies of organisations. In particular, what membership does this older person have of organisations for older people, and how do they perceive their own age in relation to other older people? What kind of assessment would a representative of an older people's club or organisation be suggesting in this case – or a 'grey power' organisation (Ginn, 1993)? A high level of knowledge, skill and values is clearly pertinent to making complex assessments which are sensitive to interacting social systems and the position of users, carers and workers within them (Smale et al., 1993, p.40).

Power

The concept of power as a constituent part of the CA/B framework is discussed not only in the first part of this book as a theoretical concept, where the general implications for practice are listed, but also in Chapter 7, in the discussion of needs, risks and strengths. It is the complexity of power relationships which forms the context for the development of needs, risks and strengths in peoples lives.

In assessing older people, therefore, power has to be analysed in the developing inequalities of their life-course, as they become older, creating situations of need and risk. It also has to be analysed in the opposite way, where the powers and strengths of particular individuals and groups help to maintain opportunities and activities – for good or otherwise. For example, an older white male may have accrued pension rights and power within a profession, enabling him to play an important social role and have influence long after official retirement. This may be beneficial for him, and possibly for others too. Alternatively, as a male adult, he may be, as some grandfathers have been, able to continue to abuse his grandchildren into older age because of his power, health and social and financial position. On the other hand, an older disabled woman may be triply oppressed, not having had equal chances to have a career and accrue wages or pension rights, but she may have developed some strengths in areas connected with her experiences and relationships. She may also be at risk, as a disabled older woman, from carers, professionals and relatives – but she may need and demand the right to as much autonomy as possible, and thus constitute a risk, whether she is dependent on someone or not. The assessment of power relationships between users, carers and family is thus a complex issue in itself.

In order to make judgements about such complex possibilities, the concept of power also has to be assessed in relation to the differing levels and areas where it operates, including in the relationship between the users and worker in the process of assessment. Here, the powers of the worker – both as a younger, employed professional, and as representative of a powerful agency – have to be taken into account in negotiating the levels of participation of users, carers and others in making a social assessment. Listening to the user's life stories, and hearing the wants and needs that may be half-expressed, requires awareness of power differentials, and skill in overcoming them. However, there is also the whole question of the politics of the agency – its position in relation to law and social policy, *and* the politics of both personal and organisational relationships within and between multi-professional agencies. In other words, any naive notion of empowerment of users has to be firmly rejected in view of the complexity of power relationships on both the user side of the equation and on the worker's, as well as between them, and in relation to third parties such as carers and other professionals. This makes assessment even more difficult in terms of the ethical and political dilemmas which have to be negotiated.

Power involves personal membership of social divisions as well as organisational politics, bringing together macro-social structural matters with local micro-social differences. This is not simply a theoretical issue but a reality of practice. Hughes's model of comprehensive assessment of older people recognises, for instance: 'the tension between professional aspirations and managerial imperatives' (Hughes, 1993). She rightly calls for fundamental debate about assessment, involving the status of professional and academic judgements about the nature of assessment in relation to the power of legal and administrative systems operating under political mandates (cf. Davis, Ellis and Rummery, 1997, p.18). Neither do the management issues only concern financial and resource questions for senior staff. The devolution of budgets, and the management of the worker's limited amount of time, and how that is distributed between different users and carers involves the worker immediately in resource allocation and administrative issues, including financial assessment (Bradley, and Manthorpe, 1997). Power thus operates in *and* through the worker's activities in assessment.

The decisions to be made about participation of users and carers which are now accepted and recommended in official guidelines cannot always be made easily. The principle of anti-oppressive practice implies opposition to power structures and practices which deprive individuals and groups of equal opportunities and conditions. But the organisations which employ assessing workers, and the methods they use (including biographical methods), are themselves implicated in social control and oppression, and participation in their official processes may be window-dressing or worse: the rhetoric of need 'appears to have little meaning outside the prioritization of criteria local authorities construct to stay within budget' (Davis, Ellis and Rummery, 1997, p.17).

The strategies for participation and giving a voice cannot therefore be reduced to a simple direction such as 'promote participation', or 'design pro formas to allow participation' (DoH, 1991, pp.47 and 55). The individualisation of assessment and the danger of incorporation requires continual review of tactics for attempting to achieve the least oppressive outcomes: for example, the use of independent advocates (Littlechild and Blakeney, 1996). The use of risk checklists is an important aid to judgement, and part of the practitioner's knowledge, but it cannot substitute for the ethical evaluation of interests and issues between all the parties involved in relationships with the user. Similarly, risk frameworks and multi-professional meetings are essential aspects of good practice for older people (Lawson, 1996), but in the end practitioners need to be 'responsible for their own decisions/actions' (Lawson, 1996, p.64), and aware of the disciplines of power to which they contribute.

Conclusion

The practical issues about assessing older people cannot be separated from the theory and values involved. Therefore, the first practical requirement is that any assessment needs to be reviewed in the light of the principles of method and values that have been set out in Part One of this book, taking them together, as an inter-related set. At the very least this would mean using them as a template for review of both written schedules or pro formas, or of case studies in the process of supervision (see below for a case study discussion).

In more complex or lengthy cases, it would mean actively using the principles to make the assessment, using various techniques to elicit life histories, to encourage co-operation of users, carers, advocates and professionals in constructing accounts of situations. It would in the end imply the worker taking responsibility for making evaluations which would acknowledge their reflexive involvement in the process, yet be in a position to claim that the basic principles of social assessment had been followed, for example in relation to the involvement of organisations and social networks (Smale et al., 1993, p.40). This does not guarantee any sort of solution to difficult problems, but it clarifies the *social* issues, comprehensively covering the sociological requirements for a social research method, and should leave open to the reader of the assessment a way of interpreting how and why the assessment has been made, acknowledging the contested nature of the needs and risks, and the inevitably partial and incomplete nature of social assessment (Ellis, 1993, p.39).

The general implications for social assessment using CA/B method are listed at the end of most of the chapters in Part One. The general implications for assessing risk and need are set out in Chapter 7. Both need to be applied to the specific area of assessing older people, and in this chapter the discussion has been about how recent theories of ageing, and recent discussions of assessing older people can be explained and understood from the perspective of CA/B theory (see also the following case study discussion). It is built into the theory that in time there will be further development of methods and theories, but it appears that at this point in time the problem is the absence of a theoretical basis for assessment which will support and guide practitioners on fundamental issues of evaluation and research. The CA/B framework is intended to contribute to that, reflecting current thinking across practitioner and theoretical discourses.

Case study discussion: Older people

Note: See Figure 3, and compare with the practice questions at the end of the chapters in Part One. The following is only intended to be indicative of issues that should be considered. The comments are fragmentary and incomplete.

In relation to Freda, the grandmother in the case study, using the CA/B framework requires an examination of the following issues:

Social difference

This must be examined not only in relation to her, but also to others involved. She herself is female, white, disabled, working-class and in a specific age group usually viewed in negative terms. Being born in 1920 means that she is long past her initial retirement age, and (at the time this is being written) is nearing the stage of being part of the 'very old', although her own and her family's perception of this may be different from the wider society.

Her particular location in these groups is additionally influenced by her disabilities relating to hearing and mobility: only her sexuality is not apparent. She thus occupies an extremely vulnerable position in relation to almost everyone around her, including the health workers, the hospital social worker and her own daughter. She will also have many strengths, drawing from her long experience of life, and her tenancy of a house where she may have developed some useful social networks.

Historical location

The nature and meaning of these needs, risks and strengths will only be fully understood by means of a life history in which her social and psychological development can be traced in order to illuminate her present situation, including her relationship with her daughter and grandchildren.

The depth of this interview may be dependent on negotiations with the user and her carer, and on the ability of the grandmother to understand and speak for herself, and what will then be agreed to be appropriate. The changing status of the assessment itself over time will be influenced by initial negotiations as to eligibility for any kind of service from the agency, but then again, as the assessment proceeds (if it does), by the extent and seriousness of the problems revealed. The life history information gathered from documents, carers and other workers will also be part of the construction of narratives about the development of her needs up to and including the present. Her experience of major social changes during her lifetime will provide the backdrop for this exploration of her world, but will also impinge significantly on the process of her personal life-course.

When further resource-providers become involved, assessment does not end, since changes over time and in circumstances call for revision and review. In addition, the social assessment may also indicate the need for therapeutic reminiscence work which builds on the social and historical narratives which have begun to be developed as part of the assessment.

Interacting social systems

The assessment needs to analyse the impact on her in the past, and continuing into the present, of the various social systems of family, local neighbourhood and agencies which have been involved with her, and wider systems also have to be examined to understand her situation. Her own social and psychological state has to be related to this wider context, and in Freda's case there are plenty of issues to consider. The family system is recently reconstituted, and some understanding of its dynamics is important, including the various sub-systems, recent traumas of loss, and extended membership. The changing neighbourhood over time and the arrival of Debbie's family within it will be significant in relation to understanding the way local social networks function, local attitudes to 'race' and class, and the allegations that neighbours have made.

Freda has obviously had involvement with health workers and hospital social workers. The story of this involvement is bound to affect present interactions. The organisation of the agency systems into purchasers and providers, and the insistence that care managers work within limited agency resources efficiently raise questions of how much time can be spent for the purpose of an adequate assessment, and whether her needs in this respect might be met. This is an ethical dilemma for the worker, who needs to balance the needs of one user against the others that s/he and the agency must try to meet. In Freda's case, complexities arise because of her vulnerabilities and the traumas in recent family history – which may be missed by a simple pro forma assessment.

In the absence of a comprehensive assessment of the needs and risks, the workers' responsibilities extend to considering strategies to alert managers to the situation, to re-orient agency policies, linking with social networks and community action, recording unmet need and different perspectives on need and risk; finding innovative means of meeting needs, and (always) making difficult choices about the allocation of time and resources, financial and otherwise. These difficult decisions can be assisted by using the CA/B principles to ensure that the key issues have been considered comprehensively enough.

Reflexivity

The social and health workers will need to assess their own personal membership of social divisions in relation to this older woman and the carer, her daughter, and the impact of the involvement of their own agency.

In relation to Freda, they will both be younger and lack the experience of impoverished, disabled old age. They will benefit from the support of informed comment and the perspectives of other older people in organisations which support them and advocate on their behalf. In addition, the disability issues may be an area where specialist advice and informed disabled perspectives may be highly relevant, rather than treating these issues as an inevitable part of old age. The issue of race and ethnicity might need to be explored in terms of the grandmother's membership of a white ethnic group, and conversely, her understanding and tolerance of difference in others, when she is negotiating with the black social worker, or in relation to black neighbours, or if she might at some stage need to attend day centres or other resources where she will be in close contact with people different from herself.

Power

The power issues in this case involve consideration of cross-cutting power structures at various personal and social levels. This is Freda's house, so she will have had some initial authority over what happens within it. How long this will last will depend on what kind of relationship she has developed with her daughter, Joan, and the grandchildren, and also her current level of mental functioning, and any supportive friendship or social network systems she has in the neighbourhood. If some of these are problematic, then she is potentially vulnerable to an abusive relationship.

The teenage grandson or Joan might be impatient or neglectful of Freda's needs, especially if there could be practical or financial advantages for themselves.

Daughters are stereotypically expected to care for their ageing parents, but there are countervailing factors clearly indicated by the CA/B framework. Joan is in a position to use her skills and status as a 'young middle-aged' adult to her own ends if she chooses. The structural lack of esteem of and for older women mean that Freda may even defer to her wishes.

Conversely, it may be the case that the family has many strengths to offer at different practical and psychological levels, in which case the powers of Joan and her son may be effectively supporting Freda, and the question will be to what extent the powers of the agency will be able to effectively support *them*.

The involvement of the agencies is not to be seen as an unmixed blessing, but as a complex pattern of powerful forces, pulling in different directions. The worker is likely to be a relatively powerful adult in relation to Freda, and to represent a threat to Freda's world, but may personally try to be supportive. The agency may publicise the assessment as 'needs-led', but there may be a drive towards avoiding expenditure, or a built-in push towards pathology rather than empowerment, assessing Freda as physically and mentally weak, in order to maximise resources. The workers may have an ambivalent relation to the agencies, since managers have power over them. There is therefore a level of personal accounting of power by workers when making recommendations, but there is also an organisational level of power, towards which the worker may take a pro-active stance on behalf of a particular user or group of users. *Both* levels have to be considered in relation to the ethics and politics of decisions made (and of the process), both in relation to the needs of the individual, the carer(s) and *other* users and carers. This existential use of power is a basic premise of CA/B methodology. It requires the systematic use of CA/B principles in continual review of individual and organisational procedures and policies, and the adoption of tactics and strategies to achieve ends as consistent as possible with those principles.

Methodology

Many of these practical strategies have been already undertaken by women experienced in working with older people in the community and in residential homes (cf. Pritchard, 1997). This methodology is an attempt to summarise and systematise some of what they have been doing, partly in order to help justify and further their efforts, partly to clarify and stimulate people's thinking in new ways.

This methodology suggests that workers assess in the light of basic principles relevant to understanding people's lives, drawing upon the perspectives of older people, as well as the methods of contemporary social research. It specifically includes taking account of possible alternative views of people's needs and strengths, as well as different views as to the strategies which would be beneficial to this service user group, as well as to individuals within it. The following diagram (Figure 7) attempts to summarise the relationship of CA/B principles to the case study, with a focus on Freda as an older woman.

Interconnected assessment principles in Figure 7

1   Identify the membership of all major *social divisions*, as far as possible, of all relevant individuals. Consider the possibility of non-visible social divisions. Take account of specific social differences within and across major social divisions, and their interconnection in this particular older person's life.

2   Examine your own membership of social divisions in relation to this older woman and her carer. Consider the impact of *yourself* on the user's situation. Where possible, share perspectives, including views on purpose,

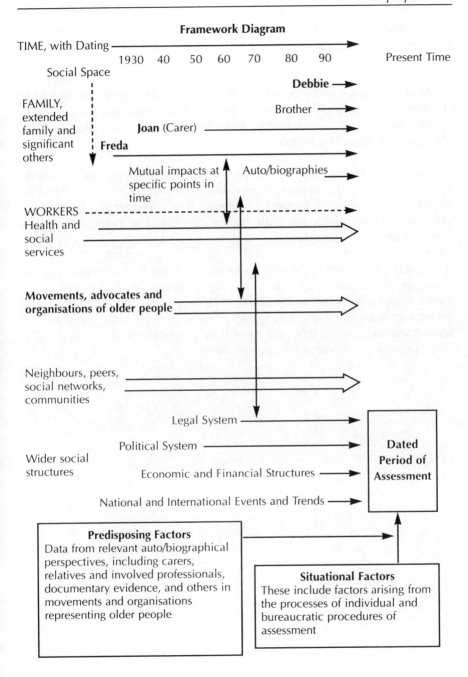

Figure 7 **Critical auto/biographical assessment with older people**

content and procedure of assessment. Acknowledge the agency's function in relation to yourself, and assess the implications with service user, relatives and carers.

3   Note the timing and place of significant events and processes, social and developmental factors in personal and family *histories*. Review life stories within concrete historical contexts, including histories of organisations and changes affecting older people.

4   Connect personal lives to various levels of *social systems* and assess the degree of positive and negative interaction in the social environment and the likelihood of continuing support, or danger of increasing stress, including in the processes of interaction with organisations and workers, in changing family and social networks.

5   Looking both vertically and horizontally at the framework, assess the changing differentials of structural, organisational and personal *power*. Identify, as far as possible, the shifting vulnerabilities and strengths of the person concerned. Note changing agency policies and structures in assessment of older people, and consider the outcome and impact with the older person – and with relatives and carers.

12 Disabled people

Introduction

Although this chapter deals with very different conditions of people's lives, it will be argued that the approach to social assessment offered here is consistent with the contemporary disability movement's approach towards seeing disability of any kind as (to a degree) significantly defined and created by social factors. I will be particularly drawing on the writings of disabled people, in view of my own able-bodied status. It will further be suggested that the auto/biographical approach to social assessment can be applied in ways that are sensitive to the great variety of disabilities, the real difficulties that arise disproportionately at different points in the life-course, and with an awareness of the power differentials that exist in this area, including the strengths and abilities of disabled people. Particular consideration will be given in this chapter to the connection between the much-discussed social model of disability and CA/B method, including issues such as communication and user views of dependence and independence.

It will be suggested throughout that the methodology is compatible with the perspectives of disabled people, and some of the points made will be similar to issues raised in previous chapters about other oppressed groups. However, there is a distinctive twist to the way in which CA/B may appear *not* to be relevant to the disabled. The point is applicable to other service users and oppressed groups but is one way in which disabled people have been especially vulnerable, mainly because of the medical dominance of disability issues, and the medical practice of taking histories. This point is about the way in which professionals (and not only health workers) have objectified people through the construction of case histories.

A recent paper has pointed out in relation to people with learning difficulties that they have usually been unable to contribute to the construction of their own life histories. There has been a lack of personal historical material in official records, and what has appeared has been a 'professional' version of their lives. It is argued that 'information constructed through professional discourse has a tendency to be problem-saturated and pathologising' (Gilman, Swan and Heyman, 1997, p.682).

This objection to constructing life histories is well directed, but is nevertheless compatible with a CA/B methodology which explicitly raises the issues of whose story is being told, and who has control over it. The importance of partnership and dialogue within the complex parameters of risks, needs and powers has been emphasised above. The need for a rounded dialogical *social* history of a life is implicit in the authors' demands for:

1   recognition of the subjects of case histories as 'stakeholders' with rights to see and contribute their perspectives to their own life histories as they appear in official records;
2   the use of life story books as 'an opportunity for "deconstructing" the objectified and subjugated identity of an individual';
3   the use of narrative research methods to construct life histories, drawing on the commonalities as well as the differences (Gilman, Swan and Heyman, 1997, p.688).

The points made are relevant to all user groups and, although they appear to be against the idea of life histories, in fact illustrate the importance of this approach to social assessment, but taking all the CA/B principles together, and finding ways of taking them seriously in practice.

Disability and social difference

The CA/B framework's view of social division is consistent with the kind of view that has been developed by the disability movement in recent years. Although there is considerable debate about the 'social concept of disability' (Abberley, 1987), there is now wide agreement that disability is similar to other forms of oppression in many ways, although it is a fuzzy concept (as with many contested social concepts) that sometimes shades into its opposite (Harris, 1996), and its official definition covers a very large number of conditions, including mental health, learning difficulties and many older people suffering from conditions which 'substantially and permanently' affect their lives – even though, as Morris points out, they may not themselves accept the term 'disabled' (Morris, 1997, p.6).

In the past, disability has conventionally been attributed to individual biological differences, but disabled people have argued that it is a society dominated by the vested interests of able-bodied people that disables them, by not taking account of the needs and rights of disabled people. They have distinguished between the various kinds of physical 'impairment' from which they suffer on the one hand, and on the other, the 'disability' that is socially imposed upon them (Oliver, 1996, p.22). This does not preclude recognition of the variety of kinds and degrees of both impairment and disability. Indeed, many disabled people have been well aware of differences between themselves, as well as between the disabled and others (e.g. Morris, 1989).

Differences are multiplied in so far as the disabled are also divided by all the other major social differences. The recognition of disability as a form of social oppression does not inhibit the appreciation of these other forms of oppression, although Oliver accepts that in practice some forms of disability training based on the social model of disability may sometimes have had that effect (Oliver, 1996, p.40). Women especially have contested the over-emphasis of the social model on social attitudes and environmental barriers (Morris, 1992a), and, along with others, has questioned the way the social model of disability deals with impairment, illness and death.

The debate is usefully summarised by Oliver, who argues that the social model of disability cannot explain disability in total – it is not a complete theory of either disability or impairment, but it remains useful as reference point for 'personal experience and professional practice' in the area of disability (Oliver, 1996, p.41).

In terms of social assessment, therefore, the individual life of a disabled person needs to be studied in socially structured contexts, where social divisions are seen to connect and interconnect in specific, time-related ways. The social dimension of disability is fundamental, resembling the way the social dimension of CA/B methodology is fundamental in social assessment.

The specific kinds of impairment, and the particular social disabilities that have impacted on a given life require an awareness of the complex social interactions that occur at different social systems levels, at different times and places – not a stereotyping generalisation about disability into which individual experiences are made to fit. This means that all variations of social division and all variations of disability are relevant, and have to be assessed *both* separately and together, taking into account the particular person and their social divisions membership in relation to those with whom they have direct and indirect contact. An assessment that fails to have this as a basic underpinning principle will ignore the particular quality of social oppression as it impinges on the disabled person.

It is always necessary to consider the full range of possible social divisions which cut across disability in complex ways, as well as the interwoven complications arising from the specific nature of the impairment, and how that is socially constructed as a disability.

Locating the disabled historically

If the full social context of a disabled person's life is essential to an understanding of their circumstances, then that must include – in principle – full reference to the personal, family and social histories within which the social context changes and continues to change as the social assessment is made.

The CA/B linking of oral and life history with critical developmental psychology is designed to provide an adequate basis for grasping the full range of factors involved, including the voice(s) of the disabled. There is a convergence of ideas between disabled writing and CA/B method here. Oliver has long argued for the importance of seeing disability in sociological terms as a 'career', emphasising the time-related factors in a disabled person's life (Oliver, 1983). The aim of his approach was to help to contextualise the disability in terms of personal and social history, taking account of when the disability began in someone's life, how it developed and interacted with other aspects of their life, and its impact on the different transitions in their life-course.

In addition, there has been a concern to join the history of individual lives to the history of the disability movements (Campbell and Oliver, 1996), as well as an increasing interest in recording the voices of various groups of disabled people talking about their own histories, and histories of the institutions and organisations in which they have lived and worked (Fido and Potts, 1989; Potts and Fido, 1991; Walmsley, 1995; Goodley, 1996). The importance of this is relevant both for professional social assessment and for self-assessment within the self-advocacy movement. A good example is the importance of 'People with learning difficulties ... writing their own histories and setting out their agendas for the future' (Goodley, 1996, p.345).

A recent development has been the use of auto/biographical methods in researching people with learning difficulties (Atkinson, 1997), which makes a connection between developing research methods and developing self-advocacy (Atkinson, 1997, pp.15–16). This connection also fits with the argument in this book about the parallels between research and assessment, since one of the self-advocacy productions quoted is the aptly entitled *Oi, It's My Assessment* (People First, 1993), reflecting the issue of mutual involvement and power relationships between the user and assessor/researcher.

For the purpose of social assessment, CA/B method means that in principle there needs to be the collection of historical data about the personal and family history of the disabled person, and that this should in turn be contextualised within the histories of the community and wider social history, including the movements of disabled people resisting oppression. This data potentially includes not only the oral evidence of the disabled person, giving their own perspective on how they have reached their present situation, but also the evidence of other disabled people on their position in society, including the specific local community. Of course, this is not to make the assumption that all this information is available, or even if it is, that it should necessarily be collected and used in a particular case. The point is that, in principle, it is applicable information, and should be considered. Similarly, the evidence of psychological development over the lifespan, placed within the social and historical context, is also pertinent. Even more critical is the evidence of third parties such as carers, doctors and other professionals, and historical and other documentary records which may be (and are) used both positively and negatively. All this evidence is potentially relevant, and would need to be sifted, discussed and analysed in accordance with CA/B principles (see 'Reflexivity in assessing disabled persons', below).

The concept of a disabled 'career' is used by Oliver to take account of this socio-historical dimension of disabled people's lives. The term derives from interactionist sociology, and is said to be useful in that: 'it focuses not only on the experience of disability, but also on the interaction between this and other aspects of an individual's total life experience' (Oliver, 1996, p.138). It especially makes it easy to link disability with age, for example, so that the particular impairment can be examined at key life transitions, within a specific social-historical context. For example, the transition from school to work is of crucial importance to disabled people, and is a key site where socially disabling discrimination structures their lives.

How a person has been disabled by that social context needs to be grasped in specific historical detail, in relation to the chronological age and psychological development of the person concerned. Specific life events, including the onset of impairment and disabled status (which may or may not occur at the beginning or during the course of a life), can be examined both for their negative and positive impact on individual circumstances.

The CA/B study of life history goes beyond interactionist analysis of interpersonal relationships, but includes them. It also takes account of wider social structures, including organisational and social power that may only be indirectly apparent in local social practices, and refers explicitly to other intervening factors, such as power and reflexivity in the process of assessment.

In addition, the assessment itself is both located at a point in time and is itself a process through time. The assessment is part of history itself, and interconnects with histories of individuals, families, agencies and groups. It is certainly part of the life history of the assessor, and the assessor's biography enters into the assessment process (see below, and Bradley and Manthorpe, 1997, p.23).

The assessment is traditionally viewed as a process in which it is necessary to: 'build continuously on earlier work and require responses to changing circumstances and previously concealed problems' (Smale et al., 1993, p.29). The changing lives of those involved are thus bound together in the historical process of assessment itself.

Assessing interacting social systems of disabled people

The psychology of inter-personal relationships at the family level has conventionally been an important lever of analysis in understanding disabled people. However, the use of middle-range theories of psychological adjustment to disability has served as a way of ignoring wider sociological factors. Oliver has pointed out the similarity of function between interactionist psychological approaches to adjustment in disabled people with disengagement theory in ageing (Oliver, 1996, pp.134–5). Both have had their origins in medical models of pathology, requiring individuals to make psychological adjustments to life events and conditions. Both have been broadened out to include interpersonal aspects of social psychology, but both are limited to explaining disability and ageing in relatively narrow terms, and do not adequately include the wider social factors and power relationships which surround and construct the disability and ageing in specific societies at specific times. For example, poverty and its consequences is an obvious factor which impacts on both disability and ageing, but is a broad social structural factor which powerfully conditions individual experience.

Whether an aspect of a person's life needs to be understood in terms of one social system or another cannot therefore be taken for granted, and may be the result of several factors. The relevance of a psychological understanding of a disabled person's life is not ruled out, but it has to be understood within the context of a social assessment, where other explanatory possibilities are considered. Problems or strengths will often be the result of interacting social systems, where analysis of the family as a social system has to be integrated with the impact of various other social systems at micro-, mezzo- and macro-levels. This is specially relevant to community care issues, normalisation and 'social role valorisation', where the interaction between different social systems at different levels of society impinges in complex ways on the individual. The aim of professionals to integrate segregated disabled people into a neighbourhood where they might play a socially valued role has been critically discussed (Ramon, 1991), and the possible supportive social networks analysed (McGrath and Grant, 1993). The point here is that the interactions of different social systems and networks at differing levels are all potentially of direct and indirect relevance.

The CA/B approach to research and assessment is based on the importance of capturing both the personal and the social, and this applies to disability just as much as to other social divisions: 'life history provides a link between public and private worlds, giving substance to the social worlds of the tellers – social worlds which are often concealed and mystified by the social sciences' (Goodley, 1996, p.337). This disability research view concurs with black women's views on the value of catching the 'multi-layered' levels of private and public in life history narratives (Etter-Lewis, 1991). Research evidence into the needs of disabled people using life history methods also shows clearly how lives 'were shaped by institutional interventions (schools and hospitals) which ultimately defined their behaviour as adults' (Preece, 1996, p.195), and auto/biographical research methods are also now being used to reveal the interacting social systems that circumscribe their lives (Atkinson, 1997). For the professional social assessment, there needs to be a critical awareness of the inter-relationship between the various interacting social systems and the perception of their impact in personal lives which is evident in life history narratives.

CA/B social assessment aims to be inclusive of the *range* of interacting social systems. It is important to see that the wider social systems are not simply 'background' issues, which can be safely held in abeyance whilst foreground issues of intra-personal and inter-personal systems are analysed. The concept of systems interaction relevant in CA/B social assessment means that the individual experience of disability is constructed daily by social practices which are based on, but also contribute to, continuing power relationships between the disabled and non-disabled – in addition to the other social divisions which fashion social life. The immediate family and caring systems, including the professional assessor, and the organisational and bureaucratic systems, as well as the wider social structures of oppression – and the resistance of movements of disabled people – have to be correlated with the unique life that is being considered.

It is important, therefore, to 'make a "holistic" assessment of the social situation, and not just of the referred individual' (Smale et al., 1993, p.45), in which a range of social systems – including carer, voluntary, community and statutory systems, and especially organisations of disabled people – are drawn into the assessment and planning.

Reflexivity in assessing disabled persons

The concept of reflexivity drawn from research methodology stresses the importance of the assessor, or observer, as also the participant and actor, and the social assessment is therefore seen as very much an actively negotiated product in which the voices of various participants, including the assessor, are more – or less – heard. In the field of disability, this concept has a particular importance, since the voices of disabled people have often not been heard. Sometimes the problems of communication for the disabled are such that it has been difficult for them to convey their thoughts in the absence of specific aids that some need in order to communicate. However, the most common reason for the silencing of the disabled is simply that researchers – and assessors – have themselves *not* been disabled. If there is added to this the assumption that not being disabled has no relevance to the production of an 'objective' account of a disabled person's life or their needs, then there is a likelihood that the disabled voice will not be heard, however clear the articulation of the messages.

One specific example of this concerns people with learning difficulties and the way in which the researcher needs to be very careful about communication – and especially about their *own* deficiencies, and not just the limitations of the person being interviewed. One paper on producing narratives of people with learning difficulties quotes Plummer's view that in the production of life histories, 'the informant should be fairly articulate [and] able to verbalise' (Plummer, 1983, p.90), arguing that this is a serious objection to working with people with learning difficulties, and may lead to the accusation that what the researcher or assessor produces may be 'unsubstantiated anecdotes' (Goodley, 1996, p.341). However, other researchers with the same user group contend that 'researchers should attend more to their own deficiencies than to the limitations of their informants', and they have produced a series of recommendations about how to get a life history from an inarticulate subject (Booth and Booth, 1996, p.67). They indicate that intellectual limitation is only part of the problem: inarticulacy is also caused by low self-esteem, and other social and emotional factors which are commonly found in the subjects of social assessment. Their argument and their recommendations therefore have a much wider relevance, and relate, for example, to the discussion of the depressed concepts of need internalised by older people (see Chapter 11). The importance of 'hearing' the voice of the disabled and attempting to engage in a shared understanding requires the assessor to develop considerable skills of communication. It also needs the assessor to consider that: 'Fluency is not the only key to communication. Silence may be as telling as talk' (Booth and Booth, 1996, p.57). Developing non-verbal communication and more sensitive methods of research is essential for all researchers, and equally for social assessments, if significant voices are to be heard, and valuable insights are not to be lost (Pitcairn, 1994).

The development of arguments about reflexivity in research methodology more generally has highlighted the fact that, especially in relation to the various social divisions, the social construction of the product of research by the researcher has a crucial impact on the construction of the lives of those researched. Women researchers have long argued that male concepts have used to interpret and/or silence women's voices and experience in a range of fields, and their aim in recent years has been to undo that kind of oppressive social practice (see Chapter 1). Disabled researchers have echoed this in their own writings, protesting strongly about the dominance of research into disability by non-disabled researchers (Morris, 1991 and 1992b; Oliver, 1992a). The implications for social assessment are not to automatically invalidate assessments done by non-disabled people, but to spotlight the issue of exactly *who* is the assessor. The objections to non-disabled research and/or assessment need to be considered at different *levels*. At the level of the employing organisation, there are questions about the access of disabled people to employment: how many disabled people are there in the organisation who can contribute to social assessment of disabled people? There is a similar issue in relation to the employment of black people in health, social and legal services. When steps are taken to employ black and/or disabled people, there are then also issues of retention, and fair treatment within the organisation.

As far as the actual process of assessment is concerned, the reflexive issues cannot be restricted to disability, but in assessing disabled people, the relationship of the assessor to disability and to the disabled communities must be accounted for in the assessment. If the assessor is not disabled, then questions immediately arise about the assessor's ability to communicate with, understand and hear the disabled person being assessed – in both the physical and intellectual senses of 'hearing'. This includes important issues relating to disability cultures, for example, in the use of sign language by deaf people. Secondly, there are questions to be asked about the availability of disabled advisors within the organisation upon whom s/he may call for advice. Thirdly, there are issues about the connections between the assessor, the employing organisation and the disabled communities – particularly communities of people with the kinds of disability relevant to the person being assessed, and the role they may be able to play either at the organisational level, or in relation to this specific assessment.

Some of the same issues may arise even if the *assessor* is disabled, since no one can have expertise or experience of the whole range of disabilities. However, there are likely to be advantages to a disabled assessor in being able to recognise quickly various reactions and behaviours that are not pathological problems of the individual, but are patterns resulting from discrimination and oppression experienced frequently by disabled people.

There are also issues of reflexivity that will cut across the disability issues. All the social divisions are relevant to reflexivity, and are part of the CA/B theoretical framework for social assessment, and in principle, it is therefore essential that they are all considered. Some of this accounting may take place in supervision with a senior; with colleagues from the relevant social division; with outside consultants or community members, but above all in dialogue with the person being assessed, and in reflective self-analysis by the assessor.

The last two parts of this accounting process relate specifically to the auto/biographical principle which underlies this book. The understanding of the life of the other is negotiated within the context of an understanding of the life of the self, the two processes intersecting simultaneously. The most difficult aspect of reflexivity in this process is the authoritative, employed position of the assessor as representative of an agency, and the service user being in a subordinate position in relation to the agency. This raises issues concerning the power structure of assessment situations with disabled people.

The assessment of power and disability

Nothing can alter the fact that the assessor is not only a person with specific social attributes and history, but is an actor with defined responsibilities to assess on behalf of an organisation. How the individual assessor plays that powerful role affects how the person being assessed responds to them in the assessment process. How the organisation is perceived over-determines that personal relationship. The perceptions of disabled people of individual assessment by large organisations are inevitably varied, and are not always going to be positive. The assessor may see their own role as potentially 'empowering', but the user may see it quite differently, even when the assessing professional behaves in the most 'empowering' way they possibly can, because the powerful structures of central and local government heavily influence the boundaries of the possible in the assessment process.

Morris has argued rather optimistically that the officially promoted concept of 'needs-led assessments' is 'essentially based on a social model of disability' (Morris, 1997). However, recent research seems to support strongly the conclusion that: 'The policy rhetoric is of needs-led assessments offering choice and empowerment to disabled people. In reality however, the concept of 'need' appears to have little meaning outside the prioritization criteria that local authorities construct to stay within budget'

(Davis, Ellis and Rummery, 1997). Similarly, a Rowntree research project concluded that: 'those needs which had not been addressed or even on the agenda were frequently the most significant' (Ellis, 1993, p.41). The issues involved in meeting the needs of people not just as individuals, but as members of an oppressed group, are not *necessarily* resolved by the concept of a needs-led assessment (see Chapter 8).

The structure of the assessment situation within the framework of community care is such that despite rhetoric about needs-led assessment, the professional has to decide in terms of policies and priorities set out by the employing organisation, and in line with government advice (DoH, 1991), what are the 'needs' which these powerful but resource-strapped organisations are prepared to consider. Those needs are defined in relation to individual circumstances, and the assessment is of individual need expressed by the service user, but within the framework of definitions of need by local agencies. The contention of French and Swain has already been cited concerning the assumption made in official guidance about the individual nature of 'voice' and the individual model of disability, and their strongly argued case that anti-disablist values would involve the *collective* voice of disabled people: 'the recognition of disability culture, the inclusion of the representative voice of disabled people in formal decision-making, and the promotion of a social model of disability as integral to the processes, relationships and content' (French and Swain, 1997, p.203). The whole emphasis of official guidance for needs-led assessment tailored to individuals is presented as a humane approach which should be preferred to agency responses based on available resources. However, the focus on the individual model, the use of eligibility criteria to eliminate some claims, and the devolution of financial responsibility onto workers effectively means that individual assessors are automatically restricting the definition and resourcing of needs. The overall effect is not necessarily better than any previous system.

The assessor should therefore consider how far the collective voice(s) of the disabled can be brought to bear in a particular situation in procedures and policies. The individual consciousness of a disabled person needs to be understood in the context of the contemporary disability movement (Campbell and Oliver, 1996, Chapter 6), and ethical and political strategies have to be developed in the awareness of how power structures have repercussions for individual decisions.

The CA/B framework supports a rigorous analysis of power, including that which underlies social practices such as assessment. In principle, the assessment will therefore include a thorough consideration of all aspects of power relationships, covering all the social divisions, and applied to all the interacting social systems in a specific case. This means, for instance, taking account systematically of the various vulnerabilities and strengths that exist in the relationships in which disabled people are involved. This may include the consideration that some other people may be vulnerable *to* disabled people in certain specific situations. For example, children may be vulnerable to disabled adults. This has led to some debate recently over the issues of 'young carers' and the disabled adults they may be looking after (Keith and Morris, 1995). Other carers may also be in vulnerable positions, either in relation to a disabled person or towards the same organisations or social systems that oppress the disabled. Their needs, risks and relative power also have to be evaluated (Ross and Waterson, 1996, p.85). Conversely, there is evidence that disabled children are particularly vulnerable, and the child protection services have not in the past been sufficiently aware of the specific dynamics of power which leave them exposed to abuse by others (Marchant and Page, 1992).

The comprehensive understanding of the multiple dimensions of power which is central to the CA/B method requires detailed examination of the specifics of power in individual situations, where both positive and negative aspects of power are viewed both in the context of social structures and specific personal and family histories.

The involvement of the professional health or social welfare worker in the assessment process is a key component of the power structure of this social practice, and connects with the discussion of reflexivity. The issue for assessors is how far in practice are they able and/or willing to support the disability movement perspective on what a specific disabled person might need, in the light of that person's own views. This might be up to and including support for self-advocacy, and control of their own budgets. There is a parallel debate between researchers into disability as to how far they should or should not be ethically and politically committed to the perspectives and needs of the disabled people they research (Barnes, 1996; Bury, 1996; Shakespeare, 1996). There is debate about how far a researcher should also have a commitment to research ideals, and whether these should have priority over other commitments, or if the first and primary issue is whether researchers are 'with the oppressors or with the oppressed' (Barnes, 1996, p.110).

The CA/B framework makes it clear that this is a similar issue to that which the assessor has to decide in principle every time an assessment is made. This is an aspect of the way in which the production of both knowledge and power in the assessment process occurs (see Chapter 1). It is an unavoidable dilemma: even in apparently straightforward assessments, the potential for reinforcing dominant concepts always exists.

The practical problem is to find strategies which resist managerially controlled procedural models of assessment which have the effect of 'limiting access to assessment at the earliest possible stage' (Davis, Ellis and Rummery, 1997, p.73), leading to 'preoccupation with eligibility and the establishment of risk, rather than disabled people's and carer's needs' (Davis, Ellis and Rummery, 1997, p.75).

For the CA/B method, the practitioner – or researcher – has to reflexively examine and question their own understanding of the power relationships involved, moving forward in ways that are consistent not only with disability perspectives, but also other issues relating to power and social division.

As with other social divisions, the exercise is not only a matter for the individual professional, but equally for the employing organisation and wider social systems. The politics of local organisations and community groups will impact on what strategies and alliances a professional can make in order to realise the aim of a needs-led assessment as 'a key way of ensuring that community care services change to meet the needs of people who have historically not been very well provided for' (Morris, 1997, p.6). This is an aim to aspire to when assessment is linked to the input of representatives of oppressed user groups, so that the way services are delivered, and the kind of services offered, can be influenced by them, rather than be the outcome of an individualised assessment based on managerially controlled and narrowly prescribed criteria and procedures. However, it would be naive to think that the internal politics of local agencies and authorities are anything but difficult, and the CA/B concepts of social difference and power indicate the complex factors that are implicated. Professionals thus have a difficult task, but with some guidelines for direction.

Conclusion

It is the contention of this book that assessing disabled people needs to be founded on CA/B principles, with modifications that are appropriate to particular settings and circumstances.

All the basic principles operate from the point of receiving a referral. The relationship between the assessor and the disabled person and carer has to be negotiated ethically and politically from the start. In relation to disabled people especially, the danger is that without a reflexive negotiation of the whole purpose of the assessment with the user, and an open negotiation of priorities (Ellis, 1993, p.40), there will be an unjustifiable intrusion into the life of the disabled person, and an undermining of their autonomy. Even if it is only a long pro forma or questionnaire that is used, unnecessary questions may be asked as part of the standard bureaucratic process of assessment, some questions that should be asked may not be, and the whole exercise will proceed without questioning the individual model of voice or of need.

Should there be time and space available for further assessment, then another of the issues that needs to be agreed is whether further assessment is desirable, and especially whether the taking of detailed social histories is appropriate. Often, the situation is that there is not enough time, and further assessment would be appropriate, but clearly not always. Disabled people with straightforward requests for a material resource (say, for a ramp) should not need to reveal their whole life history to obtain it. There is always an ethical and political issue concerning the amount of information that it is necessary for making an adequate assessment, and one of the criticisms of disability writers regarding needs assessment is precisely the 'invasions of privacy by a veritable army of professionals' (Oliver, 1996, p.69). And this is despite official guidance that an assessment should 'strike a balance between privacy and obtaining sufficient information to gain an understanding of need' (Smale et al., 1993, p.54). The CA/B framework suggests that the power issues have to be taken very seriously in relation to this matter.

The professional making a social assessment of disabled people cannot take up a neutral position since s/he is implicated as a key actor. It has been argued that the assessor needs to 'develop a relatively neutral "outside" perspective' (Smale et al., 1993, p.55), based on 'their lack of vested interest and ability to see the point-of-view of all parties' (Smale et al., 1993, p.57). This is certainly not in line with CA/B concepts of power and difference, since the assessor is not 'outside' the assessment, and does have vested interests and values that need to be scrutinised. This is consistent with recent research evidence that professionals need to 'address issues of both values and power in their assessments, particularly the way in which their implicit operation presently disadvantages the other participants' (Ellis, 1993, p.40). Workers have many vested interests, including to survive in a pressurised job, and have developed defensive techniques, such as the 'art of edging towards the door' (Ellis, 1993, p.20).

Questions remain as to how far either the agency or the individual professional can meet the demands of disabled people for self-advocacy and/or control of budgets, and the contested definitions of need. It is a 'circle which cannot be squared, [but] differing interests and levels of influence have to be openly acknowledged before a negotiated solution can be reached' (Ellis, 1993, p.39).

CA/B principles thus bring the key issues to the forefront in the social assessment of disabled people.

Case study discussion

Note: See Figure 3, and compare with the practice questions at the ends of the chapters in Part One. The following is only intended to be indicative of issues that should be considered. The comments are fragmentary and incomplete.

Social difference

In this case study, there are at least two people who have some form of disability, but there are also hidden disabilities (as well as a shortage of information). It is possible that any person identified on the framework may have another disability, including the professional workers. Service users who have a disability need to be assessed in the light of the considerations discussed in this chapter.

As already discussed above, disability as a social division is itself a fuzzy concept, and in addition to the specific way their disability is constructed, disabled people are also members of other social divisions. In this case, Debbie is also female, a young child, and of mixed race. She is said to have a speech delay and behavioural problems. How far either of these may be regarded as a disability is itself an issue which may be affected by further information about the causes of these problems, which may be more or less serious, depending on causation. Certainly, she is a vulnerable child with many needs, which are mutually exacerbated by disabilities which may or may not be long-lasting, but inability to express herself except through difficult behaviour is also readable as a sign of possible child abuse.

The grandmother also has disabilities of hearing and mobility, at least. Again, the concept of disability is fuzzy: are her mobility problems temporary as a result of the fall? These particular problems are often associated with old age, but they should also be seen as problems of disability, and subject to discrimination and oppressive structures as other disabled people are. The combination of old age, gender and disability make her very vulnerable, including to abuse.

Further information about the grandmother and Debbie is needed to establish the nature and level of their problems, what their prognosis is, and to what extent social factors influence their origins, development and likely future course. The social construction of specific disabilities thus needs to be examined, both in itself and related to interconnecting social divisions of age, gender, class, 'race', and gay and lesbian issues.

Historical location

A fundamental part of this process will be listening to the life stories that will be told by and about the people concerned. In both cases, the workers will have to consider their own communication skills in working with two very differently vulnerable people. In addition, they will need to consider carefully how to interpret the life histories they may be able to get from others, including the main carer, who has her own continuing needs as a working-class woman with major problems in her own life.

She is clearly the most likely potential source of continuing support, but is also a possible contributor to neglect and abuse, who may yet in some respects be at risk herself, especially in view of her own recent traumatic past. The history of their family relationships, as well as the histories of their disabilities, need to be placed in the context of wider histories, to understand the place and timing of disability in their lives.

Interacting social systems

The impact on Freda and Debbie in the past, and continuing into the present, of the various social systems of family, local neighbourhood, and agencies which have been involved needs to be examined. The way local social systems and networks are accommodating the needs of people with disabilities, or are exacerbating those needs, or even creating them, will be a key issue.

The accessibility and sensitivity of health and social service organisations towards disabled people and how that impacts on Debbie and Freda is obviously important. Equally, the organisations which represent disabled people, and their connections with local agencies may be negatively or positively significant, depending on whether they are able to input their perspectives and policies about supporting disabled people.

The understanding the family itself has of disability, especially the carer, Joan, and the place the disabled members have within it will be important factors in family dynamics.

Reflexivity

The social and health workers will need to assess their own personal membership of social divisions in relation to the grandmother, Freda, the granddaughter, Debbie, and the carer, Joan, and the impact of the involvement of their own agencies.

If the workers are able-bodied (and possibly even if they are not), they will need to draw on the knowledge and advice of other disabled people and organisations having expertise and experience of these specific disabilities.

They may also have to make difficult judgements where dilemmas arise as to the competing vulnerabilities and risks (balanced against varied strengths and abilities) of the different people in this situation, whilst being aware of their own personal vested interests and values, and the expectations of their employing agency.

Power

The power issues in this case involve consideration of two lots of intersecting relations of power deriving from the two people with disabilities, interconnected with differing forms of power and status derived from other sources of social division.

Both Freda and Debbie are relatively powerless, but Debbie is also a child of mixed parentage, and Freda's reported strange behaviour may be threatening to her, depending partly on Freda's past relations with Joan and with Debbie's black father. If she had disapproved of her daughter's relationship, she may view Debbie in a negative light. This is speculation until some interviewing is done, but the reality of racism affects power both at social structural and personal levels, and awareness of the possible repercussions in this case is part of the analysis of power structures.

Equally, the vulnerability of Debbie as a young child is magnified by a disabling speech delay, which may make her even more powerless – unable to express her needs or complain effectively about her treatment. This may be due to those who have power over her not listening to her, not helping her learn how to express herself, or even treating her abusively and threatening her if she tells.

Again, the specific power structures are complexly producing a situation where age, disability, gender and race are all involved: only further interviewing and investigation of the history of events and relationships will help to distinguish which of these is the most salient, to what extent they are all involved, and whether there may be other disability issues affecting the structure of situational politics in this case.

Methodology

This methodology requires workers to assess in the light of basic principles relevant to understanding people's lives, drawing upon the perspectives of disabled people.

The case illustrates that the perspectives of other oppressed social groups are intertwined with the issues of disability, there being two very different people in the case with different disabilities.

The methodology includes taking account of possible alternative views of what people's needs and strengths, in addition to different views as to the strategies which would be beneficial to this service user group in general, as well as to individuals within it, particularly in view of the complexities that arise from the specific situation. It therefore supports negotiation of the purpose and priorities of the assessment with the users and carers.

Thus, although CA/B method does not provide neat answers, it does help to take account of fundamental properties of social assessment, and their complexity in any given circumstance. The following diagram (Figure 8) attempts to summarise the relationship of CA/B principles to the case example with special reference to disability issues.

Interconnected assessment principles in Figure 8

1   Identify the membership of all major *social divisions*, as far as possible, of all relevant individuals. Consider the possibility of non-visible social divisions. Take account of specific social differences within and across major social divisions, and their interconnection in any particular disabled person's life.

2   Examine your own membership of social divisions in relation to these individuals. Consider the impact of *yourself* on the user's situation. Where possible, share perspectives, including views on purpose, content and procedure of assessment. Acknowledge the agency's function in relation to yourself, and assess the implications with users and carers.

3   Note the timing and place of significant events and processes, social and developmental factors in personal and family *histories*. Review life stories of the person within concrete historical contexts, including histories of relevant disability movements and organisations.

4   Connect personal lives to various levels of *social systems*, and assess the degree of positive and negative interaction in the social environment, and the likelihood of continuing support, or danger of increasing stress, including in the processes of interaction with organisations and workers, in changing family and social networks.

5   Looking both vertically and horizontally at the framework, assess the changing differentials of structural, organisational and personal *power*. Identify, as far as possible, the shifting vulnerabilities and strengths of the person concerned. Note the changing agency policies and structures in assessment of disability, and consider the outcome and impact with the disabled user – and carer(s), if any.

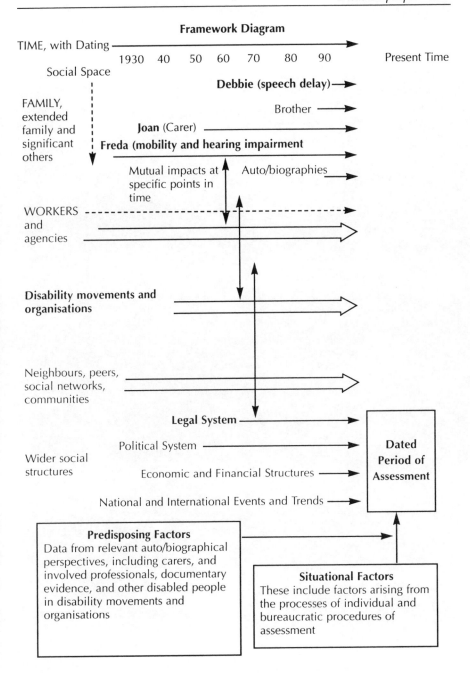

Framework Diagram

TIME, with Dating ————————————————————→

1930 40 50 60 70 80 90   Present Time

Social Space

Debbie (speech delay) ——▶

FAMILY, extended family and significant others

Brother ——▶

Joan (Carer) ————————————————→

Freda (mobility and hearing impairment

Mutual impacts at specific points in time   Auto/biographies

WORKERS and agencies

Disability movements and organisations

Neighbours, peers, social networks, communities

Legal System ————————————→

Political System ————————————→   **Dated Period of Assessment**

Wider social structures

Economic and Financial Structures ——▶

National and International Events and Trends ——▶

Predisposing Factors
Data from relevant auto/biographical perspectives, including carers, and involved professionals, documentary evidence, and other disabled people in disability movements and organisations

Situational Factors
These include factors arising from the processes of individual and bureaucratic procedures of assessment

Figure 8 Critical auto/biographical assessment with disabled people

Part Three

Conclusion

13 Towards effective social assessment

The aim of this book has been to present a concept of social assessment as relatively distinct from other kinds of assessment that can be made in relation to human individuals and groups. It is based on the perspectives of user and oppressed groups, but also draws on the experience of practitioners, and multi-disciplinary perspectives of social research. It does not require that assessment be regarded as a 'scientific' enterprise in the old empiricist sense of the word. Nor does this denial mean that assessment must in the end be based on values which are merely subjective. It is clearly a practical intervention in the social world, and as such must include elements of personal skill, judgement and art. Yet it is also a theoretical issue, which must take account of knowledge, empirical evidence and theoretical coherence in the social sciences (see Chapter 1). In sum, assessment has to partake of scientific, theoretical, artistic, ethical and practical elements – something which has long been recognised by practitioners, and regarded as traditional in social work and all the helping professions (Reamer, 1993, p.191).

The empiricist concept of science in the social sciences has been widely challenged, yet it has retained its influence in health and welfare, partly as a result of the strength of medical and psychological models. For instance, the advice of a very recent textbook on assessment in counselling explicitly appeals to the model of psychiatry as 'a very young science', which psychotherapy and counselling have only followed 'in more recent years', and similarly 'begun to be subjected to scrutiny' (Ruddell, 1997, p.11). This approach recommends diagnosis and biopsychosocial assessment as two parts of a scientific approach to assessment in counselling. The first links signs and symptoms to standard classifications, as in psychiatry, and the second focuses on the individual as a particular system with unique characteristics, drawing on conventional systems theory.

Chapter 7 discussed some of the issues that relate to psychology and social assessment, and the first conclusion is to regard this approach as insufficiently informed by social theory to justify it as a basis for a social assessment. Secondly, a consideration of the extent to which the interpersonal and the social necessarily intrude upon individual psychology suggests that the approach is also questionable even for counselling and psychological assessment, which needs to be contextualised by social assessment.

As a practical task, social assessment can be seen in problem-solving terms. There is currently a trend towards seeing assessment as a straightforward administrative task, especially in the community care field, where the influence of management science is strong. There is certainly a valid concern here for rationalising and limiting assessment interventions, so that they are accountable financially, and have a clearly defined function in relation to the organisation. They also need to be accountable to the user, and user groups, whose interests may also be in having a methodical way of expressing demands for services, explicitly related to agreed objectives, and without hidden agendas or intrusive surveillance. Such common aims may be particularly appropriate for a significant range of assessments done across various fields of health and welfare, where relatively uncomplicated or 'simple' forms of assessment need to be carried out. Even where more complex assessment is needed, these considerations need to be kept in view.

However, where simple kinds of assessment are apparently required, there still needs to be a review, and supervision of workers, of pro formas and assessment forms, using CA/B principles as a check on the methods and values being used. In Chapter 12, the danger of individualised needs-led assessment has been shown to be its openness to bureaucratic manipulation. There needs to be careful evaluation of the extent to which management and global market pressures tend to reduce assessment to the rigid application of formulae which are not sensitive to the complexities or range of needs, but are sensitive to cost considerations (Dominelli, 1996a), and where further skilled and complex assessment is in fact needed. This may require consideration, both at personal and professional levels, between worker, user and supervisor, and also at organisational and/or political levels, where guidelines and constraints are drawn which preclude adequate assessment being done. The drive towards training based on competencies, (CCETSW, 1989) has been criticised for its reduction of human services, including assessment, to measurable, management-defined tasks, and its failure to understand the importance of professional judgement drawing on theory and values (Jordan, 1991; Dominelli, 1996b). Obviously, in both assessment of service users and in training assessors, much depends on who defines the competencies, and exactly how they are judged.

A more practical approach, drawing on art rather than management science, regards social assessment as a skill or craft which relies on the personal qualities of the assessor, together with the traditions of good assessment developed within the profession. The history of social work is full of examples of this approach, from Mary Richmond at the beginning of the century (Reamer, 1993, pp.155–6) to the most recent times (Fook, Ryan and Hawkins, 1997). The acceptability of this approach has ironically also been gaining ground at the same time as the more instrumental problem-solving approach, partly as a result of the widely quoted works of Schon, who regards 'reflection in action' in a wide range of professions as 'central to the "art" by which practitioners sometimes deal well with situations of uncertainty, instability, uniqueness and value conflict' (Schon, 1983, p.50). A recent social work paper similarly regards the quality of assessment 'as dependent on the skill and thoroughness of the assessor', and regrets the development of the 'dangerous belief that the quality of assessment owes more to the quality of the assessment tools in use, or worse still, to the quantity of data collected' (Middleton, 1997, p.8).

There are thus good reasons for believing that this perspective is important, and I have tried to present CA/B theory as supporting and developing from skilful practice. CA/B has an inbuilt commitment to the significant role of professional ethical and social judgement, and an awareness of the craft of narrative construction in writing critical auto/biographies, and presentation to audiences (Polkinghorne, 1995). The CA/B method supports that element of professional judgement, but in a way that recognises the rights and roles of users, carers and related social groups whose interests and values are relevant to, and affected by professional interventions.

The art of the assessor is an important element in social assessment because of the reflexive and meaningful nature of the content and process, which inevitably implicates the assessor in a relationship with obligations for action. However, it is not necessary to oppose science and administration on the one hand with art, values and craft on the other. It has been argued above that an adequate theoretical basis for assessment is also necessary to guide and support assessors in understanding the nature of a social assessment. The focus has been upon a sociological approach which draws upon cognate social science fields, especially in psychology and history. This requires a grasp of contemporary social concepts and research methods relevant to the process of social assessment, and CA/B theory attempts to draw them together in as coherent a way as possible.

The result is an approach to assessment which is *both* 'scientific' and 'artistic', compatible with the view that social work as a whole 'is both an art and a science' (Dominelli, 1997, p.68), and that a critical, sociologically based theory provides an appropriately flexible but distinct framework.

There has been much debate over the way sociology as a discipline relates to the helping professions generally, and to social work in particular, and the position advocated here is by no means universal. It depends partly on how both sociology and social work are conceptualised. Some have argued that the radical enterprise of seeing the helping professions as informed by applied sociology (amongst other applied social sciences) is a 'misguided conceit' (Davies, 1991b, p.7), and that social workers have used structural sociological concepts inappropriately (Sibeon, 1990 and 1991). This contention implicitly supports a more instrumental and modest approach to social assessment. However, it does not take into account the practical needs of professionals in the circumstances described by Schon (see above), and is criticised by others, who point to the variety of sociological and psychological explanations that need to be considered: 'Social workers ... need to be open to a range of [sociological] explanations and theories among which the contribution of the more critical theories should play an important part' (Corby, 1995, p.103). It clearly remains a discipline of central importance to feminists and anti-racists (Dominelli, 1997), and to anyone concerned with the issues of power and ethics in the process of assessment.

Any position adopted has ethical and political implications, and the way that CA/B concepts have been marshalled in this book has tried to be explicit about its relationship to the values and perspectives relevant to user and oppressed groups. However, it is a complex issue that has not been fully discussed here, but some indication of the rationale has been given throughout the first part of the book.

The CA/B approach draws on social theory and social research methodology as a framework for social assessment practice. It does not prescribe all the details of practice, and the application of sociology is necessarily oblique and complex, given the integration of conflicting values and theory in both sociology and social assessment. The attempt to combine the reflexive positioning of the assessor within a theoretical framework that also includes 'reference' to 'realities' could require another book. The intention is to allow for both the possibility of 'empirical' research into serious issues of (for example) elder abuse or mental distress, *and* for a way of understanding the different perspectives involved, so that user and oppressed values are critically grasped rather than brushed over by dominant academic and/or professional perspectives.

It is openly accepted within this framework that values and uncertainty are unavoidable, yet precisely for that reason, they have to be dealt with as intelligently as possible. Debate should be reduced neither to ordinary empirical verification or disconfirmation, nor to a concept of reflexive social positioning which focuses solely on narrative interpretation, but this is a difficult and debated balance (Hammersley, 1993 and 1995; Humphries, 1997 and 1998; see also Chapter 1). Social assessment needs *both* if it is to succeed in making reasonable judgements about events and trends that have caused (or may cause) serious harm to vulnerable people, and to be able to develop any dialogue between the disparate perspectives that persist between professionals, and between professionals and service users.

Critical auto/biography: A framework for social assessment practice

Reflection in action requires the kind of knowledge of general principles that has been proposed here: 'really useful learning yields a comprehension of a few general principles with thorough grounding in the way they apply' (Whitehead, 1929, p.41).

Each of the CA/B principles in Part One involves a debate about social concepts which are themselves drawn from the perspectives of oppressed groups, as well as connecting with the experience of practitioners, and the debates of social theorists and researchers. But to carry credence for practitioners, 'the practice relevance of theories must be made explicit' (Dominelli, 1997, p.83). Detailed guidance for the application of the methodology to practice can be found throughout Part Two, and also in the summaries at the ends of most chapters in Part One.

The following paragraphs summarise the general practical implications of the CA/B framework for the different levels of assessment.

Although in reality assessments are rarely systematic or comprehensive, the full complement of basic CA/B principles has to be understood as underpinning each and every assessment, however brief or long. *In principle*, each concept has to be applied to each assessment, but they also have to be taken together as a whole, since they are inter-related parts of CA/B theory. The importance of systematically using the principles and categories both together *and* separately cannot be overemphasised. User groups identified by agencies particularly need to be assessed with this in mind. For example, in the case study, the grandmother, Freda, is discussed from the perspective of the mental health services in Chapter 9, and then again as an older woman in Chapter 10. Given the interconnected principles of the CA/B framework, any assessment of her should consider *all* the angles differentially, including her role as a carer of children, her membership of other social divisions and so on.

The continual practical task is to work out strategies for application of the principles, and to develop techniques and methods which are consistent with them. For practitioners to be able to make the best use of this theoretical framework to improve their assessments, the following levels or stages are essential.

Stage 1

In the case of all assessments, the initial task is to negotiate with users and carers the nature of the intervention in their lives that is proposed, as far as this is possible. There is nothing new about this: it is already a part of good practice in assessment. However, CA/B theory underscores its importance and assists the process by providing a checklist of concepts for evaluating practical, ethical and theoretical issues. The question of whether there needs to be an assessment at all, and if so, what kind and level of assessment, should be debated at this stage, and reviewed as the assessment proceeds.

Stage 2

In the case of simple or brief assessments, including the application of eligibility criteria, there may not be time or reason even for conscious consideration of basic principles, but they should be internalised in good practice. There also will need to be conscious, periodic reviews and monitoring of practice in supervision, reviews of pro formas, rating schedules and other written material, and reviews of organisational policy and practice relating to assessment. All these reviews should use the basic principles as guides for scrutinising and reassessing current practice, policy, publicity and procedures.

These reviews should be a required part of the organisational process, and they should contribute to the development of policy and practice across the organisation.

Stage 3

In the case of more complex assessments, each of the basic principles needs to be addressed, though it is inevitable that it will not be possible to answer all the questions relating to each principle. However, the absence of information *or* the deliberately negotiated decision not to proceed further (because of issues of intrusiveness or user resistance or other ethical and political issues raised in the course of initial negotiation) needs to be recorded and explained. In addition, the principles should be used to actively interrogate specific techniques and methods, pro formas and rating scales that are used as part of a complex assessment, as well as the organisational policies and processes that impinge on complex assessment.

It is common to use an eclectic variety of methods to assess a complex situation, drawing selectively on a range of potentially relevant theory (Milner and O'Byrne, 1998, p.50): these should be coherently and critically drawn together in relation to the basic social assessment principles. The worker should thus ensure that all their own methods and techniques are triangulated together in terms of the CA/B principles.

In particular (provided that there is informed consent – as far as possible), there should *normally* be (amongst other methods) a social (critical auto/biographical) history which draws on:

1 the autobiographical accounts of users and carers, as told in oral history interviews (these may need to be taken separately, but family interviews may also be part of the process);
2 the biography of users and carers, as understood by the assessor, drawing on the autobiographical accounts, but also other oral and documentary evidence;
3 the autobiography of the assessor, drawing on their understanding of their own personal social background, and how it impinges on this situation, but also drawing on an analysis of the process of the assessment through time, and their own involvement and changing understanding of it;
4 assessment of the process of assessment over time.

Given the auto/biographical nature of the assessment, there is always an interventive element in the assessment process. In a more complex assessment, this aspect *may* become a particular and planned focus, with evaluation of the impact of the assessment process over time on the functioning of people and groups (e.g. parents – see Chapter 9). Such a critical auto/biographical process is central to understanding and assessing social situations, and should be discussed with a supervisor. Assessments over longer periods of time may also benefit from the use of a journal to record changing assessor perceptions, which can later be reviewed and analysed.

Stage 4

If a 'comprehensive' assessment is to be made, *in addition* to the requirements for a complex assessment, there must be reference to three criteria of comprehensiveness:

1 It will be comprehensive, firstly because it has explicitly covered all the requirements of an adequate social assessment methodology – all the basic CA/B principles have been thoroughly considered, and a full CA/B history has been constructed. It will include consideration of the interests of the users and the agency in the full range of risks, needs and strengths.
2 It will have integrated all the available information from all the other

relevant professional sources. It is assumed that a comprehensive *social* assessment that does not include active multi-professional involvement will nevertheless require access to information from other professions, and that the comprehensive social assessment must take account of the range of professions involved in social situations, including doctors, teachers, nurses the police, and so on. This should give the social assessment information on medical, psychological, educational, criminal and other histories which can be integrated into the construction of social histories.

3   It will be thus based on a detailed knowledge of current and past circumstances, drawing on multiple observations, life history interviews, documentary evidence and the varied perspectives of users, carers and colleagues. This detail should be made evident by means of estimates of the number and kind of visits and contacts made since referral, and by reference to recording, minutes or previous summaries or reports.

4   It will have met any other specific requirements of a 'comprehensive assessment' which are required in a particular setting, where assessment needs to be set out in a certain way and cover particular points of relevance. These requirements are logically secondary, and must be consistent with the basic principles. They will inevitably include some degree of focus that is pertinent to the objectives of the assessment and functions of the agencies involved, and should reference any organisational policy, legal or academic guidelines that are relevant.

Stage 5

In multi-professional assessments, *in addition* to the above, the principles should be used to assess how compatible the concepts of contributing professionals are with CA/B social assessment and to help negotiate theoretical issues with them (see Chapter 7). If colleagues in other professions are attempting to contextualise their disciplinary concepts within a critical social framework, then a triangulation of interpretation and evidence may be possible, with special emphasis on shared data concerning health and psychological development and a shared CA/B social history. Otherwise (and/or in addition), bridging practices need to be utilised which make clear that different professionals are using different starting points or perspectives (see Chapter 7).

A social assessment should be defended as a separately based discipline, with its own methodology, but with overlaps and links to other disciplines and professions. However, a CA/B social history should be utilised not only as a basis for making a social assessment but also (simultaneously) as a means of critically contextualising other professional assessments. Furthermore, the social assessment has to include the process of assessment itself, including the liason and teamwork which exists between the professions involved (e.g. the police, health workers, psychologists and teachers), and their relationships with users – and obviously, any planned interventive assessment, and the interactions that are thus engendered. This will also take account of the local history of relationships between the different groups, as well as the roles of individual personalities and their impact on the process.

The general implications for practice of CA/B principles need to be continually and critically reconsidered in the process of application. In particular, they should not be applied in a stereotypical or casual way, but with an awareness of their internal complexity. Ideally, they should be used with some awareness of the continuing debates about their meaning amongst oppressed social and user groups and in the social sciences, and of the developing social research methods and concepts relevant to social assessment (although I recognise that practitioners will normally not be in a position to keep up with theoretical developments).

Practitioners and academics thus need to work together with social and user groups to develop these concepts and the theoretical framework as a whole. Practitioners have much to offer in terms of reflection upon their experience and the experience of others with whom they come into contact. They are increasingly being asked to engage in 'critical evaluation and development of their own professional practice' (Slater, 1996, p.206). It is also progressively being recognised that users and carers need to be drawn into discussions about how assessment is carried out. It is important that the perspectives of both users, carers and practitioners be actively sought to critically evaluate assessment processes, with special reference to the implications for the concepts and theory, as well as the process itself and any specific methods used. They may well see oppressive assumptions and/or behaviours which will not have occurred to practitioners or academics.

Using critical auto/biography as a basis for supporting social assessments does not guarantee that assessments will necessarily be more ethical or succeed in challenging the social oppressions that daily grind service users' lives. What it does is to ensure that a social dimension which takes users' perspectives seriously is central to the process of assessment. For example, from the start of the disability movement's interest in the social model of disability, the aim of one disabled writer was precisely to ensure that 'social model assessments' were done by social workers – not by doctors (Oliver, 1983, pp.58–9).

The CA/B framework builds on these social concepts (see Chapter 12), and thus provides a strong basis for a skilful social practitioner to present the case for understanding vulnerable users and carers in terms which take full account of the circumstances which constrain and condition their lives. But it does this with a clear awareness of the complexity and productive relativity of power. It also means that there is a consistent basis for working together with both users and professional colleagues. Users can be confident that the worker has some understanding of the power issues in their relationship, their right to a stake in the process, as well as being committed to listening to their life stories, and interpreting them in the light of social realities of discrimination and oppression.

Other professionals can appreciate that there is a coherent body of concepts at the core of social assessment. This means that their co-professionals can consistently articulate the social concepts in specific cases, offering a challenging perspective which can incorporate both users and carers' views. It will give social workers and others who make social assessments the confidence to assert their autonomy, as providers of a distinctive theoretical perspective that does actually reflect what they are trying to do, whilst confronting them with their own interests and involvement in processes which are always flawed and potentially dangerous to the very users whose interests they (sometimes) 'serve'.

Afterword

In self-review of the writing of this book, I am conscious of its many assertions, the limited justification and evidence that has been offered, and the relatively narrow experience upon which it is based: this must necessarily be the case, given authorship by a single person.

The disadvantage of single authorship in this respect should be compensated for to some degree by the coherence of the position advocated. The intention from the beginning has been to make clear statements of position, and to propose arguments which could make a difference to the way social assessment is done and the status in which it is held, whilst recognising what has been valuable in the past. If the book therefore appears more contentious and less tentative than it properly should, the aim is that this will help to focus discussion and move some of the issues forward. If it achieves this to any degree, it will have served both a theoretical and a practical end.

The process of research upon which the book is based has been a mixture of involvement in teaching, research and practice, some of the details of which are indicated in the 'Autobiographical notes and acknowledgements'. The book therefore does not draw upon one specific piece of research, but on different involvements in empirical and theoretical research, as well as the practical experience of teaching and discussion with students and staff on the Diploma in Social Work course (including practice teachers in the field), and the earlier involvements in social work practice. This is in some ways a messy background for this text, but given the need to encompass both theory and practice, it is the only possible one. The ideas have thus been tested out in various ways, and reflect developing concepts for which no single person could possibly take credit. I hope this has been sufficiently acknowledged in the Preface and in the 'Autobiographical notes and acknowledgements', and that the book draws together as constructively as possible current ideas about social research and assessment which reflect the impressive work of many of those referenced, especially authors whose life experience and understanding exceed my own.

The book has not been written primarily for or from the perspective of users: this would have needed a totally different approach, and one for which I am not well positioned. It should be clear that taking user and oppressed groups' views into account is central to the book, but is approached through the lens of the professional tasks of doing a social assessment and undertaking research. This is a task to which I can easily relate, having had to do it many times.

My contention is that the difficulties of taking user and oppressed views into account are paralleled in doing both assessment and research. It will always be subject to dispute and uncertainty, but it is well worth the effort to try to optimise methods of assessment and intervention in social life which make this a key objective. It has both theoretical and practical advantages, which should include more sensitive and inclusive conceptual tools, and less oppressive methods and processes in social assessment.

References

Abberley, P. (1987) 'The concept of oppression and the development of a social theory of disability', *Disability, Handicap and Society*, Vol. 2, No. 1.

Abbott, P. and Wallace, C. (1979) *An Introduction to Sociology: Feminist Perspectives* (2nd edn), London: Routledge.

Adams, R. (1990) *Self-help, Social Work and Empowerment*, London: Macmillan.

Adams, R. (1996) *Social Work and Empowerment*, London: Macmillan.

Adcock, M. with Lake, R. and Small, A. (1988) 'Assessing children's needs', in Aldgate, J. and Simmonds, J. (eds) *Direct Work With Children*, London: Batsford.

Ahmad, B. (1990) *Black Perspectives in Social Work*, London: Venture Press.

Ahmad-Aziz, A. et al. (1992) *Improving Practice with Elders: A Training Manual*, Northern Curriculum Development Project 3, Leeds: Central Council for Education and Training in Social Work.

Ahmed, S. (1997) '"It's a suntan isn't it?": Auto-biography as an identificatory practice', in Mirza, H.S. (ed.) *Black British Feminism*, London: Routledge.

Alaszewski, A. and Manthorpe, J. (1991) 'Literature review: Measuring and managing risk in social welfare', *British Journal of Social Work*, Vol. 21, No. 3, June.

Aldgate, J. and Tunstill, J. (1995) *Making Sense of Section 17*, London: HMSO.

Allat, P. et al. (1987) *Women and the Life Cycle*, London: Macmillan.

Allen, A. (1996) 'Foucault on power: A theory for feminists', in Hekman, S. (ed.) *Feminist Interpretations of Foucault*, University Park, PA: Pennsylvania State University Press.

Althusser, L. (1969) *For Marx*, London: Allen Lane.

Althusser, L. (1971) *Lenin and Philosophy and Other Essays*, London: New Left Books.

Amos, V., Lewis, G., Mama, A. and Parmar, P. (1984) 'Many voices, one chant: Black feminist perspectives', *Feminist Review*, No. 17.

Anderson, J.E. and Brown, R.A. (1980) 'Notes for practice: Life history grid for adolescents', *Social Work*, July.

Anderson, K. and Jack, D.C. (1991) 'Learning to listen: Interview techniques and analyses', in Gluck, S.B. and Patai, D. (eds) *Women's Words: The Feminist Practice of Oral History*, London: Routledge.

Ang-Lygate, M. (1997) 'Charting the spaces of (un)location: On theorizing diaspora', in Mirza, H.S. (ed.) *Black British Feminism*, London: Routledge.

Anthias, F. and Yuval-Davis, N. (1990) 'Contextualising feminism – gender, ethnic and class divisions', in Lovell, T. (ed.) *British Feminist Thought*, London: Blackwell.

Anthias, F. and Yuval-Davis, N. (1992) *Racialised Boundaries: Race, Nation, Gender, Colour and Class and the Anti-racist Struggle*, London: Routledge.

Apter, T. and Garnsey, E. (1994) 'Enacting inequality: structure, agency and gender', *Women's Studies International Forum*, Vol. 17, No. 1.

Arber, S. and Evandrou, M. (eds) (1992) *Ageing, Independence and the Life Course*, London: Jessica Kingsley.

Arber, S. and Ginn, J. (eds) (1995) *Connecting Gender and Ageing*, Milton Keynes: Open University Press.

Archard, D. (1993) *Children: Rights and Childhood*, London: Routledge.

Archer, L. (1990) 'Research and practice as related activities', in Whitaker, D.S., Archer, L. and Greve, S. (eds) *Research Practice and Service Delivery: The Contribution of Research by Practitioners*, London: CCETSW / University of York.

Aries, P. (1962) *Centuries of Childhood*, Harmondsworth: Penguin.

Atkinson, D. (1997) *An Auto/biographical Approach to Learning Disability*, Aldershot: Ashgate.

Baistow, K. (1994/5) 'Liberation and regulation? Some paradoxes of empowerment', *Critical Social Policy*, No. 42.

Banks, S. (1995) *Ethics and Values in Social Work*, London: Macmillan.

Barker, R. and Roberts, H. (1993) 'The uses of the concept of power', in Morgan, D. and Stanley, L. (eds) *Debates in Sociology*, Manchester University Press.

Barkham, M. (1989) 'Exploratory therapy in two-plus one sessions. IL: Rationale for a brief psychotherapy model', *British Journal of Psychotherapy*, No. 6, pp.81–8.

Barmby, P.J. (1991) 'In the beginning: Initial investigations of non-accidental injury', *Practice*, Vol. 5, No. 4.

Barnes, B. (1993) 'Power', in Bellamy, R. (ed.) *Theories and Concepts of Politics*, London: Routledge.

Barnes, C. (1996) 'Disability and the myth of the independent researcher', *Disability and Society*, Vol. 11, No. 1.

Barret, M. (1989) 'Some different meanings of the concept of "difference"', in Meeses, E. and Parker, A. (eds) *The Difference Within: Feminism and Critical Theory*, Amsterdam: John Benjamin.

Baumhover, L.A. and Beal, S.C. (eds) (1996) *Abuse, Neglect and Exploitation of Older Persons: Strategies for Assessment and Intervention*, London: Jessica Kingsley.

Beattie, K. (1997) 'Risk, domestic violence and probation practice', in Kemshall, H. and Pritchard, J. (eds) *Good Practice in Risk Assessment and Risk Management*, Vol. 2, London: Jessica Kingsley.

Beck, U. (1992) *Risk Society: Towards a New Modernity*, London: Sage.

Benjamin, J. (1990) *The Bonds of Love: Psychoanalysis, Feminism, and the Problem of Domination*, London: Virago.

Benton, T. (1981) '"Objective interests" and the sociology of power', *Sociology*, No. 15, pp.161–84.

Bertaux, D. (ed.) (1981) *Biography and Society: The Life History Approach in the Social Sciences*, London: Sage.

Bertaux, D. (1982) 'The life course approach as a challenge to the social sciences', in Harevan, T.K. and Adams, K.J. (eds) *Ageing and Life Course Transitions: An Interdisciplinary Perspective*, New York: Tavistock.

Beste, H.M. and Richardson, R.G. (1981) 'Developing a life story program for foster children', *Child Welfare*, Vol. 60, No. 8, September/October.

Bhaskar, R. (1986) *Scientific Realism and Human Emancipation*, London: Verso.

Bhavnani, K. (1986) 'Race, women and class: Integrating theory and practice', *Critical Social Policy*, April.

Bhavnani, K. (1990) '"What's power got to do with it?": Empowerment and social research', in Parker, I. and Shotter, J. (eds) *Deconstructing Social Psychology*, London: Routledge.

Bhavnani, K. (1993) 'Tracing the contours: Feminist research and feminist objectivity', *Women's Studies International Forum*, Vol. 16, No. 2.

Biggs, S. et al. (1995) *Elder Abuse in Perspective*, Milton Keynes: Open University Press.

Birren, J. et al. (eds) (1995) *Ageing and Biography*, Milton Keynes: Open University Press.

Blakemore, K. and Boneham, M. (1995) *Age, Race and Ethnicity*, Milton Keynes: Open University Press.

Blom-Cooper, L., Hally, H. and Murphy, E. (1995) *The Falling Shadow: One Patient's Mental Health Care 1978–1993*, London: Duckworth.

Booth, T. and Booth, W. (1996) 'Sounds of silence: Narrative research with inarticulate subjects', *Disability and Society*, Vol. 11, No. 1.

Borland, K. (1991) '"That's not what I said": Interpretative conflict in oral narrative research', in Gluck, S.B. and Patai, D. (eds) *Women's Words: The Feminist Practice of Oral History*, London: Routledge.

Bornat, J. (1989) 'Oral history as a social movement: Reminiscence and older people', *Oral History*, Vol. 17, No. 2, pp.16–24.

Bornat, J. (ed.) (1994) *Reminiscence Reviewed: Perspective, Evaluations, Achievements*, Milton Keynes: Open University Press.

Boulton, J. Gully, V., Matthews, L. and Gearing B. (1989) 'Developing the biographical approach in practice with older people', project paper No. 7, Gloucester Care of Elderly People at Home Project, Open University.

Boushel, M. (1994) 'The protective environment of children: Towards a framework for anti-oppressive, cross-cultural and cross-national understanding', *British Journal of Social Work*, Vol. 24, No. 2.

Boushel, M. (1995) 'Keeping safe: Strengthening the protective environment of children in foster care', *Adoption and Fostering*, Vol. 18, No. 1.

Bowlby, J. (1978) *Attachment and Loss, Vol II: Separation – Anxiety and Anger*, London: Penguin.

Bowlby, J. (1991) 'Postscript', in Parkes, M., Stevenson-Hinde, J. and Marris, P. (eds) *Attachment Across the Life Cycle*, London: Routledge.

Bradley, G. and Manthorpe, J. (1997) *Dilemmas of Financial Assessment*, Birmingham: Venture Press.

Bradley, H. (1996) *Fractured Identities: Changing Patterns of Inequality*, Cambridge: Polity Press.

Bradshaw, J. (1994) 'The conceptualisation and measurement of need: A social policy perspective', in Popay, J. and Williams, G. (eds) *Researching People's Health*, London: Routledge.

Braye, S. and Preston-Shoot, M. (1992) *Practising Social Work Law*, London: Macmillan.

Braye, S. and Preston-Shoot, M. (1995) *Empowering Practice in Social Care*, Milton Keynes: Open University Press.

Brearley, C.P. (1979) 'Gambling with their lives? Calculating the odds?', *Community Care*, No. 290, pp.24–5.

Brearley, C.P. (1982) *Risk and Social Work*, London: Routledge.

Bretherton, I. (1991) 'The roots and growing points of attachment theory', in Parkes, M., Stevenson-Hinde, J. and Marris, P. (eds) *Attachment Across the Life Cycle*, London: Routledge.

Broad, B. (1994) 'Social work and research processes', in Humphries, B. and Truman, C. (eds) *Rethinking Social Research*, Aldershot: Avebury.

Brodzki, B. and Schenck, C. (eds) (1988) *Life/Lines: Theorising Women's Autobiography*, Ithaca, NY: Cornell University Press.

Brown, H.C. (1992) 'Gender, sex, and sexuality in the assessment of prospective carers', *Fostering and Adoption*, Vol. 16, No. 2.

Browne, K. (1995) 'Predicting maltreatment', in Reder, P. and Lucey, C. (eds) *Assessment of Parenting: Psychiatric and Psychological Contributions*, London: Routledge.

Browne, K.D. and Hollin, C.R. (1995) 'Life span development', in Hollin, C.

(ed.) *Contemporary Psychology: An Introduction*, London: Taylor and Francis.

Browne, M. (1996) 'Needs assessment in community care', in Percy-Smith, J. (ed.) *Needs Assessments in Public Policy*, Milton Keynes: Open University Press.

Brummer, N. (1988) 'White social workers/black children: Issues of identity', in Aldgate, J. and Simmons J. (eds) *Direct Work With Children*, London: Batsford.

Bryan, B., Dadzie, S. and Scarfe, S. (1985) *The Heart of the Race: Black Women's Lives in Britain*, London: Virago.

Buchanan, K. and Middleton, D. (1994) 'Reminiscence reviewed: A discourse analytic perspective', in Bornat, J. (ed.) *Reminiscence Reviewed: Perspective, Evaluations, Achievements*, Milton Keynes: Open University Press.

Buck, M. (1997) 'Mental health and gender', *Critical Social Policy*, Vol. 17, No. 1.

Burgoyne, J. (1987) 'Change, gender, and the life course', in Cohen, G. (ed.) *Social Change and the Life Course*, London: Tavistock.

Burke, B. with Clifford, D., Cox, P. and Hardwick, L. (1995) 'The theory and practice of risk assessment', Conference Paper, ESRC Risk and Human Behaviour Programme at the University of York, London, 16 and 17 May.

Burman, E. (1990a) *Feminists and Psychological Practice*, London: Sage.

Burman, E. (1990b) 'Differing with deconstruction: A feminist critique', in Parker, I. and Shotter, J. (eds) *Deconstructing Social Psychology*, London: Routledge.

Burman, E. (1997) 'Developmental psychology and its discontents', in Fox, D. and Prilleltensky, I. (eds) *Critical Psychology: An Introduction*, London: Sage.

Burman, E. et al. (1995) *Challenging Women: Psychology's Exclusions, Feminist Possibilities*, Milton Keynes: Open University Press.

Bury, M. (1995), 'Ageing, gender and sociological theory', in Arber, S. and Ginn, J. (eds) *Connecting Gender and Aging*, Milton Keynes: Open University Press.

Bury, M. (1996) 'Disability and the myth of the independent researcher: A reply', *Disability and Society*, Vol. 11, No. 1.

Bury, M. and Holme, A. (1991) *Life After Ninety*, London: Routledge.

Butler, I. and Shaw, I. (1996) *A Case of Neglect? Children's Experience and the Sociology of Childhood*, Aldershot: Avebury.

Butler, R. (1963) 'The life review: An interpretation of reminiscence in the aged', *Psychiatry*, No. 26.

Byrne, S. (1997) 'Risk in adoption and fostering', in Kemshall, H. and Pritchard, J. (eds) *Good Practice in Risk Assessment and Risk Management, Vol. 2: Protection, Rights and Responsibilities*, London: Jessica Kingsley.

Bytheway, B. (1989) 'Beginning with life histories', in Unrah, D. and Livings

G. (eds) *Current Perspectives on Ageing and the Life Cycle*, Vol. 3, New Haven, CT: JAI Press.

Bytheway, B. (1990) 'Age', in Peace, S. (ed.) *Researching Social Gerontology*, London: Sage.

Bytheway, B. (1995) *Ageism*, Milton Keynes: Open University Press.

Cain, P. (1992) 'Objectivity and assessment', *Adoption and Fostering*, Vol. 15, No. 2.

Caine, B. (1994) 'Feminist biography and feminist history', *Women's History Review*, Vol. 3, No. 2.

Callinicos, A. (1989) *Against Postmodernism: A Marxist Critique*, Cambridge: Polity.

Campbell, J. and Oliver, M. (1996) *Disability Politics: Understanding Our Past, Changing Our Future*, London: Routledge.

Campbell, J.C. (ed.) (1995) *Assessing Dangerousness: Violence by Sexual Offenders, Batterers and Child Abusers*, London: Sage.

Campbell, R. (1995) 'Weaving a new tapestry of research: A bibliography of selected readings on feminist research', *Women's Studies International Forum*, Vol. 18, No. 2.

Cant, B. and Hemmings, S. (eds) (1988) *Radical Records: Thirty Years of Lesbian and Gay History*, London: Routledge.

Carby, H. (1982) 'White woman listen! Black feminism and the boundaries of sisterhood', in Centre for Contemporary Cultural Studies (eds) *The Empire Strikes Back: Race and Racism in 70's Britain*, London: Hutchinson.

Carmichael, S. and Hamilton, C. (1969) *Black Power*, Harmondsworth: Penguin.

Carson, D. (1994), 'Dangerous people: Through a broader conception of "risk" and "danger" to better decisions', *Expert Opinion*, Vol. 3, No. 2, pp.51–69.

Carson, D. (1996) 'Risking legal repercussions', in Kemshall, H. and Pritchard, J. (eds) *Good Practice in Risk Assessment and Risk Management*, London: Jessica Kingsley.

Casement, P. (1990) *On Learning from the Patient*, London: Routledge.

Caspi, H., Elder, G.H. and Herbener, E.S. (1990) 'Childhood personality and the prediction of the life-course pattern', in Robins, L.N. and Rutter, M. (eds) *Straight and Devious Pathways from Childhood*, Cambridge: Cambridge University Press.

Cassell, P. (ed.) (1993) *The Giddens Reader*, London: Macmillan.

Cavan, R.S. (1929) 'Interviewing for life history material', *American Journal of Sociology*, Vol. 35, No. 1.

CCETSW (1989) *Rules and Regulations for the Diploma in Social Work* (revised in 1995), London: CCETSW.

Charmaz, K. (1994) 'Grounded theory', in Smith, J.A., Harre, R. and Van Langenhove, L. (eds) *Rethinking Methods in Psychology*, London: Sage.

Clandinin, D.J. and Connelly, F.M. (1994) 'Personal experience methods', in Denzin, N.K. and Lincoln, Y.S. (eds) *Handbook of Qualitative Research*, London: Sage.

Clifford, D.J. (1982) 'Philosophy and social work: The legitimation of a professional ideology', *Radical Philosophy*, Summer.

Clifford, D.J. (1984) 'Concept formation in radical theories of need', *Critical Social Policy*, No. 11, Winter.

Clifford, D.J. (1992–93) 'Towards an anti-oppressive social work assessment method', *Practice*, Vol. 6, No. 3.

Clifford, D.J. (1994) 'Critical life histories: A key anti-oppressive research method', in Humphries, B. and Trueman, C. (eds) *Rethinking Social Research*, Aldershot: Avebury.

Clifford, D.J. (1995) 'Methods in oral history and social work', *Oral History*, Vol. 24, No. 2.

Clifford, D.J. and Cropper, A. (1994) 'Applying auto/biography: Researching the assessment of life experiences', *Auto/Biography*, Vol. 3, No. 2.

Clifford, D.J. and Cropper, A. (1997a) 'Individual assessment of potential carers: theory and practice', *Practice*, Vol. 9, No. 1.

Clifford, D.J. and Cropper, A. (1997b) 'Parallel processes in researching and assessing potential carers', *Child and Family Social Work*, Vol. 2, No. 1.

Cohen, G. (ed.) (1987) *Social Change and the Life Course*, London: Tavistock.

Cohler, B.J. (1982) 'Personal narrative and life course', in Baltes, P.B. and Brim, O.G. (eds) *Life-Span Development and Behavior*, Vol. 4, New York: Academic Press.

Coleman, P. (1986) *Aging and Reminiscence Processes: Social and Clinical Implications*, Chichester: John Wiley.

Coleman, P. (1991) 'Aging and life history: The meaning of reminiscence in late life', in Dex, S. (ed.) *Life and Work History Analyses*, London: Routledge.

Coleman, P. (1994) 'Reminiscence within the study of ageing', in Bornat, J. (ed.) *Reminiscence Reviewed: Perspectives, Evaluations, Achievements*, Milton Keynes: Open University Press.

Collins, P.H. (1990) *Black Feminism*, London: Unwin.

Colton, M., Drury, C. and Williams, M. (1995) 'Children in need: Definition, identification and support', *British Journal of Social Work*, No. 25, pp.711–28.

Conway, M.A. (1990) *Autobiographical Memory*, Buckingham: Open University Press.

Cooper, D. (1995) *Power in Struggle: Feminism, Sexuality and the State*, Milton Keynes: Open University Press.

Corby, B. (1989) 'Alternative theory bases in child abuse', in Rogers, W.S., Hevey, D. and Ash, E. (eds) *Child Abuse and Neglect: Facing the Challenge*, Milton Keynes: Open University Press.

Corby, B. (1991) 'Sociology, social work and child protection', in Davies, M. (ed.) *The Sociology of Social Work*, London: Routledge.

Corby, B. (1995) 'Risk assessment in child protection work', in Kemshall, H. and Pritchard, J. (eds) *Good Practice in Risk Assessment and Risk Management*, London: Jessica Kingsley.

Cornwell, J. and Gearing, B. (1989) 'Biographical interviews with older people', *Oral History*, Vol. 17, No. 1, pp.36–43.

Croft, S. (1986) 'Women, caring and the recasting of need', in *Critical Social Policy*, No. 16.

Curnock, K. and Hardiker, P. (1979) *Towards Practice Theory: Skills and Methods in Social Assessments*, London: Routledge.

Dahl, R.A. (1970) *Modern Political Analysis*, Englewood Cliffs, NJ: Prentice-Hall.

Dale, P., Davies, M., Morrison, T. and Waters, J. (1986) *Dangerous Families: Assessment and Treatment of Child Abuse*, London: Tavistock.

Dalrymple, J. and Burke, B. (1995) *Anti-oppressive Practice: Social Care and the Law*, Milton Keynes: Open University Press.

Davies, K. (1996) 'Capturing women's lives: A discussion of time and methodological issues', *Women's Studies International Forum*, Vol. 19, No. 6, pp.579–88.

Davies, M. (ed.) (1991a) *The Sociology of Social Work*, London: Routledge.

Davies, M. (1991b) 'Sociology and social work: A misunderstood relationship', in Davies, M. (ed.) *The Sociology of Social Work*, London: Routledge.

Davis, A. (1982) *Women, Race and Class*, London: Women's Press.

Davis, A. (1992) 'A structural approach to social work', in Lishman, J. (ed.) *Handbook of Theory for Practice Teachers in Social Work*, London: Jessica Kingsley.

Davis, A. (1996) 'Risk work and mental health', in Kemshall, H. and Pritchard, J. (eds) *Good Practice in Risk Assessment and Risk Management*, London: Jessica Kingsley.

Davis, A., Ellis, K. and Rummery, K. (1997) *Access to Assessment: Perspectives of Practitioners, Disabled People and Carers*, Bristol: Policy Press and Joseph Rowntree Foundation.

Davis, K., Leijanaar, M. and Oldersma, J. (1991) *The Gender of Power*, London: Sage.

Davis, M. and Kennedy, E. (1991) 'Oral history and the study of sexuality in the lesbian community', in Dubermann, M. et al., *Hidden from History*, London: Penguin.

Denzin, N.K. (1978) *Sociological Methods: A Sourcebook*, New York: McGraw-Hill.

Denzin, N.K. (1989) *Interpretative Biography*, London: Sage.

Denzin, N.K. (1992) 'Deconstructing the biographical method', paper presented at the 1992 American Educational Research Association, San Francisco.

Denzin, N.K. and Lincoln, Y.S. (eds) (1994) *Handbook of Qualitative Research*, London: Sage.

DHSS (1985) *Social Work Decisions in Child Care*, London: HMSO.

DHSS (1988) *Working Together: A Guide to Inter-agency Co-operation for the Protection of Children from Abuse*, London: HMSO.

Dingwall, R. (1989) 'Some problems about predicting child abuse and neglect', in Stevenson, O. (ed.) *Public Policy and Professional Practice*, Hemel Hempstead: Harvester Wheatsheaf.

DoH (1988) *Protecting Children: A Guide for Social Workers Undertaking a Comprehensive Assessment* ('The Orange Book'), London: HMSO.

DoH (1989a) *Doing it Better Together: Multi-disciplinary Assessment of the Needs of Elderly People*, London: Social Services Inspectorate.

DoH (1989b) *Caring for People*, Cmd 849, London: HMSO.

DoH (1990) *Care Programme Approach*, Health Circular (90)23/Local Authority Social Services Letter (90)11, London: HMSO.

DoH (1991) *Care Management and Assessment: Practitioner's Guide*, London: HMSO.

DoH (1993) *White Paper on Adoption*, London: HMSO.

DoH (1994) *Guidance on Discharge of Mentally Disordered People and Their Continuing Care in the Community: Health Service Guidelines*, Local Authority Social Services Letter LASSL (94)4, London: HMSO.

DoH, Dartington Social Research Unit (1995) *Child Protection and Child Abuse: Messages from Research*, London: HMSO.

Dominelli, L. (1996a) 'Globalization and the technocratization of social work', *Critical Social Policy*, Vol. 16, No. 2.

Dominelli, L. (1996b) 'Deprofessionalising social work: Anti-oppressive practice, competencies, and postmodernism', *British Journal of Social Work*, Vol. 26, No. 2.

Dominelli, L. (1997) *Sociology for Social Work*, London: Macmillan.

Douglas, M. (1986) *Risk Assessment According to the Social Sciences*, London: Routledge.

Douglas, M. (1992) *Risk and Blame: Essays in Cultural Theory*, London: Routledge.

Downie, R.S. (1977) *Roles and Values*, London: Methuen.

Downie, R.S. and Calman, K.C. (1987) *Healthy Respect: Ethics in Health Care*, London: Faber and Faber.

Downie, R.S. and Telfer, E. (1980) *Caring and Curing*, London: Methuen.

Doyal, L. (1993) 'Human need and the moral right to optimum community care', in Bornat, J. et al., *Community Care: A Reader*, London: Macmillan.

Doyal, L. and Gough, I. (1991) *A Theory of Human Need*, London: Macmillan.

Doyle, C. (1996) 'Current issues in child protection: An overview of the debates in contemporary journals', *British Journal of Social Work*, Vol. 26, No. 4.

Doyle, C. (1997) 'Protection studies: Challenging oppression and discrimination', *Social Work Education*, Vol. 16, No. 2.

Easton, D. (1953) *The Political System*, New York: Knopf.

Easton, D. (1965) *A Framework for Political Analysis*, Englewood Cliffs, NJ: Prentice-Hall.

Edgell, S. (1993) *Class*, London: Routledge.

Eisenberg, N.C. (1992) 'Child Sexual Abuse: Making Sense of the Abuse of Power and Control', unpublished PhD thesis, City of London Polytechnic.

Elder, G.H. (1974) *Children of the Great Depression*, Chicago, IL: University of Chicago Press.

Elder, G.H. (1978) 'Family history and the life course', in Harevan, T.K. (ed.) *Transitions: The Family and the Life Course in Historical Perspective*, New York: Academic Press.

Elder Jnr, G.H., Modell, J. and Park, R.D. (eds) (1995a) *Children in Time and Place: Developmental and Historical Insights*, Cambridge: Cambridge University Press.

Elder Jnr, G.H., Modell, J. and Park, R.D. (1995b) 'Epilogue: An emerging framework for dialogue between history and developmental psychology', in Elder Jnr, G.H., Modell, J. and Park, R.D. (eds) *Children in Time and Place: Developmental and Historical Insights*, Cambridge: Cambridge University Press.

Ellis, K. (1993) *Squaring the Circle: User and Carer Participation in Needs Assessment*, York: Joseph Rowntree Foundation.

Erikson, E. (1958) *Young Man Luther: A Study in Psychoanalysis and History*, New York: Norton.

Erikson, E. (1959) *Identity and the Life Cycle*, New York: International Universities Press.

Erikson, E. (1975) *Life History and the Historical Moment*, New York: Norton.

Erikson, E. (1977) *Childhood and Society*, St Albans: Triad/Paladin.

Erikson, E. et al. (1986) *Vital Involvement in Old Age: The Experience of Old Age in Our Time*, New York: Norton.

Etter-Lewis, G. (1991) 'Black women's stories: Reclaiming self in narrative texts', in Gluck, S.B. and Patai, D. (eds) *Women's Words: The Feminist Practice of Oral History*, London: Routledge.

Etter-Lewis, G. (1993) *My Soul is My Own: Oral Narratives of African Women in the Professions*, London: Routledge.

Etter-Lewis, G. and Foster, G. (1996) *Unrelated Kin: Race and Gender in Women's Personal Narratives*, London: Routledge.

Everitt, A. et al. (1992) *Applied Research for Better Practice*, London: Macmillan.

Fahlberg, V. (1981) *Helping Children When They Must Move*, London: British Association for Adoption and Fostering.

Fahlberg, V. (1982a) *Attachment and Separation*, London: British Association for Adoption and Fostering.

Fahlberg, V. (1982b) *Child Development*, London: British Association for Adoption and Fostering.

Fahlberg, V. (1988) *Fitting the Pieces Together*, London: British Association for Adoption and Fostering.

Fahlberg, V. (1994) *A Child's Journey Through Placement*, London: British Association for Adoption and Fostering.

Farmer, E. (1997) 'Protection and child welfare: Striking the balance', in Parton, N. (ed.) *Child Protection and Family Support*, London: Routledge.

Farmer, E. and Owen, M. (1995) *Child Protection Practice: Private Risks and Public Remedies*, London: HMSO.

Fawcett, B. (1996) 'Women, mental health and community care: An abusive combination?', in Fawcett, B., Featherstone, B., Hearn, J. and Toft, C. (eds) *Violence and Gender Relations*, London: Sage.

Fawcett, B., Featherstone, B., Hearn, J. and Toft, C. (eds) (1996) *Violence and Gender Relations*, London: Sage.

Featherstone, B. (1997) 'What has gender got to do with it? Exploring physically abusive behaviour towards children', *British Journal of Social Work*, Vol. 27, No. 3.

Featherstone, B. and Fawcett, B. (1995a) 'Feminism and child abuse: Opening up some possibilities', *Critical Social Policy*, No. 42.

Featherstone, B. and Fawcett, B. (1995b) 'Oh no! Not more isms: Feminism, postmodernism, poststructuralism and social work education', *Social Work Education*, Vol. 14, No. 3.

Featherstone, M. and Hepworth, M. (1990) 'Images of ageing', in Bond, J. and Coleman, P. (eds) *Ageing in Society: An Introduction to Social Gerontology*, London: Sage.

Featherstone, M. and Lancaster, E. (1997) 'Contemplating the unthinkable: Men who sexually abuse children', *Critical Social Policy*, Vol. 17, No. 4.

Fennell, G. et al. (1988) *The Sociology of Old Age*, Milton Keynes: Open University Press.

Ferard, M.L and Hunnybun, N.K. (1962) *The Caseworker's Use of Relationships*, London: Tavistock.

Fergueson, M. and Wicke, J. (eds) (1994) *Feminism and Postmodernism*, Durham and London: Duke University Press.

Fernando, S. (ed.) (1995) *Mental Health in a Multi-Ethnic Society*, London: Routledge.

Fido, R. and Potts, M. (1989) '"It's not true what was written down!" Experiences of life in a mental handicap institution', *Oral History*, Vol. 17, No. 2, pp.31–4.

Fielden, M. (1990) 'Reminiscence therapy and group work', *British Journal of Social Work*, Vol. 20, No. 1.

Fine, M. (1994) 'Working the hyphens: Reinventing self and other in qualitative research', in Denzin, N.K. and Lincoln, Y.S. (eds) *Handbook of Qualitative Research*, London: Sage.

Fook, J., Ryan, M. and Hawkins, L. (1997) 'Towards a theory of social work expertise', *British Journal of Social Work*, Vol. 27, No. 3.

Foucault, M. (1980) *Power/Knowledge*, Brighton: Harvester Wheatsheaf.

Fox, D. (1997) 'Psychology and law: Justice diverted', in Fox, D. and Prilleltensky, I. (eds) *Critical Psychology: An Introduction*, London: Sage.

Fox, D. and Prilleltensky, I. (eds) (1997) *Critical Psychology: An Introduction*, London: Sage.

Franklin, B. (ed.) (1986) *The Rights of Children*, Oxford: Blackwell.

Fraser, N. (1989) *Unruly Practices: Power, Discourse and Gender in Contemporary Social Theory*, London: Polity Press.

French, S. and Swain, J. (1997) 'Young disabled people', in Roche, J., and Tucker, S. (eds) *Youth in Society*, London: Sage.

Friere, P. (1972) *Pedagogy of the Oppressed*, London: Penguin.

Fuentes, C.R. (1997) 'Two stories, three lovers, and the creation of meaning in a black lesbian autobiography', in Mirza, H.S. (ed.) *Black British Feminism*, London: Routledge.

Furlong, A. and Cartmel, F. (1997) *Young People and Social Change: Individualisation and Risk in Late Modernity*, Milton Keynes: Open University Press.

Gallagher, B., Creighton, S. and Gibbons, J. (1995) 'Ethical dilemmas in social research: No easy solutions', *British Journal of Social Work*, No. 25, pp.295–311.

Gallie, W.B. (1964) *Philosophy and the Historical Understanding*, London: Chatto and Windus.

Galper, J. (1975) *The Politics of Social Service*, New York: Prentice Hall.

Galper, J. (1980) *Social Work Practice: A Radical Perspective*, New York: Prentice Hall.

Gay Men's Oral History Group (1989) *Walking After Midnight: Gay Men's Life Stories*, London: Routledge.

Gearing, B. and Coleman P. (1995) 'Biographical assessment in community care', in Birren, J. et al. (eds) *Ageing and Biography: Explorations in Adult Development*, New York: Springer.

Geertz, C. (1973) *The Interpretation of Cultures*, New York: Basic Books.

Germain, C. (1979) *Social Work Practice: An Ecological Perspective*, New York: Columbia University Press.

Germain, C. and Gitterman, A. (1980) *The Life Model of Social Work Practice*, New York: Columbia University Press.

Gesell, A. and Ilg, F. (1946) *The Child From Five to Ten*, New York: Harper and Row.

Gesell, A. et al. (1940) *The First Five Years of Life*, New York: Harper and Row.

Gibson, A. (1991) 'Erikson's life cycle approach to development', in Lishman,

J. (ed.) (1991) *Handbook of Theory for Practice Teachers in Social Work,* London: Jessica Kingsley.

Giddens, A. (1976) *New Rules of Sociological Method,* London: Hutchinson.

Giddens, A. (1982) *Profiles and Critiques in Social Theory,* London: Macmillan.

Giddens, A. (1984) *The Constitution of Society: Outline of a Theory of Structuration,* Cambridge: Polity Press.

Giddens, A. (1991) *Modernity and Self-identity: Self and Society in the Late Modern Age,* Cambridge: Polity Press.

Gilligan, C. (1982) *In a Different Voice,* Cambridge, MA: Harvard University Press.

Gilligan, C. (1987) 'Women's place in man's life-cycle', in Harding, S. (ed.) *Feminism and Methodology,* Milton Keynes: Open University Press.

Gilman, M., Swan, J. and Heyman, B. (1997) 'Life history or "case" history: The objectification of people with learning difficulties through the tyranny of professional discourses', *Disability Studies,* Vol. 12, No. 2.

Ginn, J. (1993) 'Grey power: Age-based organisations' response to structured inequalities', in *Critical Social Policy,* No. 38.

Gluck, S.B. and Patai, D. (1991) *Women's Words: The Feminist Practice of Oral History,* London: Routledge.

Goldner, V. (1991) 'Feminism and systemic practice: Two critical traditions in transition', *Journal of Family Therapy,* Vol. 13, pp.95–104.

Goldstein, H. (1973) *Social Work Practice: A Unitary Approach,* Columbia, SC: University of South Carolina Press.

Goodley, D. (1996) 'Tales of hidden lives: A critical examination of life history research with people who have learning difficulties', *Disability and Society,* Vol. 11, No. 3, pp.333–48.

Goodson, I. (1995 'The story so far: Personal knowledge and the political', in Hatch, J.A. and Wisniewski, R. (eds) *Life History and Narrative,* London: Falmer Press.

Gould, K.H. (1987) 'Life model versus conflict model: A feminist perspective', *Social Work,* Vol. 37, No. 4.

Gould, N. and Taylor, I. (1996) *Reflective Learning for Social Work,* Aldershot: Arena.

Greenland, C. (1987) *Preventing CAN Deaths: An International Study of Deaths Due to Child Abuse and Neglect,* London: Tavistock.

Griffiths, M. (1995) *Feminisms and the Self: The Web of Identity,* London: Routledge.

Guba, E.G. and Lincoln, Y.S. (1994) 'Competing paradigms in qualitative research', in Denzin, N.K and Lincoln, Y.S. (eds) *Handbook of Qualitative Research,* London: Sage.

Gubrium, J. (1994) *Constructing the Life Course,* Dix Hills, NY: General Hall Inc. Publications.

Gwaltney, L. (1980) *Drylongso,* New York: Random House.

Hallett, C. and Birchall, E. (1992) *Co-ordination and Child Protection*, Edinburgh: HMSO.

Halperin, D.M. (1995) *Saint Foucault: Towards a Gay Hagiography*, Oxford: Oxford University Press.

Hammersley, M. (1993) 'Research and anti-racism', *British Journal of Sociology*, Vol. 44, No. 3.

Hammersley, M. (1995) *The Politics of Social Research*, London: Sage.

Hammersley, M. (1997) 'A reply to Humphries', *Sociological Research Online*, Vol. 2, No. 4.

Hammersley, M. and Gomm, R. (1997a) 'Bias in social research', *Sociological Research Online*, Vol. 2, No. 1.

Hammersley, M. and Gomm, R. (1997b) 'A response to Romm', *Sociological Research Online*, Vol. 2, No. 4.

Hanson, B.G. (1995) *General Systems Theory: Beginning with Wholes*, London: Taylor and Francis.

Haraway, D. (1988) 'Situated knowledges: The science question in feminism and the privilege of partial perspective', *Feminist Studies*, Vol. 14, No. 3.

Hare-Mustin, R. and Maracek, J. (1997) 'Abnormal and clinical psychology', in Fox, D. and Prilleltensky, I. (eds) *Critical Psychology: An Introduction*, London: Sage.

Harevan, T.K. (1977) 'Family time and historical time', *Daedalus*, Spring, pp.57–70.

Harevan, T.K. (ed.) (1978) *Transitions: The Family and the Life Course in Historical Perspective*, New York: Academic Press.

Harris, B. (1997) 'Repoliticizing the history of psychology', in Fox, D. and Prilleltensky, I. (eds) *Critical Psychology: An Introduction*, London: Sage.

Harris, P. (1996) 'Who am I? Concepts of disability and their implications for people with learning difficulties', *Disability and Society*, Vol. 10, No. 1.

Harrison, B. and Lyon, E.S. (1993) 'A note on ethical issues in the use of auto/biography in sociological research', *Sociology*, Vol. 27, No. 1.

Hart, E. and Bond, M. (1995) *Action Research for Health and Social Care*, Milton Keynes: Open University Press.

Hartmann, A. (1979) *Finding Families: An Ecological Approach to Family Assessment in Adoption*, London: Sage.

Hartsock, N. (1990) 'Foucault on power: A theory for women?', in Nicholson, L.J. (ed.) *Feminism/Postmodernism*, London: Routledge.

Harvey, L. (1990) *Critical Social Research*, London: Unwin Hyman.

Hatch, J.A. and Wiesnewsky, R. (eds) (1995a) *Life History and Narrative*, London: Falmer Press.

Hatch, J.A. and Wiesnewsky, R. (1995b) 'Life history and narrative: Questions, issues and exemplary works', in Hatch, J.A. and Wiesnewsky, R. (eds) *Life History and Narrative*, London: Falmer Press.

Hay, C. (1995) 'Structure and agency', in Marsh, D. and Stoker, G. (eds) *Theory and Methods in Political Science*, London: Macmillan.

Hearn, B. (1997) 'Putting child and family support and protection into practice', in Parton, N. (ed.) *Child Protection and Family Support*, London: Routledge.

Hekman, S. (ed.) (1996) *Feminist Interpretations of Foucault*, University Park, PA: Pennsylvania State University Press.

Hewitt, M. (1993) 'Social movements and social need: Problems with postmodern political theory', *Critical Social Policy*, No. 37.

Hill, M. (1990) 'The manifest and latent lessons of child abuse inquiries', *British Journal of Social Work*, Vol. 20, No. 3.

Hoff, J. (1994a) 'Gender as a postmodern category of paralysis', *Women's Studies International Forum*, Vol. 17, No. 4.

Hoff, J. (1994b) 'Gender as a postmodern category of paralysis', *Women's History Review*, Vol. 3, No. 2.

Hoff, J. (1996) 'A reply to my critics', *Women's History Review*, Vol. 5, No. 1.

Holland, S. (1990) 'Psychotherapy, oppression and social action: Gender, race and class in black women's oppression', in Perelberg, R.J. and Miller, A.C. (eds) *Gender and Power in Families*, London: Routledge.

Hollis, F. (1964) *Casework: A Psychosocial Therapy*, New York: Random House.

Holloway, W. (1996) 'Gender and power in organisations', in Fawcett, B., Featherstone, B., Hearn, J. and Toft, C. (eds) *Violence and Gender Relations*, London: Sage.

Holmes, J. (1995) 'How I assess for psychoanalytic psychotherapy', in Mace, C. (ed.) *The Art and Science of Assessment in Psychotherapy*, London: Routledge.

hooks, b. (1982) *Ain't I a Woman?: Black Women and Feminism*, London: Pluto Press.

hooks, b. (1984) *Feminist Theory: From Margin to Center*, Boston, MA: South End Press.

hooks, b. (1991) *Yearning: Race, Gender and Cultural Politics*, London: Turnaround.

hooks, b. (1994) *Outlaw Culture: Resisting Representations*, London: Routledge.

Hopton, J. (1997) 'Anti-discriminatory practice and anti-oppressive practice: A radical humanist psychology perspective', *Critical Socal Policy*, Vol. 17, No. 3.

Hossack, A. and Jackson, H.F. (1991) 'Grounded reminiscence and recall therapy – a case history', *Counselling, The Journal of the British Association of Counselling*, Vol. 2, No. 1.

Howe, D. (1989) *An Introduction to Social Work Theory*, Aldershot: Wildwood House.

Howe, D. (1995) *Attachment Theory for Social Work Practice*, London: Macmillan.

Howell, D. and Ryman, M. (1987) 'New Zealand: New ways to choose adopters', *Adoption and Fostering*, Vol. 11, No. 4.

Hughes, B. (1993) 'A model for the comprehensive assessment of older people and their carers', *British Journal of Social Work*, Vol. 23, pp.345–64.

Hughes, B. (1995) *Older People and Community Care: Towards an Anti-discriminatory Approach*, Milton Keynes: Open University Press.

Hughes, B. and Mtezuka, E.M. (1992) 'Social work and older women', in Langan, M. and Day, L. (eds) *Women, Oppression and Social Work*, London: Routledge.

Hugman, R. and Smith, D. (eds) (1995) *Ethical Issues in Social Work*, London: Routledge.

Humphries, B. (1994) 'Empowerment and social research', in Humphries, B. and Truman, C. (eds) *Re-thinking Social Research*, Aldershot: Avebury.

Humphries, B. (ed.) (1996a) *Critical Perspectives on Empowerment*, Birmingham: Venture Press.

Humphries, B. (1996b) 'Contradictions in the culture of empowerment', in Humphries, B. (ed.) (1996) *Critical Perspectives on Empowerment*, Birmingham: Venture Press.

Humphries, B. (1997) 'From critical thought to emancipatory action: Contradictory research goals?' *Sociology Research Online*, Vol. 2, No. 1.

Ifekwunigwe, J. (1997) 'Diaspora's daughters, Africa's orphans?: On lineage, authenticity and "mixed race" identity', in Mirza, H.S. (ed.) *Black British Feminism*, London: Routledge.

Irigaray, L. (1981) 'This sex which is not one', in Marks, E. and De Courtivron, I. (eds) *New French Feminisms*, Brighton: Harvester.

Jackson, S. (1998) 'Looking After Children: a new approach or an exercise in form filling? A response to Knight and Caveney', *British Journal of Social Work*, Vol. 28, No. 1.

James, S. and Busia, A. (eds) (1993) *Theorising Black Feminisms*, London: Routledge.

Jay, M. (1973) *The Dialectical Imagination*, Boston, MA: Little, Brown.

Jenkins, K. (1991) *Re-thinking History*, London: Routledge.

Jenkins, K. (1995) *On 'What is History?'*, London: Routledge.

Jenks, C. (1996) *Childhood*, London: Routledge.

Jessop, B. (1990) *State Theory: Putting the Capitalist State in Its Place*, Cambridge: Polity Press.

Johnson, M.L. (1988) 'Biographical influences on mental health in old age', in Gearing, B., Heller, T. and Johnson, M.L. (eds) *Mental Health Problems in Old Age*, Chichester: John Wiley.

Johnson, M.L. et al. (1989) 'A biographically based health and social diagnostic technique: A research report', *Project Paper No. 4*, Milton Keynes: Open University Press.

Johnson, T. (1993) 'Expertise and the state', in Gane, M. and Johnson, T. (eds) *Foucault's New Domains*, London: Routledge.

Johnstone, P. (1997) 'Throughcare practice, risk and contact with victims', in Kemshall, H. and Pritchard, J. (eds) *Good Practice in Risk Assessment and Risk Management*, Vol. 2, London: Jessica Kingsley.

Jones, C. (1983) *State Social Work and the Working Class*, London: Macmillan.

Jordan, B. (1991) 'Competencies and values', *Social Work Education*, Vol. 10, No. 1.

Josselson, R. and Lieblich, A. (eds) (1993) *The Narrative Study of Lives*, London: Sage.

Josselson, R. (ed.) (1996) *Ethics and Process in The Narrative Study of Lives*, London: Sage.

Juckes, T.J. and Baresi, J. (1993) 'The subjective–objective dimension in the individual–society connection: A duality perspective', *Journal for the Theory of Social Behaviour*, Vol. 23, No. 2.

Katz, C. and Monk, J. (eds) (1993) *Full Circles: Geographies of Women Over the Life Course*, London: Routledge.

Katz, I. (1995) 'Anti-racism and modernity', in Yelloly, M. and Henkel, M. (eds) *Learning and Teaching in Social Work: Towards Reflective Practice*, London: Jessica Kingsley.

Katz, I. (1996) *The Construction of Racial Identity in Children of Mixed Parentage*, London: Jessica Kingsley.

Katz, L. (1996) 'Permanency action through concurrent planning', *Adoption and Fostering*, Vol. 20, No. 2, pp.8–13.

Keith, L. and Morris, J. (1995) 'Easy targets? A disability rights perspective on the "children as carers" debate', *Critical Social Policy*, No. 44/5.

Kelly, G. (1996) 'Competence in risk assessment', in O'Hagan, K. (ed.) *Competence in Social Work Practice*, London: Jessica Kingsley.

Kemshall, H. (1995) 'Responses to offender risk: Probation practice, organisational setting and the risk society', paper presented to the ESRC 'Risk in Organisational Settings' Conference, London.

Kemshall, H. (1996) 'Offender risk and probation practice', in Kemshall, H. and Pritchard, J. (eds) *Good Practice in Risk Assessment and Risk Management*, London: Jessica Kingsley.

Kemshall, H. (1997) 'Risk and parole: Issues in risk assessment for release', in Kemshall, H. and Pritchard, J. (eds) *Good Practice in Risk Assessment and Risk Management*, Vol. 2, London: Jessica Kingsley.

Kemshall, H. and Pritchard, J. (eds) (1996) *Good Practice in Risk Assessment and Risk Management*, London: Jessica Kingsley.

Kemshall, H. and Pritchard, J. (eds) (1997) *Good Practice in Risk Assessment and Risk Management, Vol. 2: Protection, Rights and Responsibilities*, London: Jessica Kingsley.

Kent, S.K. (1996) 'Mistrials and diatribulations', *Women's History Review*, Vol. 5, No. 1.

Key, M. (1989) 'The practice of assessing elders', in Stevenson, O. (ed.) *Age and Vulnerability*, London: Arnold.

Kincheloe, J.L. and McLaren, P.L. (1994) 'Rethinking critical theory', in Denzin, N.K. and Lincoln, Y.S. (eds) *Handbook of Qualitative Research*, London: Sage.

Knight, T. and Caveney, S. (1998) 'Assessment and action records: will they promote good practice?', *British Journal of Social Work*, Vol. 28, No. 1.

Knorr-Cetina, K. (1981) 'Introduction: The micro-sociological challenge of macro-sociology – Towards a reconstruction of social theory and methodology', in Knorr-Cetina, K. (ed.) *Advances in Social Theory and Methodology: Towards an Integration of Micro- and Macro-Sociologies*, London: Routledge.

Knowles, C. (1994) 'Biographical explanations of blackness and schizophrenia', in Stanley, L. (ed.) *Lives and Works, Auto/Biography*, Vol. 3, Nos 1–2 (double issue).

Kofodinos, J. (1990) 'Using biographical methods to understand managerial style', *Journal of Applied Behavioural Science*, Vol. 26, No. 4.

Konopka, G. (1958) *E.C. Lindemann and Social Work Philosophy*, Minneapolis, MN: University of Minnesota Press.

Langan, M. (1985) 'The unitary approach: A feminist critique', in Brook, E. and Davis, A. (eds) *Women, the Family and Social Work*, London: Tavistock.

Larrabee, M.J. (ed.) (1993) *An Ethic of Care: Feminist and Interdisciplinary Perspectives*, London: Routledge.

Lather, P. (1986) 'Research as praxis', *Harvard Educational Review*, Vol. 56, No. 3, pp.257–77.

Lather, P. (1988) 'Feminist research perspectives on empowering research methodologies', *Women's Studies International Forum*, Vol. 11, No. 6.

Lawson. J, (1996) 'A framework of risk assessment and management for older people', in Kemshall, H. and Pritchard, J. (eds) *Good Practice in Risk Assessment and Risk Management*, London: Jessica Kingsley.

Lee, J.H. and Holland, T.P. (1991) 'Evaluating the effectiveness of foster parent training', *Social Work Practice*, Vol. 1, No. 2.

Lesbian History Group (1989) *Not a Passing Phase*, London: Women's Press.

Lesbian Oral History Group (1989) *Inventing Ourselves: Lesbian Life Stories*, London: Routledge.

Lightbown, C. (1979) 'Life story books', *Adoption and Fostering*, Vol. 3, No. 3, pp.9–15

Lightfoot, J. (1995) 'Identifying needs and setting priorities: Issues of theory policy and practice', *Health and Social Care in the Community*, Vol. 3, No. 2, pp.105–14.

Lipscombe, S. (1997) 'Homelessness and mental health', in Kemshall, H. and Pritchard, J. (eds) *Good Practice in Risk Assessment and Risk Management, Vol. 2: Protection, Rights and Responsibilities*, London: Jessica Kingsley.

Little, M. (1997) 'The refocussing of children's services: The contribution of research', in Parton, N. (ed.) *Child Protection and Family Support*, London: Routledge.

Littlechild, R. and Blakeney, J. (1996) 'Risk and older people', in Kemshall, H. and Pritchard, J. (eds) *Good Practice in Risk Assessment and Risk Management*, Jessica Kingsley.

Lloyd, M. and Taylor, C. (1995) 'From Hollis to the Orange Book: developing a holistic model of social work assessment in the 1990's', *British Journal of Social Work*, Vol. 25, No. 6.

Lorde, A. (1984a) *Sister Outsider*, New York: The Crossing Press.

Lorde, A. (1984b) *Zami: A New Spelling of My Name*, London: Sheba Feminist Publishers.

Lucey, C. and Reder, P. (1995) 'Balanced opinions', in Reder, P. and Lucey C. (eds) *Assessment of Parenting: Psychiatric and Psychological Contributions*, London: Routledge.

Lukes, S. (1974) *Power: A Radical View*, London: Macmillan.

Lukes, S. (1985) *Marxism and Morality*, Oxford: Oxford University Press.

Macallum, S. and Prilleltensky, I. (1996) 'Empowerment and child protection work: Values, practice and caveats', *Children and Society*, Vol. 10, No. 1, pp.40–50.

Mace, C. (ed.) (1996) *The Art and Science of Assessment in Psychotherapy*, London: Routledge.

Maclaren, P. and Lankshear, C. (1994) *Politics of Liberation*, London: Routledge.

MacIntyre, A. (1973) 'The essential contestability of some social concepts', *Ethics*, Vol. 84.

Malik, K. (1996) *The Meaning of Race: Race History and Culture in Western Society*, London: Macmillan.

Marchant, R. and Page, M. (1992) *Bridging the Gap: Child Protection Work with Children with Multiple Disabilities*, London: NSPCC.

Marcus, G.E. (1994) 'What comes (just) after "post"? The case of ethnography', in Denzin, N.K. and Lincoln, Y.S. (eds) *Handbook of Qualitative Research*, London: Sage.

Marcus, L. (1995) 'Border crossings: Recent feminist auto/biographical theory', in Leydesdorff, S., Passerini, L. and Thompson, P. (eds) *Gender and Memory International Yearbook of Oral History and Life Stories*, Vol. IV, Oxford: Oxford University Press.

Marcuse, H. (1964) *One Dimensional Man*, London: Routledge and Kegan Paul.

Marris, P. (1991) 'The social construction of uncertainty', in Parkes, M., Stevenson-Hinde, J. and Marris, P. (eds) *Attachment Across the Life Cycle*, London: Routledge.

Marshall, A. (1994) 'Sensuous sapphires: A study of black female sexuality', in Maynard, M. and Purvis, J. (eds) *Researching Women's Lives*, London: Taylor and Francis.

Martin, B. (1988) 'Lesbian identity and autobiographical difference(s)', in Brodzki, B. and Schenck, C. (eds) *Life/Lines: Theorising Women's Autobiography*, Ithaca, NY: Cornell University Press.

Martin, R. (1995) *Oral History in Social Work*, London: Sage.

Marwick, A. (1989) *The Nature of History* (3rd edn), London: Macmillan.

Maslow, A. (1970) *Motivation and Personality*, New York: Harper.

Maynard, M. (1994a) '"Race", gender and "difference" in feminist thought', in Afshar, H. and Maynard, M. (eds) *The Dynamics of 'Race' and Gender*, London: Taylor and Francis.

Maynard, M. (1994b) 'Methods, practice and epistemology', in Maynard, M. and Purvis, J. (eds) *Researching Women's Lives from a Feminist Perspective*, London: Taylor and Francis.

Maynard, M. and Purvis, J. (eds) (1994) *Researching Women's Lives from a Feminist Perspective*, London: Taylor and Francis.

Mbilinyi, M. (1989) '"I'd have been a man": Politics and the labour process in producing personal narratives', in Personal Narratives Group, *Interpreting Women's Lives*, Bloomington, IN: Indiana University Press.

McCluskey, K.A. and Reese, H.W. (eds) (1984) *Life-span Developmental Psychology: Historical and Generational Effects*, New York: Academic Press.

McCurdy, K. (1995) 'Risk assessment in child abuse prevention programmes', *Social Work Research*, Vol. 19, No. 2.

McEwan, S. and Sullivan, J. (1996) 'Sex offender risk assessment', in Kemshall, H. and Pritchard, J. (eds) *Good Practice in Risk Assessment and Risk Management*, London: Jessica Kingsley.

McGrath, M. and Grant, M. (1993) 'The life cycle and support networks of families with a person with a learning disability', *Disability Handicap and Society*, Vol. 8, No. 1.

McMurren, M. and Hodge, J. (1994) *The Assessment of Criminal Behaviours of Clients in Secure Settings*, London: Jessica Kingsley.

McNay, L. (1992) *Foucault and Feminism*, London: Routledge.

Middleton, L. (1997) *The Art of Assessment*, Birmingham: Venture Press.

Miller, G. (1997a) 'Building bridges: The possibility of analytic dialogue between ethnography, conversation analysis and Foucault', in Silverman, D. (ed.) *Qualitative Research: Theory, Method and Practice*, London: Sage.

Miller, G. (1997b) 'Systems and solutions: The discourses of brief therapy', *Family Therapy*, No. 19, March, pp.5–22.

Miller, J. (1981) 'The use of autobiography in social work education', *British Journal of Social Work*, No. 11, pp.341–8.

Milner, J.S. and Campbell, J.C. (ed.) (1995) 'Prediction issues for practitioners', in Campbell, J.C. (ed.) *Assessing Dangerousness: Violence by Sexual Offenders, Batterers and Child Abusers*, London: Sage.

Milner, J. and O'Byrne, P. (1998) *Assessment in Social Work*, London: Macmillan.

Mirza, H.S. (ed.) (1997a) *Black British Feminism*, London: Routledge.

Mirza, H.S. (1997b) 'Introduction: Mapping a Genealogy of Black British Feminism', in Mirza, H.S. (ed.) *Black British Feminism*, London: Routledge.

Morgan, D.H.J. (1985) *The Family: Politics and Social Theory*, London: Routledge.

Morgan, D.H.J. (1992) *Discovering Men*, London: Routledge.

Morris, J. (ed.) (1989) *Able Lives: Women's Experience of Paralysis*, London: Women's Press.

Morris, J. (1991) '"Us" and "them"? Feminist research, community care, and disability', *Critical Social Policy*, No. 33.

Morris, J. (1992a) *Pride Against Prejudice: Transforming Attitudes to Disability*, London: Women's Press.

Morris, J. (1992b) 'Personal and political: A feminist perspective on researching physical disability', in *Disability, Handicap and Society*, Vol. 7, No. 2.

Morris, J. (1997) *Community Care: Working in Partnership with Service Users*, Birmingham: Venture Press.

Moustakas, C. (1990) *Heuristic Research: Design, Methodology and Applications*, London: Sage.

Mullaly, R. (1993) *Structural Social Work*, Toronto: McLelland and Stewart.

Mullender, A. and Ward, D. (1991) *Self-directed Groupwork*, London: Whiting and Birch.

Munro, E. (1998) 'Improving social worker's knowledge base in child protection work, *British Journal of Social Work*, Vol. 28, No. 1.

Nain, G.T. (1991) 'Black or Anti-racist feminism?', *Feminist Review*, No. 37.

Nicholson, L.J. (ed.) (1990) *Feminism/Postmodernism*, London: Routledge.

Nicholson, P. (1995) 'Feminism and psychology', in Smith, J.A., Harre, R. and Van Langenhove, L. (eds) *Rethinking Psychology*, London: Sage.

Nonaka, T. and Takeuchi, I. (1995) *The Knowledge-creating Company*, New York: Oxford University Press.

Oakeshott, M. (1933) *Experience and Its Modes*, Oxford: Oxford University Press.

Oakeshott, M. (1962) *Rationalism in Politics*, London: Methuen.

Oleson, V. (1994) 'Feminisms and models of qualitative research', in Denzin, N.K. and Lincoln, Y. (eds) *Handbook of Qualitative Research*, London: Sage.

Oliver, J.P.J., Huxley, J.P. and Butler, A. (1989) *Mental Health Casework: Illuminations and Reflection*, Manchester University Press.

Oliver, M. (1983) *Social Work With Disabled People*, London: Macmillan.

Oliver, M. (1992a) 'Changing the social relations of research production?', in *Disability, Handicap and Society*, Vol. 7, No. 2.

Oliver, M. (ed.) (1992b) *Social Work: Disabled People and Disabling Environments*, London: Jessica Kingsley.

Oliver, M. (1996) *Understanding Disability*, London: Macmillan.

Olsen, K. and Shopes, L. (1991) 'Crossing boundaries, building bridges', in Gluck, S.B. and Patai, D. (eds) *Women's Words: The Feminist Practice of Oral History*, London: Routledge.

Opie, A. (1993) 'Qualitative research, appropriation of the "other" and empowerment', *Feminist Review*, No. 40.

Opie, A. (1997) 'Teams as author: Narrative and knowledge creation in case discussion in multi-disciplinary health teams', *Sociology Research Online*, Vol. 2, No. 3.

Owen, H. and Pritchard, J. (1993) *Good Practice in Child Protection: A Manual for Professionals*, London: Longman.

Palmer, S. and MacMahon, G. (eds) (1997) *Client Assessment*, London: Sage.

Parker, I. and Shotter, J. (eds) (1990) *Deconstructing Social Psychology*, London: Routledge.

Parker, R. et al. (1992) *Looking After Children – Assessing Outcomes in Child Care*, London: HMSO.

Parkes, M., Stevenson-Hinde, J. and Marris, P. (eds) (1991) *Attachment Across the Life Cycle*, London: Routledge.

Parmar, P. (1990) 'Black feminism: The politics of articulation', in Rutherford, J. (ed.) *Identity: Community, Culture, Difference*, London: Lawrence and Wishart.

Parsons, T. (1952) *The Social System*, London: Tavistock.

Parsons, T. et al. (1951) *Toward a General Theory of Action*, Harvard, MA: Harvard University Press.

Parton, N. (1985) *The Politics of Child Abuse*, London: Macmillan.

Parton, N. (1991) *Governing the Family*, London: Macmillan.

Parton, N. (1994a) 'The nature of social work under conditions of postmodernity', *Social Work and Social Science Review*, Vol. 5, No. 2, pp.93–112.

Parton, N. (1994b) 'Problems of government: (post) modernity and social work', *British Journal of Social Work*, No. 24, pp.9–32.

Parton, N. (ed.) (1996a) *Social Theory: Social Change and Social Work*, London: Routledge.

Parton, N. (1996b) 'Social work, risk and the "blaming system"', in Parton, N. (ed.) *Social Theory: Social Change and Social Work*, London: Routledge.

Parton, N. (1996c) 'Child protection, family support, and social work', *Child and Family Social Work*, No. 1, pp.3–11.

Parton, N. (ed.) (1997a) *Child Protection and Family Support*, London: Routledge.

Parton, N. (1997b) 'Child protection and family support: Current debates and future prospects', in Parton, N. (ed.) (1997) *Child Protection and Family Support*, London: Routledge.

Parton N. (1998) 'Risk, advanced liberalism and child welfare: the need to rediscover uncertainty and ambiguity', *British Journal of Social Work*, Vol. 28, No. 1.

Parton, N., Thorpe, D. and Wattam, C. (1997) *Child Protection, Risk and the Moral Order*, London: Macmillan.

Payne, M. (1991) *Modern Social Work Theory*, London: Macmillan.

Payne, M. (1995) *Community Care and Older People*, London: Macmillan.

Peace, S. (ed.) (1990) *Researching Social Gerontology*, London: Sage.

People First (1993) *Oi, It's My Assessment*, London: People First.

Percy-Smith, J. (ed.) (1996) *Needs Assessments in Public Policy*, Milton Keynes: Open University Press.

Perelberg, R.J. and Miller, A.C. (eds) (1993) *Gender and Power in Families*, London: Routledge.

Perks, R. and Thompson, A. (eds) (1998) *The Oral History Reader*, Routledge.

Personal Narratives Group (1989) *Interpreting Women's Lives*, Bloomington, IN: Indiana University Press.

Phillips, J. (1996) 'The future of social work with older people', in Parton, N. (ed.) (1996) *Social Theory: Social Change and Social Work*, London: Routledge.

Phillipson, C. (1982) *Capitalism and the Construction of Old Age*, London: Macmillan.

Phillipson, J. (1992) *Practising Equality: Men, Women and Social Work*, London: CETSW.

Phoenix, A. (1990) 'Theories of gender and black families', in Lovell, T. (ed.) *British Feminist Thought*, London: Blackwell.

Pilcher, J. (1995) *Age and Generation in Modern Britain*, Oxford: Oxford University Press.

Pilgrim, D. (1990) 'Researching psychotherapy', in Parker, I. and Shotter, J. (eds) *Deconstructing Social Psychology*, London: Routledge.

Pincus, A. and Minahan, A. (1973) *Social Work Practice: Model and Method*, Itasca, IL: Peacock.

Pini, M. (1997) 'Technologies of the self', in Roche, J. and Tucker, S. (eds) *Youth in Society*, London: Sage.

Pitcairn, K. (1994) 'Exploring ways of giving a voice to people with learning difficulties', in Humphries, B. and Truman, C. (eds) *Rethinking Social Research*, Aldershot: Avebury.

Plant, R. (1970) *Social and Moral Theory in Casework*, London: Routledge.

Platt, D. and Edwards A. (1997) 'Planning a comprehensive family assessment', *Practice*, Vol. 9, No. 2.

Platt, D. and Shemmings, D. (eds) (1996) *Investigations of Child Abuse and Neglect: Partnership with Families*, London: Pitman.

Plotnikoff, J. and Woolfson, R. (1996) *Reporting to Court Under the Children Act*, London: HMSO.

Plummer, K. (1983) *Documents of Life: An Introduction to the Problems and Literature of a Humanistic Method*, London: Unwin Hyman.

Plummer, K. (1995) 'Life story research', in Smith, J.A., Harre, R. and Van Langenhove, L. (eds) *Rethinking Methods in Psychology*, London: Sage.

Polkinghorne, D.E. (1995) 'Narrative configuration in qualitative analysis', in Hatch, J.A. and Wiesnewsky, R. (eds) *Life History and Narrative*, London: Falmer Press.

Popper, K. (1963) *Conjectures and Refutations*, London: Routledge and Kegan Paul.

Porter, S. (1996) 'Contra-Foucault: Soldiering, nurses and power', *Sociology*, Vol. 30, No. 1, pp.59–78.

Potter, J. and Wetherall, M. (1995) 'Discourse analysis', in Smith, J.A., Harre, R. and Van Langenhove, L. (eds) *Rethinking Psychology*, London: Sage.

Potts, M. and Fido, R. (1991) *'A Fit Person to Be Removed': Personal Accounts of Life in a Mental Deficiency Institution*, Plymouth: Northcote House Publishers.

Poulantzas, N. (1973) *Political Power and Social Classes*, London: New Left Books.

Preece, J. (1996) 'Class and disability: Influences on learning expectations', *Disability and Society*, Vol. 11, No. 2.

Preston Shoot, M. and Agass, D. (1990) *Making Sense of Social Work: Psychodynamics, Systems and Practice*, London: Macmillan.

Pritchard, J. (1997) 'Vulnerable people taking risks: Older people and residential care', in Kemshall, H. and Pritchard, J. (eds) *Good Practice in Risk Assessment and Risk Management, Vol. 2: Protection, Rights and Responsibilities*, London: Jessica Kingsley.

Ramazanoglou, C. (1989) *Feminism and the Contradictions of Oppression*, London: Routledge.

Ramazanoglou, C. (ed.) (1992) *Up Against Foucault*, London: Routledge.

Ramazanoglou, C. (1996) 'Unravelling postmodern paralysis: A response to Joan Hoff', *Women's History Review*, Vol. 5, No. 1.

Ramon, S. (ed.) (1991) *Beyond Community Care: Normalisation and Integration Work*, London: MacmIllan.

Rassool, N. (1997) 'Fractured or flexible identities? Life histories of "black" diasporic women in Britain', in Mirza, H.S. (ed.) *Black British Feminism*, London: Routledge.

Reamer, F.G. (1993) *The Philosophical Foundations of Social Work*, New York: Columbia University Press.

Reason, P. (ed.) (1988) *Human Inquiry in Action: Developments in New Paradigm Research*, London: Sage.

Reason, P. (1994) *Participation in Human Inquiry*, London: Sage.

Reason, P. and Heron, J. (1995) 'Co-operative inquiry', in Smith, J.A. et al. (eds) *Rethinking Methods in Psychology*, London: Sage.

Reason, P. and Rowan, J. (1981) *Human Inquiry: A Sourcebook of New Paradigm Research*, Chichester: John Wiley.

Reder, P. and Duncan, S. (1995) 'The meaning of the child', in Reder, P. and Lucey, C. (eds) *Assessment of Parenting: Psychiatric and Psychological Contributions*, London: Routledge.

Reder, P. and Lucey C. (1991) 'The assessment of parenting: Some interactional considerations', *Psychiatric Bulletin*, No. 15.

Reder, P. and Lucey C. (eds) (1995) *Assessment of Parenting: Psychiatric and Psychological Contributions*, London: Routledge.

Reder, P., Duncan, S. and Gray, M. (1993a) 'A new look at child abuse tragedies', *Child Abuse Review*, No. 2, pp.89–100.

Reder, P., Duncan, S. and Gray, M. (1993b) *Beyond Blame: Child Abuse Tragedies Revisited*, London: Routledge.

Rhodes, P. (1991) 'The assessment of black foster parents: The relevance of cultural skills – comparative views of social workers and applicants', *Critical Social Policy*, No. 32, Autumn, p.31.

Richardson, F.C. and Fowers, B.J. (1997) 'Critical theory, postmodernism and hermeneutics: Insights for critical psychology', in Fox, D. and Prilleltensky, I. (eds) *Critical Psychology: An Introduction*, London: Sage.

Roberts, H. (ed.) (1981) *Doing Feminist Research*, London: Routledge.

Roberts, R. (1989) *Lessons from the Past: Issues for Social Work Theory*, London: Routledge.

Robins, L.N. and Rutter, M. (eds) (1990) *Straight and Devious Pathways from Childhood to Adulthood*, Cambridge: Cambridge University Press.

Robinson, L. (1995) *Psychology for Social Workers, Black Perspectives*, London: Routledge.

Rodger, J.J. (1991) 'Discourse analysis and social relationships in social work', *British Journal of Social Work*, Vol. 21, No. 1.

Rojek, C., Peacock, G. and Collins, S. (1988) *Social Work and Received Ideas*, London: Routledge.

Rojek, C., Peacock, G. and Collins, S. (1989) *The Haunt of Misery*, London: Routledge.

Romm, E. (1997) 'Comment on Hammersley and Gomm', *Sociological Research Online*, Vol. 2, No. 3.

Ross, L. and Waterson, J. (1996) 'Risk for whom? Social work and people with physical disabilities', in Kemshall, H. and Pritchard, J. (eds) *Good Practice in Risk Assessment and Risk Management*, London: Jessica Kingsley.

Ruddell, P. (1997) 'General assessment issues', in Palmer, S. and MacMahon, G. (eds) *Client Assessment*, London: Sage.

Runyan, W.M. (1982) *Life Histories and Psycho-biography*, Oxford: Oxford University Press.

Runyan, W.M. (1988) *Psychology and Historical Interpretation*, Oxford: Oxford University Press.

Ryan, T. (1995) 'Mental illness services and the perception and management of risk', conference Paper, ESRC Risk and Human Behaviour Programme at the University of York, London, 16 and 17 May.

Ryan, T. (1996) 'Risk management and people with mental health problems', in Kemshall, H. and Pritchard, J. (eds) *Good Practice in Risk Assessment and Risk Management*, London: Jessica Kingsley

Ryan, T. and Walker, R. (1985) *Making Life Story Books*, London: British Association for Adoption and Fostering.

Ryburn, M. (1991) 'The myth of assessment', *Adoption and Fostering*, Vol. 15, No. 1.

Saleeby, D. (1994) 'Culture, theory and narrative: The interaction of meanings in practice', *Social Work*, Vol. 39, No. 4.

Samuel, R. and Thompson, P. (eds) (1990) *The Myths We Live By*, London: Routledge.

Sanderson. I. (1996) 'Needs and public services', in Percy-Smith, J. (ed.) *Needs Assessments in Public Policy*, Milton Keynes: Open University Press.

Sands, R. and Nuccio, K. (1992) 'Postmodernist feminist theory and social work', *Social Work*, Vol. 37, No. 6.

Sangster, J. (1994) 'Telling our stories: Feminist debates and the use of oral history', *Women's History Review*, Vol. 3, No. 1.

Sarup, M. (1993) *Post-structuralism and Postmodernism*, London: Harvester Wheatsheaf.

Sawicki, J. (1991a) *Disciplining Foucault*, London: Routledge.

Sawicki, J. (1991b) 'Foucault and feminism: Towards a politics of difference', in Shanley, M.L. and Pateman, C. (eds) *Feminist Interpretations and Political Theory*, London: Polity Press.

Sayers, J. (1986) *Sexual Contradictions: Psychology, Psychoanalysis and Feminism*, London: Tavistock.

Scambler, G. (1996) 'The "project of modernity" and the parameters for a critical sociology: an argument with illustrations from sociology', *Sociology*, Vol. 30, No. 3, pp.567–81.

Schon, D.A. (1983) *The Reflective Practitioner*, New York: Basic Books.

Schutz, A. (1967) *The Phenomenology of the Social World*, Evanston, IL: Northwestern University Press.

Scott, D. (1998) 'A qualitative study of social work assessment in cases of alleged child abuse and neglect', *British Journal of Social Work*, Vol. 28, No. 1.

Scott, J. (1996) *Stratification and Power: Structures of Class, Status and Command*, Cambridge: Polity Press.

Scraton, P. (ed.) (1997) *'Childhood' in 'Crisis'?*, Taylor and Francis.

Seabrook, J. (1982) *Working Class Childhood: An Oral History*, London: Gollancz.

Selwyn, J. (1991) 'Applying to adopt: the experience of rejection', *Adoption and Fostering*, Vol. 15, No. 3.

Selwyn, J. (1994) '"Spies, informants and double agents" – Adoption assessments and role ambiguity', *Adoption and Fostering*, Vol. 18, No. 4.

Shakespeare, P. et al. (1993) *Reflecting on Research Practice*, Milton Keynes: Open University Press.

Shakespeare, T. (1996) 'Rules of engagement: Doing disability research', *Disability and Society*, Vol. 11, No. 1.

Sharkey, P. (1989) 'Social networks and social service users', *British Journal of Social Work*, No. 19, pp.387–405.

Sheldon, B. and MacDonald, G. (1992–3) 'Implications for practice of recent social work effectiveness research', *Practice*, Vol. 6, No. 3.

Sheppard, M. (1990) *Mental Health Work in the Community: Theory and Practice in Social Work and Community Mental Health Nursing*, Sheffield: Joint University and Social Services Research.

Sheppard, M. (1991) 'Referral source and process of assessment: A comparative analysis of assessments for compulsory admission under the Mental Health Act 1983', *Practice*, Vol. 5, No. 4.

Sheppard, M. (1993) 'Theory for approved social work: The use of the Compulsory Admissions Assessment Schedule', *British Journal of Social Work*, No. 23, pp.231–57.

Sheppard, M. (1995) 'Social work, social science and practice wisdom', *British Journal of Social Work*, No. 25, pp.265–93.

Sherif, C. (1987) 'Bias in psychology', in Harding, S. (ed.) *Feminism and Methodology*, Milton Keynes: Open University Press.

Sibeon, R. (1990) 'Social work knowledge, social actors and de-professionalisation', in Abbott, P. and Wallace, C. (eds) *Sociology of the Caring Professions*, London: Falmer Press.

Sibeon, R. (1991) *Towards a New Sociology of Social Work*, Aldershot: Avebury.

Simpkin, M. (1979) *Trapped Within Welfare*, London: Macmillan.

Siporin, M. (1975) *Introduction to Social Work Practice*, New York: Macmillan.

Skeggs, B. (1994) 'Situating the production of feminist ethnography', in Maynard, M. and Purvis, J. (eds) *Researching Women's Lives*, London: Taylor and Francis.

Skynner, A. (1976) *One Flesh, Separate Persons*, London: Constable.

Slater, P. (1996) 'Practice teaching and self-assessment: Promoting a culture of accountability in social work', *British Journal of Social Work*, Vol. 26, No. 2.

Smale, G. and Tuson, G. with Biehal, N. and Marsh, P. (1993) *Empowerment, Assessment, Care Management and the Skilled Worker*, London: HMSO.

Smith, C. and White, S. (1997) 'Parton, Howe and postmodernity: A critical comment on mistaken identity', *British Journal of Social Work*, Vol. 27, No. 2.

Smith, J.A., Harre, R. and Van Langenhove, L. (eds) (1995a) *Rethinking Methods in Psychology*, London: Sage.

Smith, J.A., Harre, R. and Van Langenhove, L. (eds) (1995b) *Rethinking Psychology*, London: Sage.

Smith, J.A, Harre, R. and Van Langenhove, L. (1995c) 'Idiography and the case study', in Smith, J.A., Harre, R. and Van Langenhove, L. (eds) *Rethinking Psychology*, London: Sage.

Smith, L. (1994) 'Biographical method', in Denzin, N.K. and Lincoln, Y. (eds) *Handbook of Qualitative Research*, London: Sage.

Social Services Inspectorate (1993) *Evaluating Performance in Child Protection: Practice Guide*, London: HMSO.

Social Services Inspectorate, Dept of Health (1995) *The Challenge of Partnership in Child Protection: Practice Guide*, London: HMSO.

Soderqvist, T. (1991) 'Biography or ethnobiography or both? Embodied reflexivity and the deconstruction of knowledge-power', in Steier, F. (ed.) *Research and Reflexivity*, London: Sage.

Souflee, F. (1993) 'A metatheoretical framework for social work practice', *Social Work*, Vol. 38, No. 3, pp.241–360.

Specht, H. and Vickery, A. (eds) (1977) *Integrating Social Work Methods*, London: Allen and Unwin.

Squire, C. (1989) *Significant Differences: Feminism in Psychology*, London: Routledge.

Stacey, J. (1991) 'Can there be a feminist ethnography?', in Gluck, S.B. and Patai, D. (eds) *Women's Words: The Feminist Practice of Oral History*, London: Routledge.

Staffordshire County Council (1991) *The Pindown Experience and the Protection of Children*, Stoke: Staffordshire County Council.

Stanley, L. (1987) 'Biography as microscope or kaleidoscope? The case of "power" in Hannah Cullwick's relationship with Arthur Munby', *Women's Studies International Forum*, Vol. 10, No. 1, pp.19–31.

Stanley, L. (ed.) (1990) *Feminist Praxis*, London: RKP.

Stanley, L. (1992) *The Auto/biographical I: The Theory and Practice of Feminist Auto/biography*, Manchester University Press.

Stanley, L. (1993) 'On auto/biography in sociology', *Sociology*, Vol. 27, No. 1.

Stanley, L. (1994) 'Sisters under the skin? Oral histories and auto/biographies', *Oral History*, Vol. 22, No. 2.

Stanley, L. (1996) 'The mother of invention: necessity, writing and representation', in Wilkinson, S. and Kitzinger, C. (eds) *Representing the Other: A Feminism and Psychology Reader*, London: Sage.

Stanley, L. and Wise, S. (1983) *Breaking Out: Feminist Consciousness and Feminist Research*, London: Routledge.

Stanley, L. and Wise, S. (1994) *Breaking Out Again: Feminist Ontology and Epistemology*, Manchester University Press.

Steier, F. (ed.) (1991) *Research and Reflexivity*, London: Sage.

Stenson, K. (1993) 'Social work discourse and the social work interview', *Economy and Society*, Vol. 22, No. 1, pp.42–6.

Stevenson, O. (1989) *Age and Vulnerability*, London: Edward Arnold.

Stevenson, P. (1991) 'A model of self-assessment for prospective adopters', *Adoption and Fostering*, Vol. 15, No. 3, pp.30–4.

Stewart, K. (1996) 'Sexual abuse as a moral event', *British Journal of Social Work*, Vol. 26, No. 4.

Stone, L. (1981) *The Past and the Present*, London: Routledge.

Strachan R. and Tallant, C. (1997) 'Improving judgement and appreciating biases within the risk assessment process', in Kemshall, H. and Pritchard, J. (eds) *Good Practice in Risk Assessment and Risk Management, Vol. 2: Protection, Rights and Responsibilities*, London: Jessica Kingsley.

Stuart, M. (1994) 'You're a big girl now: Subjectivities, oral history and feminism', *Oral History*, Vol. 22, No. 2.

Tantam, D. (1995) 'Why assess?', in Mace, C. (ed.) *The Art and Science of Assessment in Psychotherapy*, London: Routledge.

Tao, J. and Drover, G. (1997) 'Chinese and Western notions of need', *Critical Social Policy*, Vol. 17, No. 1.

Taylor, B. and Devine, T. (1993) *Assessing Needs and Planning Care in Social Work*, Aldershot: Arena.

Taylor-Gooby, P. (1994) 'Postmodernism and social policy: A great leap backwards?' *Journal of Social Policy*, Vol. 23, No. 3.

Thoburn, J., Brandon, M. and Lewis, A. (1997) 'Need, risk and significant harm', in Parton, N. (ed.) *Child Protection and Family Support*, London: Routledge.

Thomas, R.M. (1979) *Comparing Theories of Child Development*, Belmont, CA: Wadsworth.

Thompson, N. (1993) *Anti-discriminatory Practice*, London: Macmillan.

Thompson, N. (1996) *Age and Dignity*, Aldershot: Arena.

Thompson, P. (1984) *The Voice of the Past* (2nd edn), London: Routledge.

Thorpe, D. (1996) 'Categorising referrals about children: Child protection or child welfare?', in Platt, D. and Shemmings, D. (eds) *Investigations of Child Abuse and Neglect: Partnership with Families*, London: Pitman.

Thorpe, D. (1997) 'Policing minority child-rearing practices in Australia', in Parton, N. (ed.) *Child Protection and Family Support*, London: Routledge.

Tibbles, P.N. (1992) 'Changes in depression and personal construing following assessment for dynamic psychotherapy', *British Journal of Medical Psychology*, No. 65, pp.9–15.

Timms, N. (1986) 'The fate of the counsellors', *Adoption and Fostering*, Vol. 10, No. 1, pp.12–16.

Timms, N. and Watson, D. (eds) (1976) *Talking About Welfare: Readings in Philosophy and Social Policy*, London: Routledge.

Timms, N. and Watson, D. (eds) (1979) *Philosophy in Social Work*, London: Routledge.

Tonkin, E. (1992) *Narrating Our Pasts: The Social Construction of Oral History*, Cambridge: Cambridge University Press.

Toulmin, S. (1970) 'Reasons and causes', in Borger, F. and Cioffi, F. (eds) *Explanation in the Behavioural Sciences*, Cambridge: Cambridge University Press.

Towle, C. (1965) *Common Human Needs*, New York: National Association of Social Work.

Treacher, A. and Carpenter, J. (eds) (1984) *Using Family Therapy*, Oxford: Blackwell.

Tuchman, G. (1994) 'Historical social science: Methodologies, methods and meanings', in Denzin, N.K. and Lincoln, Y. (eds) *Handbook of Qualitative Research*, London: Sage.

Tunstill, J. (1997) 'Implementing the family support clauses of the 1989 Children Act: Legislative, professional and organisational obstacles', in Parton, N. (ed.) *Child Protection and Family Support*, London: Routledge.

Tyson, K.B. (1992) 'A new approach to relevant scientific research for practitioners: The heuristic paradigm', *Social Work*, Vol. 37, No. 6, pp.541–56.

Urwin, C. (1985) 'Constructing motherhood', in Steedman, C., Urwin, C. and Walkerdine, V. (eds) *Language, Gender and Childhood*, London: Routledge and Kegan Paul.

Vetere, A. (1992) 'Working with families', in Usher, J. and Nicholson, P. (eds) *Gender Issues in Clinical Psychology*, London: Routledge.

Von Bertalannfy, L. (1968) *General Systems Theory*, New York: George Braziller.

Wachtel, P. (1977) 'Interaction cycles, unconscious processes, and the person–situation issue', in Magnusson, D. and Endler, N. (eds) *Personality at the Crossroads*, Hillsdale, NJ: Erlbaum.

Wallace, J.B. (1994) 'Life stories', in Gubrium, J. and Sankar, A. (eds) *Qualitative Methods in Ageing Research*, London: Sage.

Walmsley, J. (1995) 'Life history interviews with people with learning disabilities', *Oral History*, Vol. 23, No. 1.

Waterhouse, L. and Carnie, J. (1992) 'Assessing child protection risk', *British Journal of Social Work*, Vol. 22, No. 1.

Watson, L.C. (1976) 'Understanding a life history as a subjective document', *Ethos*, No. 4, pp.95–131.

Webb, R. and Tossell, D. (1991) *Social Issues for Carers: A Community Care Perspective*, London: Edward Arnold.

Whitaker, D.S. and Archer, L. (1994) Partnership research, and its contribution to learning and to team building', *Social Work Education*, Vol. 13, No. 3.

White, H. (1995) 'Response to Arthur Marwick', *Journal of Contemporary History*, Vol. 30, pp.233–46.

White, S. (1997) 'Beyond retroduction? Hermeneutics, reflexivity and social work practice', *British Journal of Social Work*, Vol. 23, No. 5.

White, V. (1995) 'Commonalty and diversity in feminist social work', *British Journal of Social Work*, Vol. 25, pp.143–56.

Whitehead, A.N. (1929) *Aims of Education*, London: Macmillan.

Whittaker, T. (1996) 'Violence, gender and elder abuse', in Fawcett, B., Featherstone, B., Hearn, J. and Toft, C. (eds) *Violence and Gender Relations: Theories and Interventions*, London: Sage.

Wilkin, D. (1990) 'Dependency', in Peace, S. (ed.) *Researching Social Gerontology*, London: Sage.

Wilkinson, I. (1987) 'Family assessment: A review', *Journal of Family Therapy*, No. 9, pp.367–80.

Wilkinson, S. (1997) 'Feminist psychology', in Fox, D.R. and Prilleltensky, I. (eds) *Critical Psychology*, London: Sage.

Wilkinson, S. and Kitzinger C. (1996) 'Theorizing representing the other' in Wilkinson, S. and Kitzinger, C. (eds) *Representing the Other: A Feminism and Psychology Reader*, London: Sage.

Williams, B. (1997) 'Rights versus risks: Issues in work with prisoners', in Kemshall, H. and Pritchard, J. (eds) *Good Practice in Risk Assessment and Risk Management*, Vol. 2, London: Jessica Kingsley.

Williams, F. (1989) *Social Policy: A Critical Introduction*, Cambridge: Polity Press.

Willis, P. (1977) *Learning to Labour*, Farnborough: Saxon House.

Winch, P. (1965) *The Idea of a Social Science*, London: Routledge and Kegan Paul.

Winnicott, D. (1960) 'The theory of the parent–infant relationship', *International Journal of Psycho-analysis*, No. 41.

Winnicott, D. (1971a) *Playing and Reality*, London: Tavistock.

Winnicott, D. (1971b) *Therapeutic Consultations in Child Psychiatry*, London: Hogarth Press.

Winnicott, D. (1980) *The Piggle: An Account of the Psychoanalytical Treatment of a Little Girl*, Harmondsworth: Penguin.

Wise, S. (1987) 'A framework for discussing ethical issues in feminist research', in Griffiths, V. et al. (eds) *Writing Feminist Biographies, Vol. 2: Using Life Histories, Studies in Sexual Politics*, Department of Sociology, University of Manchester.

Wittgenstein, L. (1963) *Philosophical Investigations*, Oxford: Blackwell.

Wolff, S. (1978) 'The case history in child care', in *Good Enough Parenting*, CCETSW Study No. 1, London: CCETSW.

Wright Mills, C. (1956) *The Power Elite*, London: Oxford University Press.

Yow, V.R. (1994) *Recording Oral History*, London: Sage.

Zeller, N. (1995) 'Narrative strategies for case reports', in Hatch, J.A. and Wiesnewsky, R. (eds) *Life History and Narrative*, London: Falmer Press.

Subject Index

Index of Authors Cited

Social Assessment

CD ROM CA/B COMPUTER SOFTWARE

The case study used in this book and the theoretical principles discussed here have been combined in a CD ROM to demonstrate how theory and practice can be studied together. With this software you can:

- see and hear the author give a personal introduction to the book and the software;
- see how each individual theoretical principle relates to the case study;
- investigate the details of the case study in much greater depth, using computer technology;
- scroll across a giant life map to explore social connections across time and space;
- refer back to principles, definitions and further information at the touch of a button;
- enable students to explore the case study and make their own assessments;
- illustrate principles of social assessment in training presentations.

The Social Assessment CD ROM runs on Windows 95 or Windows 3.1, and ideally requires sound and vision capabilities on your PC. It can be used without the sound to explore the case study and other diagrams, but it needs to be used with the book to understand the full implications of CA/B social assessment for theory and practice.

The Social Assessment CD ROM is for sale. To place an order or for further information please contact:

CA/B Software
Dr D.J. Clifford
School of Law and Applied Social Studies
Liverpool John Moores University
1 Myrtle Street
Liverpool L7 4DN
E-mail: <D.J.Clifford@livjm.ac.uk>